ACROSS THE CONTINENT

JEFFERSON,
LEWIS AND CLARK,
AND THE MAKING
OF AMERICA

ACROSS THE

CONTINENT

EDITED BY

Douglas Seefeldt

Jeffrey L. Hantman

Peter S. Onuf

UNIVERSITY OF VIRGINIA PRESS
CHARLOTTESVILLE AND LONDON

Publication of this volume was assisted by
a grant from the University of Virginia's
Lewis and Clark Bicentennial Project.

University of Virginia Press
Printed in the United States of America on acid-free paper

First published 2004
First paperback edition published 2006
ISBN 978-0-8139-2595-0 (paper)

9 8 7 6 5 4 3 2 1

The Library of Congress has cataloged the hardcover edition as follows:
LIBRARY OF CONGRESS CATALOGING-IN-PUBLICATION DATA

Across the continent : Jefferson, Lewis and Clark, and the making of America /
edited by Douglas Seefeldt, Jeffrey L. Hantman, and Peter S. Onuf.
     p.   cm.
  Includes bibliographical references and index.
  ISBN 0-8139-2313-1 (cloth : alk. paper)
  1. Lewis and Clark Expedition (1804–1806) 2. West (U.S.)—Discovery and exploration. 3. United States—Territorial expansion. 4. Jefferson, Thomas, 1743–1826—
Views on the West (U.S.) 5. Explorers—West (U.S.)—History—19th century.
6. West (U.S.)—History—To 1848. I. Seefeldt, Douglas, 1964–   II. Hantman,
Jeffrey L. III. Onuf, Peter S.
F592.A49 2004
917.804′2—dc22

                                                                    2004011981

To our colleagues in the
Lewis and Clark
Bicentennial Project

Contents

Preface

THE BICENTENNIAL OF THE TRANS-
continental expedition led by Meriwether Lewis and William Clark
in 1803–6 has generated tremendous interest throughout the United
States. Countless organizations and individuals are devoting extraordinary time, energy, and resources to commemorating the Corps of
Discovery's expedition from St. Louis to the mouth of the Columbia River and back.

The University of Virginia has a particular interest in the expedition. Lewis and Clark were both Virginians, and Thomas Jefferson,
the architect of the venture, is the university's founder. The Lewis
and Clark Bicentennial Project (LCBP) represents the university's
contribution to the ongoing national conversation about the expedition and to the emerging body of scholarship on its role in North
American history. Initiated and generously supported by a grant
from the office of President John T. Casteen III, the LCBP has since
its launch in summer 2000 sponsored undergraduate courses, conferences, and visiting lecturers, as well as digital resource development and the coproduction of an award-winning documentary film

on the Virginia roots of Lewis and Clark. The LCBP was directed by Jenry Morsman from 2000 to 2002 and by Douglas Seefeldt from 2002 to 2004. The project's Web site is hosted by the Virginia Center for Digital History at www.vcdh.virginia.edu/lewisandclark/lcbp/.

The LCBP engaged University of Virginia faculty from an extraordinarily wide range of disciplines in a three-year colloquium that considered Lewis and Clark and the American West. The group included Brian Balogh, John K. (Jack) Brown, William Carter, Barry Cushman, Jeffrey Hantman, Janet S. Herman, Michael F. Holt, Alan B. Howard, Lisa Lauria, Earl J. Mark, Maurie McInnis, Betsy Mendelsohn, Peter Onuf, John G. (Frank) Papovich, Kate Pierce, Stephen Plog, Stephen Railton, Douglas Seefeldt, Aaron Sheehan-Dean, Carl O. Trindle, Dell Upton, Jennings L. Wagoner, and Henry M. Wilbur. Seefeldt, Hantman, and Onuf are particularly grateful to Lisa Lauria, Kate Pierce, and the other LCBP members for valuable contributions made to the success of the new "American Wests" course they offered in 2002 and 2003.

In October 2001, Alan Taylor, David Hurst Thomas, and Kenneth Prewitt delivered earlier versions of essays in this volume in the Thomas Jefferson Foundation Distinguished Lecture Series held at the University of Virginia. Subsequently, Peter Onuf, Jeffrey Hantman, Jenry Morsman, and Doug Seefeldt were enlisted to contribute additional essays. Under the leadership of President Daniel P. Jordan, the Thomas Jefferson Foundation (Monticello) has promoted an extraordinary revival of Jefferson scholarship. We are indebted to Dan and to James Horn, former Saunders Director of the International Center for Jefferson Studies at Monticello, for their support and encouragement.

Introduction

Geopolitics, Science, and Culture Conflicts

Peter S. Onuf and Jeffrey L. Hantman

THE BICENTENNIAL COMMEMORATION of the Lewis and Clark expedition is upon us, and it won't go away for a long time. Unwilling to wait until May 2004—the real bicentennial of the expedition's departure up the river from St. Louis—commemoration organizers decided that the proper place to begin was at Monticello, or, more accurately, in the capacious mind of the expedition's sponsor, President Thomas Jefferson, on the bicentennial of its conception. If all goes according to plan, we'll still be at it during the summer of August 2006, two hundred years after the bedraggled Corps of Discovery—"almost forgotten" and generally presumed dead by their countrymen (though "the President of the U. States had yet hopes of us")—floated down the Missouri to a "harty welcom" at St. Louis.[1]

Will the intrepid explorers wear out their welcome with us in the meantime? Probably not. Indeed, the early signs are that this will be the most successful bicentennial in modern memory, eclipsing celebrations of the Revolution and Constitution that combined patriotic and commercial excess with eye-glazing exercises in civic edification;

it also promises to obliterate all memory of the rancorous quincentenary celebration of Columbus's "discovery" of America (leaving aside the much-bruited question of whether or not that "discovery" was a good thing, celebrating it seemed in bad taste). Just as Lewis and Clark successfully navigated through a treacherous zone of chronic intertribal warfare (the expedition's only fatality, Sergeant Charles Floyd, died of a ruptured appendix), they have risen triumphantly above the culture wars of our own time. Dialecticians may see this as a backlash to the trashing of Columbus; or it may be a tribute to the astute diplomacy of the commemorators, who have successfully enlisted native peoples in their new corps of rediscovery; it may also be that the Lewis and Clark expedition is so firmly entrenched in the popular imagination that the urge to celebrate is more or less spontaneous, and organizers simply have to provide appropriate opportunities for its expression. We lean toward the last explanation.

The expedition's mythic West provides a multicultural common ground for Americans of all backgrounds and persuasions, a place where white pioneers and Indians made love, not war, a place where the spirit of adventure remained unsullied by imperialistic impulses to kill, conquer, and exploit. Sacagawea, the "Indian princess" (actually the wife, and arguably—as a Shoshone captive among the Mandan—the slave of interpreter Toussaint Charbonneau) has long played a starring role in Corps mythology, and William Clark's black slave York has more recently made a strong bid for equal billing. Together, their presence gives the expedition a satisfyingly modern complexion (they are us!), while blurring the racial binaries—white over black, white over red—that dominate the new conventional wisdom (in school and college curriculums at least) about early American history.

Perhaps our next big commemoration—of Jamestown's founding in 1607—will also conjure up images of happy interracial encounters, though it will be much harder to suppress the imminent and pervasive brutality, insensitivity, and all-around nastiness of the hapless colony's early history. The great advantages of the Lewis and Clark expedition are that it lasts so long but has so little immediate impact: the first encounters, however great the intercultural divide—however we may lament our heroes' failure to learn more from the Indians about living with the land and living in the cosmos—were not tainted by the immediate aftermath. It was not until the discovery of gold in California that the "wilderness" was definitively breached: miners, railroad builders, ranchers, and federal troops rushed west, obliterating Indians and transforming the landscape. This was the "winning of the West" that once gripped the American imagination but now seems somewhat embarrassing, perhaps even shameful. We would rather win the West the way Lewis and Clark supposedly did, by getting along with the Indians. In a compensatory way, it is gratifying to imagine that Indians then held the upper hand: they easily could have wiped out this tiny, ragged, poorly equipped, and generally clueless band—rumors did occasionally reach camp that one nation or other "intended to kill us"— but held back; and, if Lewis and Clark were agents of empire, they were prudent enough not to throw their weight around—though Lewis certainly had some bad moments—and wise enough to learn some lessons in survival from their "savage" hosts.[2]

Historians love to puncture mythological hot-air balloons, though we suspect revisionism will have little impact in this case.[3] The best historians can do is to insist, as we have done above, that the expedition didn't really matter very much in its own time. But that is not to say that it doesn't matter now; its contemporary significance may, in fact, be a function of its historical irrelevance, or rather its disconnection from the larger narrative of American westward expansion. The modern West, in Patricia Limerick's influential formulation, is a "legacy of conquest"; Lewis and Clark tell us it can be something more and better than that, that its future history can recapture the spirit of their Edenic moment.[4] Who would be so churlish as to quarrel with such a Noble Lie? As myths go, this is not a bad one, and it gets better the more we reenact the journey— really and imaginatively—and immerse ourselves in the fascinating evidence now available in Gary Moulton's magnificent documentary edition of *The Journals of the Lewis and Clark Expedition*.[5] In this case, good history—the assemblage of a vast and reliable historical record—serves mythological purposes. In a perverse way, the authenticity of the record is important, for it licenses us to project ourselves into the past and to identify more fully with our heroes. We forget that "the past is a foreign country." Instead, we find ourselves with Lewis and Clark, imagining what it must have been like to encounter for the first time "this truly magnificent and sublimely grand" western landscape.

If we can't see with our explorers' eyes, if our way of seeing is now so radically different, we also are hard pressed to recapture their broader view of the world. Lewis and Clark were not sent west to satisfy Jefferson's scientific curiosity or to test their own manhood in a wilderness adventure. They were intensely aware that the trans-Mississippi was contested ground, only recently (and nominally) annexed to the United States. Much of the region up the Missouri and along the northwest coast was well known to Russian, French, British, and American traders; even where Indians had not yet seen—or "discovered"—whites, they were linked to the Euro-American world through trading and raiding networks, or by the spread of contagious diseases (smallpox devastated western Indians in the early 1780s).[6] For the Americans to establish effective control, President Jefferson had to assume the role of "Great American Father," dispensing favors, securing trade connections, and making the Indians "sensible of their dependance on the will of our government."[7] On the return trip, Lewis led a small party north into present-day Montana, hoping to prove that the Missouri River system extended to 50 degrees, thus pushing American claims north at the expense of the British. The Marias River, he earlier predicted, "was destined to become . . . an object of contention between the two great powers of America and Great Brit[a]in."[8]

Lewis and Clark were the advance guard of a new American empire. Their goal was not to subjugate the natives—in view of their numbers, this would have been a suicidal enterprise—but rather to forge a new alliance system that would eliminate European imperial rivals and establish a Pax Americana in the region. Chronic conflict among the Indians provided them an opening. High in the Rockies, Shoshone chief Cameahwait was eager to cut a deal: "If we had guns, we could then live in the country of buffaloe and eat as our enemies do and not be compelled to hide ourselves in these mountains and live on roots and berries as the bear do."[9] Needless to say,

Indians could not know what lay in store for their children and grand-children. While a few nations—usually far offstage—made ominous noises, most welcomed the expedition. In some cases, the explorers' white skin was their passport: Lewis was "overjoyed" at the first sighting of a Shoshone and "had no doubt of obtaining a friendly introduction to his nation provided I could get near enough to him to convince him of our being white men."[10] Under the circum-stances, the explorers needed all the help they could get. Geopoliti-cal considerations drove their information gathering: they needed to know as much as possible about native manpower and firepower, alliances and enmities; ethnographic observation—understanding the Indians on their own terms—was, at best, an afterthought.

The expedition was largely irrelevant because it proved prema-ture. Lewis and Clark could not fully grasp the diplomatic situation in Indian country, and their efforts at pacification had little lasting impact: they could scatter medals (inscribed with Jefferson's image) throughout the region—in one grisly case, "about the neck" of a Blackfoot Lewis had shot to death, so that his fellow Indians "might be informed who we were"—but they could not, literally, deliver the goods.[11] Instead, it was enterprising Indian traders from St. Louis—naturalized under the Louisiana Purchase treaty—who consolidated the new nation's commercial hegemony in the Missouri watershed. Meanwhile, the Rockies would remain beyond the pale of American influence; the Anglo-American struggle for empire that Lewis had predicted would not take place on the northern plains but rather on the northwest coast, culminating in the partition of the Oregon country in 1848. With all due deference to chaos theory, these devel-opments would have taken place whether or not the expedition had succeeded, or even taken place.[12]

Future generations of Americans will turn to Lewis and Clark for entertainment and inspiration, untroubled by the intermittent rumblings of academic revisionists. After all, the stock of the found-ers, with all their warts—even Jefferson, wartiest of them all—has been rising recently, not only in the "general public" but among seri-ous historians as well. By comparison, Lewis and Clark are relatively uncomplicated, even benign figures. Of course, Lewis was a tor-mented soul, ungraciously and imprudently prone to vent hostile feelings for his Indian hosts (sympathetic readers will speculate endlessly on the "issues" that bedeviled the poor man); mapmaker Clark is probably more the man for our own times, with his feet more firmly on the ground, his openness to experience, and his comparatively enlightened racial attitudes. At the end of the day, the explorers did little harm (leaving aside that Blackfoot, who may have been up to no good himself), and the Indians might agree that they even occasionally did some good, as they dispensed trade goods, medicine and medical services—word of "our skill as phisicians and the virture of our medecines have been spread it seems a great distance," Lewis noted in May 1806—and, most dubiously, political counsel that was, due to translation problems, probably unintelligible and in any case useless.[13] The harm came later, and it's comforting to think that the explorers set a higher standard then—before a later generation's reign of terror spread like wildfire across the plains—a standard that we can imagine we are living up to now.

The Lewis and Clark expedition offers a quasi-mythological touchstone for American self-understanding. Our goal in *Across the Continent* is not to demolish the myth but rather to explore the complicated ways in which the explorers' world connects to our own. Every generation gives the national narrative a distinctive inflection, discovering new experiences, new heroes, and new voices in the past. Lewis and Clark loom much larger now in the American imagination than they did in their own time, in large part because Lewis failed to publish the expedition's journals before his untimely death—probably by his own hand—in 1809. Publication made explorers like Captain James Cook and Sir Alexander Mackenzie famous, and it also buttressed the territorial ambitions of great imperial powers. Lewis and Clark thus faithfully chronicled their diplomatic encounters with the natives as they mapped their progress across the continent, demonstrating both their own and the new nation's presence in this vast, uncharted space. But the expedition's promise remained unfulfilled as long as the journals languished in their unrevised, unpublished form.

Expedition member Patrick Gass published a journal of his own in 1807 that was widely distributed in multiple versions. At Jefferson's insistence, Philadelphian Nicholas Biddle brought out a narrative based on the leaders' journals in 1814, but it was only in 1904–5, on the expedition's centennial, that the first comprehensive edition of the journals, edited by Reuben Gold Thwaites, was finally published. By this time, of course, the nation was no longer new and its continental claims had long since been consolidated: politicians and opinion makers were not now looking westward but were instead trying to make sense of America's role as an emerging power in a much larger world. In 1893, the great Wisconsin historian Frederick Jackson Turner delivered his famous address on "The Significance of the Frontier in American History," an elegiac (and premature) obituary on westward expansion: as urban-industrial civilization emerged to the east, the West faded into the past and the frontier became history. From this new perspective, publication of the expedition's journals did not represent the projection of power—demonstrating the new nation's scientific capacity to survey, classify, and control nature—but instead constituted an act of recovery, correcting a great historical injustice. It is as if Lewis's failure to publish and the expedition's relative obscurity—and, therefore, its historical irrelevance—were not his fault, but ours. Contemporaries should have known then what we know now, and as our knowledge of the expedition grows we can finally set things right. Historians thus may insist that Lewis and Clark were not all that important: in the past they had little impact on the shape of the future. But it is also equally true that they have loomed ever larger in the American historical imagination, that in the future they will increasingly shape our understanding of the past. The bicentennial celebrations confirm this long-term development and give it a powerful new impetus.

The historians' turf-conscious skepticism about the explorers' importance is both exaggerated—as Alan Taylor indicates, their exploits, unlike those of their Spanish predecessors, were not shrouded in official secrecy—and misplaced. After all, historians are taught that the agendas of their predecessors were determined by contemporaneous preoccupations and imperatives; they might like to think that they can rise above their own times as they strive for "objectivity." They can't, of course—though they shouldn't stop trying. The more constructive response is to recognize that "history" itself has a history, and that popular perceptions of the importance of Lewis and Clark need to be explained—or, as they would say, "historicized," not derided. Further, the expedition's outcome proved unimportant only in relative terms, because Jefferson had such high expectations for it (expectations that may have driven Lewis crazy), and because the broader geopolitical situation seemed so precarious as the Louisiana crisis came to a head in 1803. In his instructions, Jefferson wrote the script for Lewis and Clark to be American heroes, advance agents of American empire in a dangerous and contested frontier region. They played their parts admirably, but the story line shifted in unanticipated directions: as the Louisiana crisis passed, foreign threats receded and American traders solidified their control over the Missouri River trade. When measured by the standard of the expedition's consequences, the stature of Lewis and Clark diminishes accordingly. But in their own historical moment, the explorers themselves were rightly impressed with—at times, oppressed by—the portentous significance of their mission. In celebrating Lewis and Clark's heroism, modern admirers may lose sight of the geopolitical contingencies, substituting in their stead an outward-bound man-in-nature adventure saga. At the same time, however, they have a much better sense of the expedition's epochal importance to Jefferson and his contemporaries than nay-saying historians intent on matching consequences with causes.

Across the Continent begins with two historical essays that reconstruct the expedition's geopolitical context. Alan Taylor illuminates the strong connection between empire, science, and commerce in the heroic age of exploration prior to Lewis and Clark. The lucrative sea otter trade spurred imperial commercial rivalries along the northwestern rain coast. For Jefferson, Mackenzie's transcontinental trek across modern-day Canada in 1793 added an ominous new element of risk to the equation. British maritime supremacy combined with commercial ties with Indians across the continent, from the plains to the Pacific, threatened to encircle the United States on the north and west and jeopardize its tenuous claims to the vast region covered by the Louisiana Purchase. Jenry Morsman suggests that these security concerns were paramount for Jefferson, who recognized that unexpected difficulties in crossing the Rocky Mountains were, in fact, a boon to the new nation. Here, at last, was the kind of natural boundary that could guarantee national security. Easy passage through the mountains would certainly promote continent-spanning trade networks, but it would also open the continent to penetration from powerful imperial foes—as the Mississippi threatened to do before the Americans finally gained control of New Orleans in the Louisiana Purchase.

Taylor and Morsman remind us that Jefferson's hopes for an expansive republican empire were shadowed by profound anxieties. "Manifest destiny" was not yet a self-evident proposition; the new nation's imperial rivals—much more powerful in conventional terms and attracted by the extraordinary profits of the fur trade—might still extend their influence far into the North American hinterland. Later generations of Americans would emphasize the importance of a "natural," seemingly irresistible tide of settlement for the expansion of the union. But settlement was stretched thin in the early decades of the nineteenth century—and the loyalties of settlers themselves proved notoriously fickle in these years. In any event, the tide of settlement—spurred by the expansion of plantation slavery in the Old Southwest and of wheat farming in the Northwest—would not fill up the cis-Mississippi region or push significantly beyond the river for decades. The consolidation of American empire in the trans-Mississippi West would depend instead on the vigorous exercise of the power of the federal government: to remove or preempt imperial rivals and successor states; to pacify, domesticate, remove, or extirpate Indian nations that obstructed American access to crucial resources; to establish legal and political regimes that would promote and manage settlement, in the process privatizing the public domain—once it had been effectively cleared of conflicting claims and claimants.

Kenneth Prewitt and David Thomas show how the technologies that transformed the West emerged out of Enlightenment conceptions of science and empire. If the mythologized Lewis and Clark seem somehow disconnected from "history"—if their imperial mission has been obscured by the massive changes that followed in their wake; if, as a result, their observations and calculations, their natural history and their ethnography now seem like disinterested "science"—their sponsor Jefferson is more obviously implicated in the historical processes of nation making. Prewitt, a public policy expert who served as director of the 2000 United States Census, and Thomas, an anthropologist at the American Museum of Natural History, both bring a historical perspective to the scientific endeavors that marked, bounded, named, and counted the peoples of the American West. Both are self-conscious practitioners of social and human science disciplines that have played a crucial role in the making of America, disciplines that bear the enduring stamp of the Enlightenment generally, and of Jefferson in particular.

Jefferson and fellow practitioners of the emergent disciplines of demography and anthropology sought to impose principles of order on their new world: science served their nation-making project. With their unpublished journals and patchwork of data and observations, Lewis and Clark may not have made the grade as "scientists," but Jefferson's design for the expedition epitomized the Enlightenment quest for order and control. Enlightened natural history embraced ethnography, the study of peoples and cultures in newly discovered landscapes, as well as the identification and classification of new species and the mapping of rivers and geologic formations. Enlightened statesmen applied these same scientific principles to nation making by defining and delimiting, counting and representing, the "people" and their territory. The "natural" order of things could be deduced from the observations, specimens, and artifacts collected by Lewis and Clark and other explorers and displayed to didactic effect in museums and cabinets of curiosities. Jefferson thus transformed his main entrance hall at Monticello into one of the first natural history "museums" in America, cramming it with Indian artifacts from the expedition as well as with curiosities from around the globe. These collections and displays were byproducts of the Enlightenment's "scientific colonialism"; they helped order and define the new nation and its seemingly boundless domain.

Prewitt and Thomas both look at the historical context in which decisions about counting and ordering in the new nation were first made. The 1790 census, which Prewitt analyzes, counted Americans in an arbitrary but orderly manner. The proto-anthropology of the nineteenth and early twentieth centuries described by Thomas also ordered people, in this case Native Americans, according to the precepts of natural history. People were named, or renamed; marked by boundaries; and placed on maps that defined a cultural and political landscape. The Enlightenment legacy Prewitt and Thomas confront in their respective fields is the tendency to see these ordering systems as somehow natural, inevitable, and unproblematic. For better or worse, these ways of counting, naming, and mapping have all left their imprint on the nation and its peoples.

Dividing the nation into different kinds of people—especially along the lines of race and ethnicity—each with a distinctive historical relation to the nation's civic community, leads directly to the culture wars and identity politics surrounding the nation's anniversaries, from the Columbian quincentenary to the Lewis and Clark bicentennial. Jefferson can hardly be held accountable for racialized thinking in modern America, but Prewitt shows that counting and sorting Americans by race in the first federal census—supervised by Secretary of State Jefferson—constituted the first great effort to depict the nation in scientific terms. Ordering people by race avoided the uncertainties of multiple, ambiguous, and fluid classifications: how, for instance, could census takers distinguish farmers (who engaged in small-scale domestic manufacture) from artisans and manufacturers (who farmed)? In the dynamic circumstances of the new republic, any such effort to codify the social order was bound to fail. Racial distinctions, by contrast, proved much more compatible with the goals of nation building.

Anthropologists moved into the West well after Lewis and Clark encountered people with flexible and multiple racial and tribal identities such as the iconic Sacagawea and her son. Yet early anthropologists were more interested in ideal types, categorizing native people into distinct tribal groups with distinctive histories. Their contemporary successors question the Enlightenment legacy of conflating arbitrary systems of classification with the "natural" order of things—ironically, their unwillingness to embrace "essentialist" group definitions has on occasion been invoked to deny federal recognition to Indian communities who have historically thought of themselves as "tribes."[14] This fundamental change in anthropological thinking from Jefferson's time to our own raises questions about his iconic status as a founder of the discipline.

Some of Jefferson's questions for Lewis and Clark, his correspondence with fellow natural philosophers, and his commentaries in *Notes on the State of Virginia* all foreshadow the four-field approach of modern anthropology (cultural anthropology, archaeology, linguistics, and physical anthropology). The questions that engaged Jefferson about the origins and characteristics of the "races" would remain paramount in the pre-Darwinian world of nineteenth-century America. Some commentators speculated that the Indians were not indigenous people at all but were rather recent arrivals who had supplanted a more sophisticated race of "mound builders," creators of the massive earthworks and burial mounds that drew the colonists' attention.[15] Controversy over Indian origins and history raised further questions about the Indians who survived the onslaught of white civilization: Were they all of the same race, or of the same type? To address these questions, as well as to fill in museum cases, the practice of collecting of Indian objects and of measuring and storing Indian bones began and continued unabated well into the twentieth century, until finally outlawed by federal legislation. For more than a century, Indians, dead or living, were objects of intensive anthropological study as their remains accumulated in museum storage areas.[16] These orderings by race and by tribe are a disciplinary—and national—legacy of Enlightenment science.

The native people who occupied and continue to occupy the complex cultural landscape that Lewis and Clark encountered have not been given an equal hearing in the recounting of Western history. Thomas's essay and the concluding essay by Douglas Seefeldt bring us to a final important question: Who gets to tell the nation's history? Though the question is by now well rehearsed, it becomes particularly urgent, Seefeldt remarks, on the occasion of anniversaries, which "make excellent platforms for both commemoration and dissent." Angry critics have challenged the dominant, progressive narrative of American history—particularly the celebratory account of westward exploration and settlement in which Lewis and

Clark figure so prominently—and have begun to elaborate counternarratives from alternative perspectives.

Seefeldt focuses on two recent controversies in the Southwest that illuminate what's at stake in these memory wars. The first concerns the commemoration (and denunciation) of the Spanish colonizer Don Juan de Oñate; the second considers the scandal surrounding Ramón Gutiérrez's influential academic study *When Jesus Came, the Corn Mothers Went Away*.[17] In both cases, Indians felt their perspective had been ignored and their history disrespected. They framed their complaints in essentialist terms: only those who had lived their lives as Pueblo Indians and embraced their worldview could possibly write accurately about Pueblo encounters with the Spanish.

Anthropologists now like to think that their discipline can give voice to past generations, and particularly to those who have not been heard in the dominant national narrative. But anthropologists who study American Indians have had to wrestle with the fact that most of them have been outsiders. Indians have been objects of study, observed from a distance. Was something missing? Or was this detachment exactly what the science called for: the distance that allows for objective analysis? Was the massive compilation of supposed social facts, from kinship systems to skull measurements, offering a voice, an alternative narrative? Or was the anthropological voice simply one more facet of the dominant narrative?

Over the last generation, indigenous peoples' challenges to the scientific authority of anthropology (and social history) have become increasingly effective, in and beyond the academy. In a dramatic turnaround, federal legislation now limits access to objects that anthropologists once called "data," and that Indian people call "sacred objects," including ritual objects and bones. And the demand that Indians' perspectives on their own histories be acknowledged and incorporated in the larger narrative of American history is beginning to be met.

We can now hear many voices and competing histories, each privileged by the narrator's "positionality" or cultural identity. The danger, of course, is that these voices will become increasingly unintelligible to each other. Can oral history, tradition, and history be worked into the same capacious narrative, or do they necessarily conjure up different worlds? Does every cultural encounter engender divergent, incommensurate perspectives? The histories of our disciplines, anthropology and history, incline us to a more hopeful conclusion. No single voice can write the history that Americans will need in the future; no single group can stand in for all of us, and no group—however "people" or "tribe" may be defined or deconstructed—can ever be understood in isolation.

It is two hundred years since Lewis and Clark ventured into Indian country, and the time to hear native voices is long overdue. We Americans constantly construct new narratives, new identities, new mythical realities. The challenge is to rise above isolated and isolating histories, to find ourselves in the web of interlocking perspectives described by Seefeldt, to seek connections among the many points of observation, experience, and understanding that we share. Across the continent there are many perspectives, some still rarely and some only lately heard. These perspectives can teach us who we have been—and who we might be—as a people.

NOTES

1. William Clark entries, Sept. 17 and 23, 1806, in Gary E. Moulton, ed., *The Lewis and Clark Journals: An American Epic of Discovery* (Lincoln, Neb., 2003), 373, 375.

2. Clark, Oct. 23, 1805, ibid., 227.

3. For a game effort to offer an Indian-centered counternarrative, see Thomas P. Slaughter's recently published *Exploring Lewis and Clark: Reflections on Men and Wilderness* (New York, 2003). Slaughter plumbs the explorers' psyches in a way that can only, perversely, deepen their mythic resonance in our self-obsessed, therapeutic age.

4. Patricia Limerick, *Legacy of Conquest: The Unbroken Past of the American West* (New York, 1987).

5. Gary E. Moulton, ed., *The Journals of the Lewis and Clark Expedition*, 13 vols. (Lincoln, Neb., 1979–2001).

6. See Elizabeth A. Fenn's excellent study, *Pox Americana: The Great Smallpox Epidemic of 1775–1782* (New York, 2001), 224–58.

7. Clark, Nov. 28, 1784, and Meriwether Lewis, Aug. 17, 1805, in Moulton, *Lewis and Clark Journals*, 71, 186.

8. Lewis, June 7, 1805, ibid., 125.

9. Lewis, Aug. 14, 1805, ibid., 180.

10. Lewis, Aug. 11, 1805, ibid., 172.

11. Lewis, July 27, 1806, ibid., 345. The definitive study is James Ronda, *Lewis and Clark among the Indians* (Lincoln, Neb., 1984); on the killings, see 238–44.

12. For an excellent recent study of the Louisiana Purchase (which was very important but has attracted relatively little bicentennial attention), see Jon Kukla, *A Wilderness So Immense: The Louisiana Purchase and the Destiny of America* (New York, 2003).

13. Lewis, May 23, 1806, in Moulton, *Lewis and Clark Journals,* 318.

14. See James Clifford's discussion of the Mashpee in James Clifford, *The Predicament of Culture* (Cambridge, Mass., 1988).

15. See Robert Silverberg's overview in *Mound Builders of Ancient America: The Archaeology of a Myth* (Greenwich, Conn., 1968).

16. See David Hurst Thomas's detailed review in *Skull Wars: Kennewick Man, Archaeology, and the Battle for Native American Identity* (New York, 2000).

17. Ramón A. Gutiérrez, *When Jesus Came, the Corn Mothers Went Away: Marriage, Sexuality and Power in New Mexico, 1500–1846* (Stanford, Calif., 1991).

JEFFERSON'S PACIFIC

> The Science of
> Distant Empire,
> 1768–1811
>
> Alan Taylor

As TRADITIONALLY TOLD, THE MERI-
wether Lewis and William Clark expedition across the American
West to the Pacific was an adventure into the great unknown and a
story of national fulfillment. That version, I will argue, slights the
global context and the international significance of their exploration. We need to recover the expedition's proper place within a
prior and expanding series of European probes, both geographic
and commercial, into the North Pacific. Far from heading out blind,
Lewis and Clark sought a new American route to a Pacific world
recently delineated by Spanish, Russian, British, and French maritime explorers. Their discoveries inspired commercial mariners,
who developed a profitable and globe-spanning trade in European
metal goods, Northwest American sea otter pelts, and Chinese luxury goods during the late 1780s. The profits also attracted a British-
Canadian, Alexander Mackenzie, who led an overland party across
Canada to the Pacific in 1793—anticipating Lewis and Clark by a
decade.[1]

The various probes combined science and commerce and inspired a heated competition between rival empires for information about, and access to, the Pacific world. That competition brought the diverse peoples all around the Pacific Rim into new relationships over very long distances through the medium of European ships. And the growing integration of the Pacific into a European-managed market economy obliged the native peoples of the Pacific Rim to adapt to unprecedented and traumatic changes in their world.

The Pacific exploration by Europeans troubled the leaders of the new United States. Although their western boundary then lay at the Mississippi, American leaders assumed that their people enjoyed a natural and providential right ultimately to settle and dominate North America to the Pacific. At the end of the eighteenth century, however, as the Pacific became defined on global maps, in published journals, and in the diplomatic discourse of Europeans, Americans could not take for granted their eventual possession of the continent's west coast.[2]

No American saw the Pacific implications more clearly than Thomas Jefferson, who combined a special interest in science with a diplomatic expertise in Europe. As early as 1783, he was casting about for an American to conduct an overland exploration in search of the Pacific—and he explicitly couched that search in dread of a British alternative. Jefferson gave scant thought to the Russians, considered the French as friends, and regarded the Spanish as weak: as easy marks for an inevitable American expansion. But Jefferson obsessively feared the British empire as a formidable, relentless, and insidious foe to the American republic. He worried that the emerging web of Pacific exploration and commerce would enable the British to renew their empire in a new and especially promising quarter, one that would curtail American expansion westward. That worry imparted an urgency to Jefferson's long-standing interest in the transcontinental exploration to the Pacific.[3]

Science

Until the mid-eighteenth century, the Pacific Ocean remained the most mysterious part of the temperate earth to Europeans and their American colonists. On the far side of the planet from Europe, the Pacific was especially difficult for Europeans to reach. From the west, the only maritime access came via the distant, stormy, and rocky Strait of Magellan at the southern tip of South America. Although long hoped for, and persistently sought, the fabled Northwest Passage through northern North America remained elusive. The Pacific was also so huge—covering a third of the planet—that European mariners readily got lost for want of accurate techniques for determining longitude. Once they found a secure track across the Pacific, mariners clung to it, which discouraged new discoveries.

During the early sixteenth century, the Spanish mariner Ferdinand Magellan entered and crossed the Pacific via the strait that now bears his name. Following up on Magellan's discoveries, the Spanish founded a colony at Manila in the Philippines and, during the 1560s, initiated a trade across the Pacific to Mexico. Along the trade route, the Spanish discovered a few inhabited islands, principally Guam in the Marianas, where they established a small settlement to resupply their ships with water and provisions. Following the same narrow trade passage in one vessel once a year from the Philippines to Mexico, the Spanish preserved their ignorance of most of the Pacific. During the sixteenth century, the Spanish did probe the California coast north of Mexico, but they decided against colonization. And the northwestern coast of North America to Alaska and the Aleutians remained unknown to the Spanish—or any other Europeans—until the eighteenth century. Nonetheless, the Spanish insisted that they owned the Pacific and threatened to destroy the intruding ships of other European empires.[4]

The Spanish concealed what they did know about the Pacific, lest the information only benefit the piracy of their English and French rivals. In secret files, the Spanish buried the maps and reports of their explorers, which hurt their successors, who repeated the mistakes as well as the "discoveries" of forgotten predecessors. Beginning with Sir Francis Drake in 1578–79, English marauders occasionally broke into the Pacific to plunder Hispanic shipping and seaports. But periodic hit-and-run raids generated little new information and no lasting benefit to the rival empires.[5]

During the eighteenth century, the Russian, British, and French governments began systematically and competitively to explore the Pacific Ocean in search of imperial advantage. The decline of

Spanish naval power enabled rival vessels more securely to venture into the Pacific. New and more precise instruments—especially the chronometer—permitted mariners to ascertain their longitude in distant oceans. Better instruments also led to the development of far more accurate maps and charts, which were critical to navigating the vast reaches of the open Pacific to find and return to far-flung islands.[6]

Spain's rivals invoked service to science as their right to explore the Pacific, in defiance of Spanish protests. With the zeal of converts, the rivals treated Spanish secrecy and protectiveness as intellectual crimes against human progress. Of course, the European rivals celebrated science as a universal ideal in order to pursue their special geopolitical interests to investigate distant places and to trade with exotic peoples. Consequently, the Spanish ambassador was skeptical when a British official defended Pacific exploration on the grounds "that the English Nation is actuated merely by desiring to know as much as possible with regard to the planet which we inhabit."[7]

Part of the broad intellectual movement known as the Enlightenment, science was a new mix of ideology and methodology. Educated Europeans sought more systematically and more empirically to collect and organize new information about everything on earth (and beyond). Although certainly employed as a tool of empire, science exercised its own influence over imperial policy. A new interest group developed to urge their governments to spend money on science. For example, in Britain the Royal Society united leading scientists, prominent merchants, and some powerful aristocrats into a body with a growing political influence in Parliament and with the Crown. In 1768, when the Royal Society wanted astronomers sent to the South Pacific to view the transit of Venus, the British Admiralty was happy to provide a naval vessel and crew, at public expense. Of course, it helped that the Board of Admiralty concluded that such an expedition would also serve an important political goal: to trump the Spanish and beat the French in exploring and exploiting the unknown reaches of the Pacific.[8]

As never before, the eighteenth-century imperial explorers self-consciously wrote and acted in the name of science. Although commanded by naval officers, and worked by common sailors, the voyages also included cartographers, astronomers, naturalists, and artists to study and depict the waters, skies, soils, plants, animals, weather, and peoples of distant coasts. In 1771, when Captain James Cook returned to England from the South Pacific, his team of naturalists unloaded more than 500 bird skins, another 500 specimens of fish, more than 1,000 new species of plants, 1,300 sketches and paintings—as well as an array of Polynesian clothes, tools, weapons, musical instruments, and vocabularies.[9]

The new methods and schemes for gathering and organizing information fed a sense of imperial mastery and destiny. Historian Richard Drayton observes, "Systems of classification, as much as sextants and chronometers, allowed Europeans to perceive themselves as the magistrates of Providence, equipped by their knowledge of its laws with responsibilities over all of creation." The systematic collection of data about new plants and animals helped to identify marketable commodities for commercial exploitation. And new knowledge of distant peoples promised to facilitate their eventual pacification as imperial subjects.[10]

In eighteenth-century Europe, wealth and prowess increasingly accrued to nations that took the lead in discovering and analyzing new information about distant places and peoples. And, because scientific publications circulated throughout the learned circles of the European elite, systematic exploration became a medium for the competitive pursuit of national prestige. Indeed, the collection and publication of geographic information became critical to diplomatic claims to new lands. For example, Captain Cook urged that his Pacific findings be quickly "published by Authority to fix the prior right of discovery beyond dispute." By promptly and officially printing Cook's maps and journals, the British government reaped credit for "discovering" much of the Pacific Northwest in 1778, when, in fact, secretive Spanish expeditions had already visited that coast in 1774 and 1775. Confronted with a European diplomatic and scientific community inclined to credit Cook with primacy, the frustrated Spanish had to send more conspicuous expeditions in 1788–89 to gather evidence from the northwestern Indians that the 1774–75 voyages had, in fact, existed.[11]

Alaska and California

During the sixteenth and seventeenth centuries, as western Europeans headed across the Atlantic to colonize North America from the west, Russians expanded eastward across Siberia, reaching the Pacific by 1639. During the 1680s and 1690s, they occupied the Kamchatka Peninsula, which became their base for forays into the North Pacific. The Russians primarily came as fur traders seeking the Siberian sable, initially for the European market. But in 1689 the Russians opened an even more lucrative trade with China, via the Siberian border town of Kaikhta, where the Russians obtained, in return, Chinese porcelains, teas, and silks. To procure furs, the Russian traders, known as *promyshlenniki,* relied upon armed force to intimidate the Siberian peoples into paying an annual tribute in furs.[12]

During the early eighteenth century, the Russian imperial court at St. Petersburg organized and financed official expeditions of oceanic exploration beyond Kamchatka into the North Pacific. Sensitive that western Europeans regarded Russia as backward and marginal, Russian officials vowed to demonstrate their sophistication and relevance as a scientific power. Russian imperialists envied the western European success in geographic discovery and in developing profitable commercial colonies in North America. By joining the competition for knowledge and commerce in North America, the Russians hoped to prove that they belonged culturally, commercially, and politically to Europe. They meant to compete in the accumulation of both scientific knowledge and colonial wealth—pursuits that had become interdependent. In search of respect to the west, the Russians pursued information and colonial power to the east.

Russian geographers and officials reasoned that the northwest coast of North America could be found by ships sailing eastward from the northeast coast of Siberia. Such naval exploration might, at last, reveal the rumored and coveted maritime passage through North America, so long suspected and so vainly sought from the Atlantic side by the western Europeans. To test these possibilities, in 1729 and 1741 the Russian Crown sponsored exploration by the Danish mariner Vitus Bering and his Russian lieutenant, Alexeii Chirikov. The Crown also sent along two renowned international scientists, Georg Wilhelm Steller, a German naturalist, and Louis Delisle de la Croyere, a French astronomer. By gathering and publishing new data, the scientists would strengthen the Russian diplomatic claim to new lands.

In 1729, Bering and Chirikov determined that an extension of the Pacific Ocean, now known as the Bering Sea, bounded Asia on the east, but, shrouded by dense fogs, they failed to detect the North American shore. Twelve years later, Bering and Chirikov made it across the Bering Sea to find the rainy Aleutian Islands and the mountainous southern coast of Alaska. Separated by a storm, Chirikov and his vessel returned to Kamchatka in October, while Bering suffered shipwreck and scurvy on an uninhabited island in the Bering Sea. Compelled to spend the long, dark, frigid winter in huts dug into the earth, Bering and half his men died of some combination of frostbite, hunger, disease, and exhaustion. The following spring, the survivors rebuilt their ship and sailed back to Kamchatka, arriving in August 1742.[13]

They returned with the pelts of nine hundred sea otters, which netted high prices and keen interest from the fur traders of Kamchatka. Having depleted the sables of Siberia, the *promyshlenniki* needed a new source of luxury furs for their Chinese market. Beginning in the mid-1740s, small bands of *promyshlenniki* sailed to the western Aleutians to compel the native Aleut peoples to become market hunters. During the 1760s, as the market hunting exterminated the sea otter and reduced the Aleut, the *promyshlenniki* extended their operations eastward to Umnak, Unalaska, and Kodiak, larger islands at the eastern end of the Aleutian chain and off the southern coast of Alaska.

During the 1780s, a cartel of major Siberian merchants tried to control, regulate, and reorganize the chaotic and destructive exploitation of the sea otter and the Aleut. Led by Grigorii Ivanovich Shelikhov, in 1784 the merchants founded a small settlement on Kodiak Island, the first permanent Russian position in North America. In 1799, the Russian government rewarded Shelikhov's firm with a charter as the Russian-American Company. The charter provided a twenty-year monopoly over the Aleutian and Alaskan fur trading, and the powers to govern the little colony of Alaska. That year the company also expanded eastward to tap the sea otter pelts in the waters off the Alaska panhandle, founding a new fortified settlement at Sitka on a wooded island.[14]

During the mid-1760s, the Spanish ambassador to St. Petersburg belatedly learned about Bering's expedition, the *promyshlenniki* operations in the Aleutians, and the Russian plans to explore farther south and west. At the same time, Spanish officials worried over exaggerated reports that British fur traders from Hudson's Bay had crossed the northern Great Plains and the Rocky Mountains to approach the Pacific. In 1768, the royal inspector general in New Spain, José de Galvez, concluded, "There is no doubt that in any case we have the English very close to our towns of New Mexico, and not very far from the west coast of this continent."[15]

As a precaution meant to secure the unguarded northwestern door to precious Mexico against both the Russians and the British, in 1768 Galvez sent a small military expedition to occupy the best harbors with a system of forts, known as presidios, supported by missions run by Franciscan priests. Lacking sufficient Hispanics to colonize California, Galvez meant to turn the native Indians into Hispanics by indoctrination at missions. The expedition's commander, Captain Gaspar de Portola, fortified Monterey to, in his words, "defend us from attacks by the Russians, who were about to invade us." In fact, there were no Russians within two thousand miles. But news of Monterey alarmed the Russians, who feared that the Spanish were coming to attack them in Kamchatka and the Aleutians. Just as the Spanish overreacted to overstated reports of the Russian advance, in 1770 the Russians hastily bolstered their defenses against the supposed Spanish threat. Pacific exploration had the elements of a farce—although natives ultimately experienced it as tragedy.[16]

Neither the Spanish nor the Russians effectively occupied their vast geographic claims. By 1784, Alta California had only two agricultural towns (San Jose and Los Angeles), four presidios, and nine missions. The approximately nine hundred Hispanic colonists were stretched thin along a five-hundred-mile-long coast from San Francisco to San Diego and scattered among thousands of Indians. In 1800, Russian America had only about four hundred colonists. Confined to a few pockets on coastal islands, they avoided the vast and forbidding interior, which remained a daunting mystery.[17]

The British

During the 1760s, a third European empire—the British—began systematically to explore the Pacific. Despite their great military victory over France in the Seven Years' War that ended in 1763, the British dreaded that their imperial rival might exploit some new opportunity for trade and colonies in that great, mysterious corner of the globe, the Pacific Ocean. Defining the Pacific geography seemed a cost-effective insurance policy against a French comeback as a colonial and naval power. No British politician wished later to be accused of losing something valuable in the Pacific to their enemy. National pride and fear, as much as national interest, drove the British to explore the Pacific—just as similar anxieties had pushed the Spanish into California.[18]

In 1768, the British Admiralty and the Royal Society entrusted Pacific exploration to Captain James Cook, an especially disciplined navigator and geographer. Following Bering's example, Cook brought along a few scientists, principally the botanist Joseph Banks. In two long and celebrated voyages, in 1768–71 and 1772–75, Cook systematically crisscrossed the South Pacific and mapped the coasts of Australia and New Zealand—previously known only vaguely from hasty Dutch encounters a century before. Cook's reconnaissance facilitated subsequent British colonization of Australia, which began with an arrival of 723 convicts at Botany Bay in early 1788. The two voyages established Cook's reputation as the preeminent explorer of the eighteenth century. More methodical and thorough than any predecessor, Cook developed maps, charts, and journals of unprecedented precision, thereafter defining the Pacific in print for distant Europeans. He also set the scientific protocols emulated by subsequent explorers seeking equal credit for their empires.[19]

In 1776–79, for his third and final voyage, Cook probed the North Pacific in search of the fabled Northwest Passage around or through North America. Sailing northeast from Tahiti in January 1778, Cook was pleasantly surprised to stumble upon the Hawaiian Islands, a midoceanic and subtropical range of volcanic peaks inhabited by Polynesians who had arrived about nine hundred years before. After two weeks of mostly harmonious exchanges—both diplomatic and commercial—Cook sailed northward in renewed search of North America's northwest coast, arriving there in the spring of 1778.[20]

Cook and his crew found an elaborate native culture adapted to a mild and rainy climate abounding in timber, fish, sea otters, seals, and whales. Well fed by fishing and marine hunting, the rain coast natives developed a dense population. Although divided into at least six language groups and hundreds of villages, the rain coast peoples shared important cultural elements including complex social hierarchies, elaborate ceremonies, and a highly stylized art expressed mostly in wood carving. Almost every village was independent and organized along kinship lines, with leadership divided among multiple chiefs. In addition to waging far-ranging wars for slaves, the rain coast peoples conducted elaborate chains of trade along the coast with one another and up the major rivers with the Indians of the mountainous interior.[21]

In the spring of 1778, Cook spent a month at Nootka, an inlet on the west coast of Vancouver Island, to repair and refit his ships and to obtain fresh water and provisions. The local natives called the place Yuquot and themselves the Moachat, but Cook's misnomer "Nootka" has stuck ever since on both place and people. They had some past experience with European mariners and ships because of brief Spanish visits in 1774 and 1775. Eager to procure metal goods, the Moachat paddled out in many canoes to meet Cook's two ships and initiate trading. The rain coast peoples belied the classic stereotype of naïve natives easily cheated by European traders bearing a few beads. A scientist on Cook's expedition complained that the rain coast natives were "very keen traders, getting as much as they could for everything they had; always asking for more, give them what you would."[22]

Ultimately, Cook's crew had no reason to complain of their transactions with the Moachat and their rain coast neighbors. During that spring and summer, the mariners purchased 1,500 sea otter pelts for about six pence apiece in English goods. A year later, en route homeward, they stopped in China, where each pelt sold for goods worth about one hundred dollars. Launched as science, Cook's voyage evolved smoothly into commerce—which demonstrated the close relationship of capitalism and science in British thought and practice.[23]

Upon departing Nootka, Cook and his men spent the summer and fall of 1778 following and charting the coast northeastward to Alaska and the Bering Strait. In November 1778, the mariners sailed back to Hawaii for a warm-weather base to rest and resupply through the winter. In February 1779, however, Cook died in a violent melee provoked by a bungled attempt to arrest some Hawaiians for the theft of some iron tools and a small boat. Cook's successor, Lieutenant Charles Clerke, sailed away in March to complete their coastal survey of Alaska, before proceeding to China with a cargo of sea otter pelts.[24]

Upon returning to London, some of the crewmen published accounts of their voyage in 1781 and 1782, and Cook's official journals appeared in print in 1784. Those publications, especially their news of the profitable sea otter trade, aroused intense interest by European governments. Determined to match the British coup, in 1785 the French dispatched the Comte de La Perouse and a team of scientists on two ships to Hawaii, California, the Northwest Coast, and Alaska. Unfortunately, in 1788 off the coast of Australia a cyclone destroyed both ships, killing all on board. Even the Spanish began to experiment in the game of scientific exploration, sending a nautical expedition led by Alejandro Malaspina to the North Pacific in 1791–92. Determined to trump Cook's voyage, the Spanish team of naturalists, astronomers, and artists more closely examined the region's natives, topography, flora, and fauna of the rain coast. But Spanish secrecy died hard, ultimately frustrating the whole purpose behind the expensive expedition. Upon returning to Spain in 1794, Malaspina ran afoul of the conservative and suspicious authorities, who imprisoned the explorer and buried his report in a confidential archive, where it remained unpublished until 1885.[25]

British merchants were more successful in exploiting Cook's discoveries, dispatching some twenty-six ships laden with trade goods to Nootka and other rain coast harbors between 1785 and 1790. Proceeding on to China with sea otter pelts, the traders purchased Chinese porcelain, tea, spices, and silks for conveyance and sale in Europe.

Once the rare experience of government-sponsored explorers, circumnavigation became a commercial commonplace during the late 1780s.[26]

Americans learned of Cook's exploration from John Ledyard. Born in Connecticut, Ledyard had served as a British marine on Cook's final voyage. In 1782, Ledyard deserted from the British service, returned to the United States, and, a year later, published a journal of his Pacific voyage. Ledyard extolled the "astonishing profits" of the sea otter trade, which intrigued American merchants, who sent their first two vessels to Nootka in 1788. By the end of the decade, seven American ships had visited that coast to trade for sea otters. Many more followed during the 1790s as American shippers eclipsed the British, who were hampered by the monopoly to the China trade that the British empire had awarded to the East India Company.[27]

The new trade alarmed the Spanish authorities, who perceived yet another ominous intrusion uncomfortably close to their precious Mexico. Indeed, from a Spanish perspective, the rival probes were converging into a formidable threat. In late 1788, the viceroy of New Spain warned his superiors in Madrid:

> We should not be surprised if the English colonies of America, republican and independent, put into practice the design of discovering a safe port on the South Sea, and try to sustain it by crossing the immense land of this continent above our possessions of Texas, New Mexico, and the Californias. Much more might be expected of an active nation that bases all its hopes and resources on navigation and commerce; and, in truth, it would obtain the richest trade of Great China and India if it were to succeed in establishing a colony on the west coasts of America. Obviously, this is a feat that would take many years, but I truly believe that as of now we ought to try to elude its effects, all the more when we see that now we are threatened by the probes of Russia, and those that can be made by the English from Botany Bay, which they are populating.

A year later, the viceroy sent a naval expedition to Nootka to seize four British ships, arresting their captains and crews.[28]

In early 1790, news of the seizures reached and outraged British authorities, who threatened war and mobilized their fleet. A British emissary approached the American administration of George Washington, seeking military cooperation against the Spanish colonies. The secretary of the treasury, Alexander Hamilton, favored an alliance with the British, but the Anglophobic secretary of state, Thomas Jefferson, successfully counseled continuing neutrality. Unprepared for conflict, the Spanish backed down, releasing the British ships, cargos, and prisoners. The Spanish also paid reparations for damages and conceded Britain's right to trade with the natives of the Pacific Northwest. In 1795, the Spanish abandoned the small fort that they had erected at Nootka, and the delighted Moachat demolished the buildings to harvest the nails and hinges.[29]

Mackenzie

Cook's third voyage had roughly closed the cartographic gap between Spanish California and Russian Alaska. Cook's thorough exploration virtually killed the myth of an accessible saltwater Northwest Passage through North America. But, at the same time, he suggested a new fantasy: that a capacious inlet—now known as Cook's Inlet—on the coast of Alaska received a large river that flowed westward from the interior.[30]

Such a river promised relatively easy access to the Pacific from the center of North America, which especially intrigued British fur traders based in Montreal. After the British conquest of French Canada in 1760, British firms took control of the fur trade that extended westward via the Great Lakes into the Manitoba country around Lake Winnipeg. The British traders also assumed the former French beliefs that the Rocky Mountains were low and narrow— scant obstacle to western exploration and commerce—and that Lake Winnipeg lay near a navigable river called "Oregan," which flowed westward to the Pacific. "Oregan" seemed ever closer as the British traders probed westward in search of new Indian hunters able to supply large quantities of beaver pelts. In 1767–68, some traders reached and wintered on the Saskatchewan River, which served, a decade later, as the base for Peter Pond to open the fur trade along the beaver-rich Athabaska River and Lake to the north. From Indian informants, Pond learned of the Great Slave Lake, which emptied into an immense river—known to the Indians as the Deh-Cho—that evidently flowed westward toward the Pacific. During a 1785 visit to Montreal, Pond read accounts of Cook's third voyage and latched onto the explorer's suggestion that Cook's Inlet received an immense river, "Cook's River." Equating the Deh-Cho with Cook's River and the fabled "Oregan," Pond planned to find and descend the river to the Pacific. To systematize his discoveries and speculations and to publicize his future services as trader and explorer, Pond prepared a large and detailed map, linking Canada's interior with the Pacific coast as delineated by Cook.[31]

Pond warned British officials to act decisively before Russian and American fur traders occupied and preempted the Pacific Northwest. Endorsing Pond's scheme of western exploration and occupation, Lieutenant Governor Henry Hamilton of Quebec advised his superiors in London, "The prosecution of [Pond's discoveries] may lead to establishments, at this period (considering the active and encroaching spirit of our neighbors) particularly necessary." As always, fear of imperial rivals was the most powerful incentive for Pacific enterprise.[32]

However, in wooing support from Montreal traders and British officials, Pond had three strikes against him. First, he was poorly educated and lacked the sophistication and equipment to make accurate readings of his location or to write and publish his accomplishments in the scientific and literary style. Indeed, Pond miscalculated the longitude of the Great Slave Lake by about seven hundred miles to the west—halving its actual distance to the Pacific and rendering his theory more plausible in the short term. In a new era of exploration as science, Pond was too crude to play the game well. Second, he was an American by birth, which became a liability in the British empire after the thirteen colonies rebelled. He confirmed and compounded that distrust by giving a copy of his map to the American Congress in the vain hope that it might fund his exploration. Third, and worst of all, Pond had a violent temper that led him twice, in 1782 and 1787, to kill rival traders. Ostracized by his partners and facing prosecution, in 1788 Pond fled across the border into the United States, where he languished in poverty and obscurity.[33]

Pond's departure empowered his former protégé, a young trader named Alexander Mackenzie, who had arrived in the Athabaska country in 1787. Inheriting Pond's plan, Mackenzie led a small party of Indians and French Canadians in birch-bark canoes down the Deh-Cho during the summer of 1789. To Mackenzie's chagrin, the river turned northward, reaching the Arctic Ocean rather than the Pacific. Subsequently known as the Mackenzie River, the waterway did prove commercially valuable as a new source of furs for the Montreal cartel, and the 1,120-mile journey established Mackenzie's abilities to lead a small party deep into unknown territory possessed by jealous natives.[34]

Better educated and connected than Pond (and a Scot by birth), Mackenzie secured more official credit for his accomplishments. Attentive to Captain Cook's precedents, Mackenzie cast his reports in the forms and tropes of the new science. In a journal, he detailed observations on botany, zoology, geology, climate, native culture, and latitude and longitude. Merely going somewhere no longer sufficed, for detailed observations made en route became critical to validate exploration in Europe's literary and official circles. Upon returning to Montreal in 1790, Mackenzie continued across the Atlantic to London, where he circulated his journal and his conversation to cultivate patrons in high places: the Admiralty, Colonial Office, War Office, and Royal Society. He arrived at an auspicious moment, when the Nootka crisis with Spain enhanced official and intellectual interest in strengthening British access to the Pacific Northwest. Although Mackenzie had fallen short, he impressed his contacts with the abilities and determination to succeed on a second attempt. Recognizing his own limitations as a scientist, Mackenzie also sought out instruction and equipment to refine his ability to determine his geoposition in renewed exploration.[35]

While obliged to master the scientific style of exploration, Mackenzie also had to have a commercial objective, profitable to himself and his fellow shareholders in Montreal's Northwest Company, which subsidized his ventures. They sought a route across Canada that could enable their capital to profit from the booming sea otter trade of the Pacific Northwest. Rather than haul sea otter pelts eastward via Montreal to London, the Montreal men hoped to send British manufactures westward over land to the rain coast to purchase sea otter pelts for shipment across the Pacific to China. In other words, they hoped to compete with the British and American mariners who reached the Pacific via the long route around the southern tip of South America. A Canadian trade with China, however, would violate the monopoly granted by Parliament to the East India Company, arousing the opposition of an especially powerful interest within the British empire. Consequently, Mackenzie wanted to find the Russian traders in Alaska who had access to China via Kaikhta, in hopes of negotiating their partnership with the Montreal merchants. In prosecuting his transimperial vision of profits, Mackenzie's first loyalty was to himself; his second to the Northwest Company; and only his third lay with the more nebulous British empire with its vested interests, including the East India Company. In such a hierarchy of loyalties, Mackenzie was merely typical of his time and place.[36]

In 1792, Mackenzie returned to the Athabaska country to prepare his second expedition, this time involving about nine men, once again a mix of Indians and French Canadians. In the spring and summer of 1793, they ascended the rocky and rapid Peace River, heading westward into the Rocky Mountains, which proved far higher, wider, and more complex than anticipated. Through trial and error and ultimately with the advice of local Indians, Mackenzie found a way through the mountains to the Bella Coola River, which flowed beneath dark forests of immense trees toward the Pacific.[37]

Mackenzie just missed connecting with a British maritime expedition led by Captain George Vancouver, a protégé of Cook, who had come via Hawaii to survey the northwest coast in June. While trading with the rain coast natives, one of Vancouver's men, Thomas Manby, astutely observed, "As neither Land [n]or Water, stops the car[r]ier of commerce, I dare say, many of our articles have by this time, nearly approached, the opposite side of the Continent, as a continual chain of barter, exists between Tribe and Tribe, through this amazing track of Country, which in time, will no doubt, find their way, to our factories in Canada, or the back settlements of Hudson's bay." Indians had long traversed the mountains that were so mysterious, complicated, and daunting to Mackenzie. And just as Manby had predicted, Mackenzie began to find European metal goods among the Sekani people of the mountains, which confirmed that they knew the trade route to the Pacific. Mackenzie explained that he then set out to "pursue that chain of connexion by which these people obtain their ironwork." Once Mackenzie reached the Nuxalk people on the Bella Coola River, those trade goods proliferated, confirming his proximity to the ocean. The emerging Pacific world of trade that was Mackenzie's goal also generated the tangible clues that drew his party to its destination. The eastward and overland passage of those clues revealed a long-standing web of intertribal connections otherwise opaque to the explorer.[38]

But Vancouver's recent passage did not entirely work to Mackenzie's advantage. The British mariners had riled the Bella Bella people of the river's mouth by firing a warning shot and forcing their way into one Indian home. When Mackenzie reached the coast, his party faced harassment and threats by the irritated Bella Bella.

Obliged to act quickly, Mackenzie enacted the ceremonies of possession expected by Enlightenment exploration. First, he recorded ethnographic, botanical, faunal, and geologic information that matched what he had read in Cook's journals—to document that his party had reached the same coast. Second, Mackenzie employed his bulky navigational instruments (hauled hundreds of miles over rugged terrain for this special moment) to calculate and record latitude and longitude. He noted, "I had now determined my situation, which is the most fortunate circumstance of my long, painful, and perilous journey." Without such measurements for publication at home, Mackenzie's travel and trouble would be for naught. Third, with a paint made of vermilion and grease he inscribed a large rock: "Alexander Mackenzie, from Canada, by land, the twenty-second of July, one thousand seven hundred and ninety-three." Bella Bella people later recalled Mackenzie's behavior with sextant, chronometer, and paint as strange and threatening, as apparent acts of sorcery. Noting their alarm and anger, Mackenzie rapidly finished his inscription and retreated.[39]

Finally, in trade with the friendlier natives known as the Bella Coola, Mackenzie collected sea otter pelts: the consummate trophy proving that he had reached the Northwest Coast. Both coming and going, the goods of the Pacific trade proved essential to Mackenzie's success. Where European trade goods had led Mackenzie over an

Indian trail, an Indian trade good became critical to proving his Pacific arrival to a European audience. Indeed, the sea otter pelt had become the symbol as well as the substance of the profitable trade that drew Europeans (and Americans) into the North Pacific world with its emerging ties to the Chinese market.[40]

Ultimately, none of these ceremonies would matter unless Mackenzie safely returned to Montreal and London with his precious journal and sea otter pelts to demonstrate his accomplishment. On August 24, 1793, Mackenzie reached his Peace River base east of the Rockies, completing a circuit of 108 days (seventy-five out and thirty-three back) and 2,400 miles (about 1,200 each way). Not until the summer of 1794 could he attain Montreal, where he shrewdly plied British officials with tales of adventure, reports of science, and gifts of sea otter pelts. In return, Mackenzie reaped their enthusiastic letters to the home government, endorsing his accomplishment and praising his vision of a global trade through Canada. Obliged to attend to his tangled business concerns in Canada and the United States, Mackenzie could not travel to London until 1800. Only there, at the center of British culture and power, could Mackenzie secure credit and celebrity—as well as official support for his grand commercial plans.[41]

In late 1801 in London, Mackenzie achieved his first goal by publishing his journals with a prestigious firm and with the assistance of a consummate editor. Astutely dedicated to the king, George III, the book became a sensation—required reading for the learned, mercantile, and official classes on both sides of the English Channel and of the Atlantic Ocean. Mackenzie also benefited from the patronage of especially important men: Prince Edward Augustus and Sir Joseph Banks. The prince was the king's son (and the father of Queen Victoria). Banks was an accomplished naturalist; a veteran of Cook's first voyage; the king's preeminent scientific advisor; and the prime conduit for scientific information and patronage in the empire. Banks and Prince Edward arranged for the publication of Mackenzie's journals and for his knighthood by the king in early 1802. That winter Sir Alexander Mackenzie basked in the praise and attention of London's high society.[42]

Frequenting the Colonial Office, Mackenzie tried to convert his new intellectual and social cachet into imperial authorization and funds for his commercial scheme. By establishing fortified trading posts on the rain coast, he argued, the British could succeed where the Spanish had failed, to command the native peoples and sea otters of the Pacific Northwest. According to Mackenzie, the stakes were global: "By opening this intercourse between the Atlantic and Pacific Oceans and forming regular establishments through the interior, at both extremes, as well as along the coasts and islands, the entire command of the fur trade of North America might be obtained. . . . To this might be added the fishing in both seas and the markets of the four quarters of the globe." In particular, Mackenzie urged the construction of armed posts at Nootka Sound and at the mouth of the Columbia River, the largest navigable river in the Pacific Northwest. Otherwise, he warned, the Americans would occupy both.[43]

Unfortunately for Mackenzie, imperial officials were polite but noncommittal. The British government was exhausted of funds and imagination by a long war with France. And Britain's officials were loath to cross the powerful interests—the Hudson's Bay Company and the East India Company—which felt threatened by Mackenzie's proposed end run around their profitable monopoly rights. Even the Northwest Company turned against Mackenzie, convinced that he was insufficiently loyal to its interests. Indeed, he recognized the shorter transit and lower cost of shipping British manufactures to the Pacific Coast via Hudson's Bay rather than through Montreal. Although geographically astute, that proposal alienated Mackenzie's Montreal partners without converting the Hudson Bay Company, which did not wish to share its facilities. Finally, the book that won his fame also worked against his commercial proposal. By narrating so vividly his long and sometimes harrowing journey, Mackenzie won applause for his endurance, courage, and resourcefulness—but undermined the feasibility of his route for commercial transport. Ironically, Mackenzie's grand scheme of overland commerce sank in direct and inverse proportion to his soaring charisma as an explorer.[44]

The President

In 1802, Mackenzie's most avid—but horrified—American reader was the new president, Thomas Jefferson. Ever fearful of British intentions, the president naturally concluded that British officials would, of course, embrace Mackenzie's scheme to occupy the rain coast just to spite the United States. In fact, British officials paid far less attention to the United States than Jefferson believed. Preoccupied with more pressing matters in Europe and India, British ministers wasted relatively little time or energy on the pesky but irrelevant Americans. Moreover, the clashing economic interests within the empire deprived its policies of the coherence, determination, and malignancy that Jefferson imagined. Just as the Spanish had overreacted to the Russians—and the British to the French—so too the Americans fantasized a Pacific threat that demanded a defensive expansion.[45]

The president had long worried that the British or the French would occupy the Pacific Northwest just to frustrate America's proper destiny, as he saw it, to people the continent from coast to coast. In 1783, Jefferson learned that Montreal's traders were trumpeting Peter Pond's discoveries and lobbying the British government to fund an official expedition overland to the Pacific. In the short term, nothing came of that proposal. Instead, the traders had to finance Mackenzie, who could not begin until 1789. But in late 1783, Jefferson assumed that the British government would leap at the chance to outflank the United States. Although he never doubted the sincerity of his own scientific pretensions, Jefferson always saw through those of foreigners: "I find they have subscribed a large sum of money in England for exploring the country from the Missisipi to California. They pretend it is only to promote knolege. I am afraid they have thoughts of colonising into that quarter."[46]

As a congressman and a leader of the American Philosophical Society—Philadelphia's counterpart to London's Royal Society— Jefferson hoped to beat the British in an overland race to the Pacific. In December 1783, he tried to raise funds by a subscription among the society's members, and he hoped to interest George Rogers Clark, a veteran army officer, in leading the expedition. But neither the funds nor Clark were available.[47]

In 1784, Jefferson moved to Paris as the American ambassador to France. He found the French organizing the La Perouse expedition to the North Pacific as their riposte to Cook's third voyage. Again

Jefferson distrusted foreign science as imperialism in disguise: "They give out that the object is merely for the improvement of our knowledge of the geography of that part of the globe. Their loading . . . and some other circumstances appear to me to indicate some other design; perhaps that of colonising on the West[er]n coast of America, or perhaps only to establish one or more factories there for the fur trade."[48]

Jefferson rued that his own weak and nearly bankrupt country could not match the expensive French investment in a naval expedition to the Pacific. Instead, Jefferson could only invest his own paltry funds in a lone pedestrian without official standing. In Paris in 1785, Jefferson befriended John Ledyard, the American adventurer who had served as a marine aboard Cook's third voyage. Anticipating Mackenzie and Lewis and Clark—but in reverse—Ledyard proposed crossing North America from west to east. First, he had to return to the Pacific Northwest, which he meant to accomplish by traveling eastward across Russia to Kamchatka, where he hoped to find a vessel bound for the rain coast. Impressed by Ledyard's zeal, Jefferson advanced some money and wrote a letter of recommendation to the Russian empress, Catherine the Great. Determined to protect Russia's sea otter trade, the empress refused her permission. Ledyard tried anyway, penetrating deep into Siberia until halted by arrest in February 1788. Sent back to St. Petersburg and expelled from Russia, Ledyard returned to Paris. Jefferson urged the adventurer to proceed to the United States and "go to Kentucky and endeavour to penetrate westwardly from thence to the South Sea." Instead, Ledyard went to explore Africa and died suddenly in Cairo in early 1789.[49]

Jefferson's third attempt to sponsor a transcontinental expedition was also no charm. In 1793, returned to the United States and serving as secretary of state, Jefferson embraced an expedition proposed by André Michaux, a French botanist resident in the United States since 1785. This time Jefferson could raise a subscription among his fellow members of the American Philosophical Society and even drafted formal instructions to guide Michaux. Because the destination was a coast frequented by European and American mariners, rather than some great unknown, Jefferson advised Michaux to seek them out and procure their certificates as a proof of success.

Jefferson instructed the botanist to ascend the Missouri River to its source in the Rocky Mountains and then seek a pass through to "a river called Oregan" that flowed into the Pacific. Instead Michaux attended to his duties as a French secret agent, lingering in Kentucky to recruit prominent men, including George Rogers Clark, for a filibustering expedition to conquer Louisiana, then a Spanish possession. Foiled in that scheme by the American government, which remained committed to neutrality, Michaux returned to France in 1796.[50]

Despite his three frustrations, Jefferson continued to dream and systematically accumulated the best American collection of Pacific information. In addition to Ledyard's book, Jefferson acquired the official published journals of Captains James Cook (1784) and George Vancouver (1798). Mackenzie's second journey became known to Jefferson at least by 1797, when the American Philosophical Society obtained and displayed a sea otter pelt procured by the explorer. Five years later, Jefferson eagerly procured Mackenzie's book, which worked on both Jefferson's British fears and his transcontinental hopes. On the one hand, Jefferson felt alarmed by Mackenzie's call for the British occupation in armed force of the Pacific Northwest. On the other hand, Jefferson saw opportunity in Mackenzie's conjecture that the passage through the Rocky Mountains would be lower and easier farther south, in the American latitudes. The president hoped that an American overland expedition could reach the Pacific via the Columbia River, which had eluded Mackenzie and which was the most promising conduit for American influence and trade.[51]

In addition to helping to catalyze the Lewis and Clark expedition, Mackenzie's book provided an essential source of geographic information and exploration know-how. Jefferson gave a copy to Meriwether Lewis, who carried it across the continent. After the American expedition returned, a critic reminded a boastful Lewis:

> Mr. M'Kenzie with a party consisting of about one fourth part of the number under your command, with means which will not bear a comparison with those furnished you, and without the *authority*, the *flags*, or *medals* of his government, crossed the Rocky mountains several degrees north of your rout[e], and for the *first time* penetrated to

the Pacific Ocean. You had the advantage of the information contained in his journal, and could in some degree estimate and guard against the dangers and difficulties you were to meet.

Because Mackenzie had learned and applied the scientific forms of exploration, as well as the native protocols for trade and diplomacy, his journal was an invaluable guide to Lewis and Clark.[52]

The expedition also carried a composite map made in Philadelphia but based on the British maps of 1802 (Aaron Arrowsmith) and 1803 (Nicholas King), which recorded the information garnered by Cook, Vancouver, Pond, and Mackenzie. Thanks to the maps and the journals, Lewis and Clark had a surprisingly clear picture of their Pacific destination. Their challenge was to get there, which would fill in the geographic gap in Euro-American knowledge, south of Mackenzie's crossing and between the Mandan Indian villages of the upper Missouri (which had been frequented by French and British traders since the late 1730s) on the east and the Pacific coast to the west.[53]

In early 1803, asserting constitutional scruples, Jefferson doubted that Congress could sponsor exploration purely dedicated to science; he reasoned that only the federal power to promote and regulate commerce could justify expending public funds on a transcontinental expedition. But such a commercial purpose would alarm Spanish and British officials, who might make crippling difficulties. Consequently, the president officially told Congress that the proposed expedition was primarily commercial and only incidentally scientific. But Jefferson unofficially reassured the Spanish and British diplomats that commerce was a mere political cover for a purely scientific enterprise. He informed Congress that the expedition would enrich America by diverting the fur trade away from British Canada; but he promised Edward Thornton, the British chargé d'affaires, that "it was in no shape his wish to encourage commerce with distant or indeed with any Indian tribes." The Spanish ambassador, Carlos Martinez de Yrujo, reported that Jefferson insisted that the expedition meant only to "unite the discoveries that these men would make with those which the celebrated Makensi made in 1793." Although Yrujo vigorously urged Jefferson to desist, the president blandly assured Congress that the Spanish considered the proposed expedition as "a matter of indifference" and "as a literary pursuit, which it is in the habit of permitting within its dominions."[54]

By offering science pretending to be commerce, Jefferson seemed to invert his oft-expressed distrust of foreign exploration as imperial commerce masquerading as science. But that too was a ploy, for Jefferson knew that commerce and science were inextricably interdependent in the construction of a Pacific empire. Yrujo understood that Jefferson sought "to discover the way by which the Americans may some day extend their population and their influence up to the coasts of the South Sea."[55]

The procedures followed, and the discoveries made, by prior Pacific explorations shaped the famous instructions that Jefferson bestowed upon Captain Meriwether Lewis in June 1803. To meet scientific standards, the American explorers were to make frequent and precise celestial measurements "to fix the latitude and longitude of the places" they reached. In a journal kept in multiple copies, they were to record observations of the flora, fauna, soil, and climate. And Jefferson ordered them to collect detailed ethnographic data that would later assist American officials, traders, and missionaries in the assimilation and subordination of native peoples. Bent on immediately wresting the sea otter trade away from British mariners, Jefferson directed Lewis to investigate whether it could be "conducted through the Missouri & U. S. more beneficially than by the circumnavigation now practised." And Jefferson recognized that mercantile shipping to the Pacific Northwest had become so routine that his explorers could anticipate returning by sea—if the overland return seemed too dangerous. The president instructed Lewis to seek out "the sea-vessels of any nation" to take a passage "by sea, by the way either of cape Horn, or the cape of good Hope." In sum, the expedition's instructions presumed a European knowledge about, and presence on, the northwest coast.[56]

Although successful in crossing the continent to the Pacific (and returning by land), the Lewis and Clark expedition initially discouraged overland commerce to the Pacific by exploding the myth that the Rocky Mountains were narrow and low. Indeed, the explorers' long, hard route through the American Rockies to the Columbia proved no more commercially viable than had Mackenzie's equally tangled course through the Canadian Rockies. But the maritime route to the Pacific Northwest impressed Lewis as of critical strategic importance to American expansion. He urged Americans to occupy the mouth of the Columbia River with a trading post—to fend off other empires, principally the British. Alexander Mackenzie similarly understood the lessons of the American expedition. In 1808, with Anglo-American relations deteriorating, Mackenzie sent a new memorandum to the imperial government, reiterating the urgent importance of a British post at the Columbia's mouth. Again his preoccupied and overstretched government postponed action.[57]

Meanwhile, the Jefferson administration embraced the Columbia trading post proposed by a New York City fur merchant, John Jacob Astor, who had learned western geography and commercial prospects during dealings with his partners in Montreal. Warming to Astor's scheme, Jefferson wanted "to get the whole of this business passed into the hands of our own citizens & to oust foreign traders." Although Jefferson lacked public resources to invest in the scheme, Astor proceeded with his own capital. In 1811, two parties of Astor's men—one by sea and the other by land—established a stockaded post named "Astoria" near the mouth of the Columbia. For the time being, the Americans had pulled ahead in the race to realize the imperial possibilities of the Pacific explorations of Cook, Vancouver, Mackenzie, and Lewis and Clark.[58]

The scientific forms followed, and scientific information sought, by Lewis and Clark have long seemed to represent the unique initiative and scientific genius of Thomas Jefferson. By instead recovering the expedition's predecessors, we can see their development of the protocols and goals of exploration that Jefferson mastered and taught to Lewis. Putting the Lewis and Clark expedition in a more global and historical context, however, shifts rather than diminishes its importance. If less than an unprecedented push into the unknown, the expedition was also obliged to overcome the liabilities of a late start in the geopolitics of science. If endowed with the insights of predecessors, Lewis and Clark also faced the challenges of claiming an American place in a highly contested corner of the globe. By making the most of what had already been learned, the Lewis and

Clark expedition helped to secure a Pacific footing against formidable competitors endowed with precedence.

NOTES

1. For work that does acknowledge the international background, see James P. Ronda, *Astoria and Empire* (Lincoln, Neb., 1990), 4–36; James P. Ronda, "Dreams and Discoveries: Exploring the American West, 1760–1815," *William and Mary Quarterly*, 3d. ser., 46 (1989): 145–62. In the latter, Ronda notes, "The persistent notion that exploration was an adventure into the unknown cannot be farther from what explorers were really about" (147). For a recent and popular reiteration of the traditional nationalistic perspective, see Dayton Duncan, *Lewis and Clark: The Journey of the Corps of Discovery* (New York, 1997).

2. See, for example, Thomas Jefferson to Archibald Stuart, Jan. 25, 1786, in Donald Jackson, *Thomas Jefferson and the Stony Mountains: Exploring the West from Monticello* (1981; Norman, Okla., 1993), 61.

3. Walter LaFeber, "Jefferson and an American Foreign Policy," in *Jeffersonian Legacies*, ed. Peter S. Onuf (Charlottesville, 1993), 370–91.

4. Warren L. Cook, *Flood Tide of Empire: Spain and the Pacific Northwest, 1543–1819* (New Haven, 1973), 1–20.

5. Ibid., 4–5, 7–9, 17–20; Barry M. Gough, *Distant Dominion: Britain and the Northwest Coast of North America* (Vancouver, 1980), 8–20; Iris H. W. Engstrand, "Seekers of the 'Northern Mystery': European Exploration of California and the Pacific," in *Contested Eden: California before the Gold Rush*, ed. Ramón A. Gutiérrez and Richard J. Orsi (Berkeley, 1998), 78–110.

6. Derek Howse, ed., *Background to Discovery: Pacific Exploration from Dampier to Cook* (Berkeley, 1990); Glyndwr Williams, "The Pacific: Exploration and Exploitation," in P. J. Marshall, ed., *The Oxford History of the British Empire*, vol. 2, *The Eighteenth Century* (New York, 1998), 552–75; David Mackay, *In the Wake of Cook: Exploration, Science, and Empire, 1780–1801* (London, 1985), 16–17.

7. Gough, *Distant Dominion*, 51–52, 93.

8. Hugh Cobbe, ed., *Cook's Voyages and the Peoples of the Pacific* (London, 1979); Robin Fisher and Hugh Johnston, eds., *Captain James Cook and His Times* (Seattle, 1979); Alan Frost and Jane Samson, eds., *Pacific Empires: Essays in Honour of Glyndwr Williams* (Vancouver, 1999); Lynne Withey, *Voyages of Discovery: Captain Cook and the Exploration of the Pacific* (New York, 1987).

9. Mackay, *In the Wake of Cook*, 5–6; Lucile H. Brockway, *Science and Colonial Expansion: the Role of the British Royal Botanic Gardens* (New York, 1979), 61–76; John Gascoigne, *Science in the Service of Empire: Joseph Banks, the British State, and the Uses of Science in the Age of Revolution* (New York, 1998), 16–33; Richard Drayton, *Nature's Government: Science, Imperial Britain, and the "Improvement" of the World* (New Haven, 2000), 41–49, 66–67.

10. Caedmon A. Liburd, ed., *Enlightenment and Exploration in the North Pacific, 1741–1805* (Seattle, 1997); Drayton, *Nature's Government*, 92–93, quotation on 45.

11. Cook, *Flood Tide of Empire*, 79–84, 100; David J. Weber, *The Spanish Frontier in North America* (New Haven, 1992), 285–86.

12. Benson Bobrick, *East of the Sun: The Conquest and Settlement of Siberia* (London, 1992); William W. Fitzhugh and Aron Crowell, eds., *Crossroads of Continents: Cultures of Siberia and Alaska* (Washington, D.C., 1988), especially the essays by Lydia T. Black and William W. Fitzhugh.

13. Glynn Barratt, *Russia in Pacific Waters, 1715–1825* (Vancouver, 1981); Raymond H. Fisher, *Bering's Voyages: Whither and Why* (Seattle, 1977); William R. Hunt, *Arctic Passage: The Turbulent History of the Land and People of the Bering Sea, 1697–1975* (New York, 1975).

14. James R. Gibson, *Imperial Russia in Frontier America: The Changing Geography of Supply of Russian America, 1784–1867* (New York, 1976); Barbara Sweetland Smith and Redmond J. Barnett, eds., *Russian America: The Forgotten Frontier* (Tacoma, Wash., 1990).

15. Gough, *Distant Dominion*, 93; Cook, *Flood Tide of Empire*, 44–60; Weber, *Spanish Frontier*, 237–38.

16. Weber, *Spanish Frontier*, 236–65; Gough, *Distant Dominion*, 93–94; Cook, *Flood Tide of Empire*, 51–54; Julia G. Costell and David Hornbeck, "Alta California: An Overview," in David Hurst Thomas, ed., *Columbian Consequences*, vol. 1, *Archaeological and Historical Perspectives on the Spanish Borderland West* (Washington, D.C., 1989), 303–32.

17. Weber, *Spanish Frontier*, 258–65; Gough, *Distant Dominion*, 93–94; Cook, *Flood Tide of Empire*, 51–54; Gibson, *Imperial Russia in Frontier America;* Smith and Barnett, *Russian America.*

18. Drayton, *Nature's Government*, 68–69.

19. Gough, *Distant Dominion*, 21–24; Mackay, *In the Wake of Cook*, 7–8; Withey, *Voyages of Discovery*, 126–322.

20. Gough, *Distant Dominion*, 24–29; Withey, *Voyages of Discovery*, 323–64.

21. Gough, *Distant Dominion*, 30–32; Kenneth M. Ames and Herbert D. G. Machner, *Peoples of the Northwest Coast: Their Archaeology and Prehistory* (London, 1999), 13–20.

22. J.C.H. King, "The Nootka of Vancouver Island," in *Cook's Voyages and Peoples of the Pacific*, ed. Hugh Cobbe (London, 1979), 89–93, 100–103; Cook, *Flood Tide of Empire*, 87; Gough, *Distant Dominion*, 33–39, 42–43.

23. King, "The Nootka," 107–8; Cook, *Flood Tide of Empire*, 87–88; Mackay, *In the Wake of Cook*, 59.

24. Cobbe, *Cook's Voyages and the Peoples of the Pacific*; Robin Fisher and Hugh Johnston, eds., *Captain James Cook and His Times* (Seattle, 1979); Frost and Samson, *Pacific Empires*; Glyndwr Williams, "The Pacific: Exploration and Exploitation"; Withey, *Voyages of Discovery*, 370–400.

25. Weber, *Spanish Frontier*, 285–89; Cook, *Flood Tide of Empire*, 100–104, 111–19.

26. Jackson, *Jefferson and the Stony Mountains*, 48; Cook, *Flood Tide of Empire*, 100–104, 111–14; Gough, *Distant Dominion*, 51–71, 100.

27. Cook, *Flood Tide of Empire,* 104–7.

28. Ibid., 129–249 (Manuel Antonio Flores to Antonio Valdes, Dec. 23, 1788, quoted on 130).

29. Gough, *Distant Dominion,* 100–115, 130–31; Mackay, *In the Wake of Cook,* 85–87; Reginald C. Stuart, *The Half-Way Pacifist: Thomas Jefferson's View of War* (Toronto, 1978), 20–21.

30. Harold Innis, "Peter Pond and the Influence of Capt. James Cook on Exploration in the Interior of North America," Royal Society of Canada, *Transactions* 21 (1928), sec. 2, 139–40; Ronda, *Astoria and Empire,* 5–6.

31. Innis, "Peter Pond," 139–40; Ronda, *Astoria and Empire,* 6–13; W. J. Eccles, *Essays on New France* (Toronto, 1987), 96–109; Barry Gough, *First Across the Continent: Sir Alexander Mackenzie* (Norman, Okla., 1997), 62.

32. Hamilton quoted in Ronda, *Astoria and Empire,* 9.

33. Barry Gough, "Peter Pond," in *Dictionary of Canadian Biography* (Toronto, 1983), 5:681–83; Gough, *First Across the Continent,* 71–73, 101.

34. Gough, *First Across the Continent,* 67–98; W. Kaye Lamp, "Sir Alexander Mackenzie," in *Dictionary of Canadian Biography,* 5:538.

35. Gough, *First Across the Continent,* 94, 101–3.

36. Ibid., 105–6; Ronda, *Astoria and Empire,* 15–18.

37. Gough, *First Across the Continent,* 105–23.

38. Thomas Manby quoted in Elizabeth A. Fenn, *Pox Americana: The Great Smallpox Epidemic of 1775–82* (New York, 2001), 251; Mackenzie quoted in Gough, *First Across the Continent,* 128.

39. Gough, *First Across the Continent,* 143–56, Mackenzie quoted on 156. For the European imperial tradition of ceremonies of possession, see Patricia Seed, *Ceremonies of Possession in Europe's Conquest of the New World, 1492–1640* (New York, 1995).

40. Gough, *First Across the Continent,* 152.

41. Ibid., 160–81.

42. Ibid., 170–80.

43. Ibid., 180–86, Mackenzie quoted on 205.

44. Ibid., 4–5, 170–85.

45. Peter S. Onuf, *Jefferson's Empire: The Language of American Nationhood* (Charlottesville, 2000), 100; Robert W. Tucker and David C. Hendrickson, *Empire of Liberty: The Statecraft of Thomas Jefferson* (New York, 1990), 42–43, 62.

46. Jefferson to George Rogers Clark, Dec. 4, 1783, quoted in Jackson, *Jefferson and the Stony Mountains,* 42–43.

47. Ibid., 42–43.

48. Jefferson to John Jay, Aug. 14, 1785, quoted ibid., 48–49.

49. Ibid., 49–56; Jefferson to Rev. James Madison, July 19, 1788, quoted ibid., 56.

50. Ibid., 75–78.

51. Gary E. Moulton, ed., *The Journals of the Lewis and Clark Expedition,* 13 vols.

(Lincoln, Neb., 1979–2001), 2:1–3; Jackson, *Thomas Jefferson and the Stony Mountains,* 92–95, 197; Ronda, "Exploring the American West," 149–50.

52. David McKeehan to Meriwether Lewis, April 7, 1807, in Donald Jackson, ed., *Letters of the Lewis and Clark Expedition, with Related Documents, 1783–1854,* 2d ed., 2 vols. (Urbana, Ill., 1978), 2:401–2.

53. Jackson, *Jefferson and the Stony Mountains,* 129–34; Eccles, *Essays on New France,* 98–109.

54. Carlos Martinez de Yrujo to Pedro Cevallos, Dec. 2, 1802; Jefferson to Congress, Jan. 18, 1803; and Edward Thornton to Lord Hawkesbury, March 9, 1803, all in Jackson, *Letters,* 1:4, 11–13, and 26–27.

55. Carlos Martinez de Yrujo to Pedro Cevallos, Dec. 2, 1802, ibid., 1:4; Jackson, *Jefferson and the Stony Mountains,* 125.

56. Jefferson to Lewis, June 20, 1803, in Jackson, *Letters,* 1:61–66 (quotations on 65). For the scientific preparations for the expedition, see also William H. Goetzmann, *Exploration and Empire: The Explorer and the Scientist in the Winning of the American West* (New York, 1966), 3–7.

57. Jackson, *Thomas Jefferson and the Stony Mountains,* 280–81.

58. Ibid., 280–81 (Jefferson to Astor, April 13, 1808, quoted on 281); Ronda, *Astoria and Empire,* 38–50.

Securing America

*Jefferson's Fluid Plans
for the
Western Perimeter*

Jenry Morsman

WHEN THOMAS JEFFERSON ASSUMED
the presidency in 1801, he stated that the United States was "kindly
separated by nature and a wide ocean from the exterminating
havoc" of imperial Europe. Further, he proclaimed that America's
was "the strongest government on earth." Although such rhetoric
suited an ideal image of "a rising nation, spread over a wide and
fruitful land," it also masked Jefferson's deep concern about the real
geopolitical challenges his nation faced on the North American continent. The United States was, in fact, not so far removed from the
tangles and threats of European power, and the liabilities of the Mississippi River in the West potentially undermined the benefits of the
Atlantic Ocean in the east. Moreover, if a government's strength
depended on "every man . . . meet[ing] invasions of the public order
as his own personal concern," then where population was sparse,
the government could not be strong.[1] Along its western boundary,
neither geography nor demography—pillars of Jeffersonian defense
strategy—favored the United States. As Jefferson would later con-

cede to Secretary of the Navy Robert Smith, America was, in its western section, "miserably weak."[2]

Within two years of taking office, Jefferson presented to the "Gentlemen of the Senate and of the House of Representatives" a multifaceted plan to establish "as firm a front" on the western border of the United States "as on our Eastern border." Central to his scheme for strengthening the American periphery was the expansion of commerce with Indians, east and west of the Mississippi River. While United States citizens would develop informal trading relationships with some Indians, the United States would, he imagined, establish formal trading relationships with others. Anticipating that "at it's present session" the legislature would consider whether to continue, to amend, or to discontinue altogether "the Act for establishing trading houses with the Indian tribes," Jefferson thought it was "my duty to communicate the views which have guided me." He explained that he not only supported continuing the establishment of trading houses, but that he hoped to extend "the external commerce of the U. S." Putting commerce in the service of national defense, Jefferson argued that the effective management of the Indian trade could lead both to the acquisition of strategic Indian lands within the United States and to greater familiarity and more affectionate connections with Indians residing outside the United States. The happy consequence of such developments, he added, would be the limitation, if not the outright removal, of the threats posed by the Spanish, the French, and the British empires, each of which had maintained an interest in the North American interior.[3]

Geopolitics

By the fourth week of November 1802, Jefferson had learned that approximately one month earlier the Spanish intendant in New Orleans had terminated Americans' right of deposit at the mouth of the Mississippi.[4] Whatever the actual motivation of the intendant had been, the closure of New Orleans to American trade inflamed one of the most critical and enduring issues to challenge the new nation through its first two decades. When he recommended that legislators consider the "late occurrences on the Mississippi" in his January 18, 1803, message to Congress, Jefferson was, in fact, referring to the 1802 closure of New Orleans. Making the reference vague rather than specific invited reflection on the role of the Mississippi River throughout the geopolitical history of the United States.[5]

Perhaps more than any other issue in the first two decades of the new nation's existence, the question of navigation on the Mississippi River exposed the limits of the national government, the fragility of union, and the weakness of the western border. In 1784, Thomas Hutchins described the river as "the great passage made by the hand of nature"; it would, he suspected, "promote the happiness and benefit of mankind." Regardless of his confidence in the river's latent advantages for humanity, Hutchins was less sanguine about the benefits the Mississippi River would provide the United States of America.[6]

Hutchins recognized that the strength of the union between eastern and western Americans and the security of the western border itself would be contingent upon the Americans' "share of the navigation of the Mississippi" River. The population of Americans in the cis-Mississippi West was rapidly increasing. Their prosperity depended upon their ability to deliver agricultural products to the markets of the Atlantic world in a cost-effective manner. Transporting goods by land over the Appalachian Mountains was slow and often prohibitively expensive. Barring any artificial obstructions or political interference, floating produce down the Mississippi River to New Orleans and then to market via the Gulf of Mexico was faster and far less expensive. Moreover, without manufactures of their own, westerners depended on commercial exchange with European cities and with the emerging industrial centers of the Atlantic states. Without free navigation of the Mississippi, the "commercial prosperity" of the westerners and, by extension, the very "safety" of the republic would be at risk.[7]

Prior to the American Revolution, the Spanish controlled the Mississippi River, and the Spanish king Carlos III restricted trade along the river. Louisiana was, for him, to serve the Spanish empire chiefly as a natural, undeveloped, strategic barrier between adventuring and acquisitive Americans and the king's silver mines in New Spain. Carlos III had steadfastly sought to limit American penetration south and west of the Mississippi River since 1762. During the

American Revolution, though, the British navy had hampered the ability of Spanish ships to supply Louisiana from Caribbean posts. With limited options, the king opened the river to those Americans who wanted to float goods down the Mississippi so that they could supply the Spanish people living in Louisiana. The Mississippi River trade quickly proved prosperous both for western Americans and the Spanish merchants in New Orleans, but at the same time, the Spanish foresaw serious threats associated with the new trade and with the American settlements along the tributaries of the Mississippi.[8] Even Intendant Martin Navarro, a free-trade enthusiast, warned of "new enemies who regarded our situation with too great jealousy." The Americans to the north would one day "be harmful . . . unless we shelter ourselves in time by promoting a numerous population in this province in order to observe and even to restrain their intentions."[9]

Following the Revolution, Americans did manage to establish a legal claim to free navigation on the Mississippi River. American and English peace negotiators in Paris established the western boundary of the United States "along the middle of the . . . river Mississippi," from the latitude of the northwesternmost point of the Lake of the Woods "until it shall intersect the northernmost part of the thirty-first degree of north latitude." They further determined that "the navigation of the river Mississippi, from its source to the Ocean, shall forever remain free and open to the subjects of Great-Britain and the citizens of the United States."[10] Whatever the language of the "definitive treaty of peace," though, Hutchins warned, "treaties are not always to be depended on." Even "the most solemn," he wrote, "have been broken."[11]

As it turned out, there was a more immediate threat to American navigation on the Mississippi than a potential violation of the terms of the 1783 Treaty of Paris by the British. During the peace negotiations, from which the Spanish were excluded, the Americans and the English conspired with each other against Spain for territorial advantage. At issue was the northern boundary of the province of West Florida. Although 32° 30' north latitude had been recognized as the northern border of West Florida since 1763, the 1783 Treaty of Paris officially placed the border separating the United

States and West Florida along the thirty-first parallel, significantly farther south. The contracting nations secretly agreed, though, that if the British managed to retain control of West Florida, then both parties would recognize the 32° 30′ line. Essentially, Americans had acknowledged the legitimacy of the 32° 30′ line but arranged to extend their own national domain by pushing the border south if any power other than England held West Florida. Ultimately Spain, not England, retained control of West Florida. Spanish authorities learned of America's duplicitous efforts, and a boundary dispute erupted. Snubbed by the Americans in Paris and now in possession of both West Florida and Louisiana, the Spanish had the motive and the means to interfere with American navigation on the Mississippi.[12] So long as Spain was, Hutchins wrote, "in possession of New Orleans, which commands the entrance to the western country," for Americans "to expect the free navigation of the Mississippi [was] absurd." The Spanish, he explained, had "forts on the Mississippi, and whenever they may think it consistent with their interest, they will make use of them to prevent [Americans from] navigating on it."[13] In control of the mouth of the Mississippi, the Spanish wasted little time squeezing American commerce. Any American trader venturing below 32° 30′ in search of an Atlantic market at which to dispose of his goods risked interference from Spanish colonial authorities. At customshouses established along the river, the Spanish charged tolls, caused delays, and sometimes confiscated American trade goods, and finally, on June 24, 1784, the Spanish closed the Mississippi to American traders.[14]

Madison characterized the "attempt in Spain to shut the mouth of the Mississippi against the inhabitants above" as "impolitic and perverse." He wrote that "she can no more stop the current of trade down the river than she can that of the river itself," and that she "would never be so mad as to persist in her present ideas."[15] Madison's claims notwithstanding, the Spanish demonstrated that they possessed the power to influence the commercial prosperity of American settlers west of the Appalachian Mountains. In so doing, the Spanish laid bare the fragility of the connections between western Americans and fellow citizens on the Atlantic coast. American leaders recognized the danger quickly. In October 1784, George

Washington wrote to Virginia governor Benjamin Harrison, "insoluble bonds" between Americans would require "the cement of interest." The "flanks and rear of the United States are possessed by other powers, and formidable ones, too," wrote Washington, and he wondered, "How entirely unconnected with them shall we be, and what troubles may we not apprehend, if the Spaniards . . . , instead of throwing stumbling-blocks in their way, as they now do, should hold out lures for their trade and alliance?" The answer, he told Harrison, did not require "the gift of prophecy." Trans-Appalachian Americans would secede from the Union and offer their allegiance to whatever power controlled the Mississippi and New Orleans. "The western states . . . stand as it were upon a pivot—the touch of a feather, would turn them any way."[16] Washington was not alone in his assessment. Kentucky politician John Brown believed that the Mississippi River could easily become "the foundation for the dismemberment of the American Empire."[17] From Paris in January 1786, Jefferson wrote to Archibald Stuart, "the navigation of the Mississippi we must have."[18] A year later he wrote to his friend James Madison that "the act which abandons the navigation of the Mississippi is an act of separation between the Eastern and Western country."[19]

Lending still further credence to the possibility of disunion were the Federalists of the Northeast. Indeed, there were New Englanders, Rufus King chief among them, who were eager to relinquish American access to the Mississippi River.[20] Furthermore, in the mid-1780s Spanish officials essentially invited emigrants from the United States to settle on large tracts of land in Louisiana and provided access to the Mississippi River in exchange for a loyalty oath. Enough Americans accepted the offer that the Spanish faced the new and difficult challenges of managing a foreign population.[21] Americans increasingly pushed into the Spanish territory south and west of New Orleans.[22]

In the mid- and late 1780s, though, the frustration of westerners ran high. They felt abandoned by the national government and unfavorably compared its behavior to that of Parliament in the years preceding the Revolution. In 1786, with a rumor circulating through the West that John Jay had concluded a treaty, the terms of which would close the Mississippi River to American commerce for a period ranging from twenty-five to thirty-five years, "a copy of a letter from a gentleman at the falls of [the] Ohio, to his friend in New England" was submitted to Congress: "the late commercial treaty with Spain, in shutting up, as it is said, the navigation of the Mississippi, for the term of twenty-five years, has given this western country a universal shock, and struck its inhabitants with amazement." The writer accused Congress of selling westerners and of making them "vassals to the merciless Spaniards." Spanish policies had already "ruined" even wealthy westerners, for the customs officials had the "power . . . to take our produce at any price they please" or even to confiscate it. "The parliamentary acts which occasioned our revolt from Great Britain were not so barefaced and intolerable," he wrote. "You are as ignorant of this country," he told the members of the Congress, "as Great Britain was of America."[23]

The Louisville writer raised the twin specters of war and disunion. He wrote that westerners were preparing "to drive the Spaniards from their settlements, at the mouth of the Mississippi." He believed they could "raise twenty thousand troops this side of the Alleghany and Appalachian mountains," and that such a number would grow by two to four thousand annually. And then he warned Congress: "In case we are not countenanced and succored by the United States (if we need it) our allegiance will be thrown off, and some other power applied to. Great Britain stands ready with open arms to receive and support us. . . . When once reunited to them, 'farewell, a long farewell, to all your boasted greatness.' The province of Canada and the inhabitants of these waters, of themselves, in time, will be able to conquer you." The author softened his threats by suggesting such eventualities could be avoided if the national government took the proper steps. If they did not, however, he advised, "blame yourselves."[24] Others sought solutions outside the national government. In 1793, Revolutionary War hero George Rogers Clark accepted a commission from the French representative to the United States, Citizen Genet. As the commander-in-chief of the French Revolutionary Legions on the Mississippi, Clark's goals were to wrest control of the river from the Spanish and to open the river to free trade, but he abandoned the effort.[25] Not all developing schemes were hostile to the Spanish. James Wilkinson, of Maryland and

Kentucky, attempted to negotiate his own personal trade agreement with Estaban Miró, the acting governor of Louisiana.[26]

In 1795, Thomas Pinckney concluded the Treaty of San Lorenzo between the United States and Spain. The treaty recognized the western border of the United States to be the middle of the channel of the Mississippi River and the southern border to be the thirty-first parallel. Furthermore, the treaty provided Americans the full right of navigation on the Mississippi and the right of deposit at New Orleans.[27] Although the treaty appeared to put to rest the critical issues that aggravated westerners and thereby threatened the union, doubts remained. Writing, each to the other, on the same day in March 1796, both Jefferson and Madison expressed concern about the treaty. Madison described the agreement as a "bitter pill." Jefferson wrote, "The Spanish treaty will have some disagreeable features, seeds of chicanery and eternal broils, instead of peace and friendship."[28]

Trouble on the Mississippi would continue, but increasingly the Spanish were not to blame. The more powerful French, with whom the United States endured increasingly strained relations through the 1790s, emerged as the most immediate threat in the West. In response to the first Treaty of San Ildefonso in 1796, rumors circulated in America that Spain had returned Louisiana to France. Although not true, by 1797 a revitalized France was indeed eager to reestablish its colonial empire and made overtures to Spain for the acquisition of Louisiana.[29] Three years later, on October 1, 1800, by the second Treaty of San Ildefonso, the French finally did acquire Louisiana. Jefferson learned of the transfer approximately eight months later, in May 1801, and was overcome by the implications he foresaw for the United States. As he later wrote Robert Livingston, "the cession of Louisiana and the Floridas by Spain to France works most sorely on the U.S." Emphasizing America's growing western population, which would eventually yield more than half of the nation's produce, Jefferson argued that New Orleans was the "one single spot, the possessor of which is our natural and habitual enemy." The Spanish retrocession "reverse[d] all the political relations of the U. S."; it introduced "a new epoch in our political course." If the United States could not control New Orleans, then the unity of the entire nation would be at risk.[30]

Jefferson had long understood the importance of free navigation on the Mississippi and the right of deposit at New Orleans for the preservation of union between eastern and western Americans. In addition to serving as the major commercial avenue for American commerce west of the Appalachian Mountains, the Mississippi River was the western boundary of the United States. But rivers made for complicated boundaries. As much as the line of the river marked the separation of peoples, the movement of the river encouraged their interaction. The Mississippi River, the tributaries of which fanned out across the interior of the continent, had a particularly strong tendency to draw together the many peoples living on those tributaries. Just as the water's current carried the settlers of the Mississippi's eastern tributaries toward New Orleans, so too did the water's current carry the peoples of the great river's western tributaries to the same Gulf of Mexico port.[31] While free navigation on the Mississippi secured by the United States government may have cemented the bonds between western Americans and those of the Atlantic states, it also drew the national government deeper into the competitive international neighborhood of the Mississippi River valley.

The politics of union between the eastern states and the western states and territories and the decades of struggle for free navigation of the Mississippi River and the right of deposit in New Orleans were key factors creating a climate compelling Jefferson to approach Congress with a request for an "appropriation of two thousand five hundred dollars 'for the purpose of extending the external commerce of the U.S.'"[32] Alexander Mackenzie's *Voyages from Montreal* provided the catalyst.[33] Early in 1802, Jefferson placed an order with New York bookseller James Cheetham for the recent publication. While at Monticello that summer, Jefferson read the young Scottish explorer's account of his journeys from Canada to the Arctic Ocean and from Canada to the Pacific Ocean.[34] The second expedition was of greater interest to Jefferson. Although Mackenzie believed that his first expedition had satisfactorily "settled the dubious point" of an all-water route linking the Atlantic and Pacific oceans, he believed that his second journey demonstrated the "practicality of a commercial communication through the continent of North America." Moreover, he believed that he had identified not one, but two routes "through the continent." One of the paths included the Great River of the West—the Columbia.[35]

Mackenzie's success alone was not what caught Jefferson's attention. Rather, the meaning that the explorer ascribed to the expedition raised concern. Jefferson was alarmed by Mackenzie's description and promotion of the commercial and ultimately political possibilities to which the geography as he understood it might give rise. In his concluding pages, Mackenzie provided a "general, but short, geographical view of the country" that he saw as a "field for commercial enterprise." Effective development of trade would require "only the countenance and the support of the British government." "By opening this intercourse between the Atlantic and Pacific Oceans and forming regular establishments through the interior, and at both extremes, as well as along the coasts and islands, the entire command of the fur trade of North America might be obtained, from latitude 48 North to the pole." Mackenzie speculated on "the probable advantages that may be derived from advancing the trade. . . . When supported by the operations of the credit and capital which Great Britain so pre-eminently possess," those advantages would be both "essential" and "incalculable." Indeed, Mackenzie envisioned a British commercial empire that would reach "the markets of the four quarters of the globe."[36]

Had Mackenzie done no more than fantasize about a British commercial network of global scale, Jefferson might have been able to dismiss the journals more easily—or at least simply to appreciate their supposed contributions to geographical knowledge of North America. Mackenzie, however, addressed three other elements of particular, long-standing interest to Jefferson. First, using criteria with which Jefferson was well acquainted, Mackenzie offered a positive evaluation of the Columbia River. The river and the "level country" through which it passed constituted a "situation fit for colonization, and suitable to the residence of a civilized people." The mouth of the river, he wrote, was "capable of receiving ships," and the river itself "was navigable throughout for boats."[37] He stated plainly that "whatever course may be taken from the Atlantic, the Columbia is *the line* of communication from the Pacific Ocean" into the interior.

Second, Mackenzie took a rather dim view of the "American adventurers" who were operating in the Pacific Northwest. "Without regularity or capital, or the desire of conciliating future confidence," he wrote, they "look altogether to the interest of the moment." The Americans "collect all the skins they can procure, and in any manner that suits them, and having exchanged them at Canton for the produce of China, return to their own country." Although he had been informed that many had been "very successful," Mackenzie was sure "such adventurers . . . would instantly disappear before a well-regulated trade." Third, Mackenzie linked commerce with politics. In addition to the financial benefits that might be accrued by opening wider North American trade, there would be political advantages. Supporting his plan for an enlarged commercial system were "many political reasons" that, he wrote, "it is not necessary here to enumerate." The subtext was clear enough: as the commercial system expanded, so too did the political realm; commerce secured kingdom.[38]

So, when read in Charlottesville, Virginia, in 1802, the journal of Mackenzie's 1793 expedition—which, ironically enough, began with the ascension of the Peace River—announced a potential significant threat to the security of the western United States. At the very least, Mackenzie hinted at British designs for permanence at the mouth of the Columbia, and Jefferson feared that the Great River of the West would become the entering wedge through which the British could attempt to dominate the interior of the continent, even south of 48° north latitude. If there were an easy water or land route between the Columbia and the Missouri, Jefferson knew, the British would have access not only to the Missouri River but also to the Mississippi River and to the interior of the United States. Moreover, he could not be certain that the inhabitants of the region—Indian and American— would not welcome the British presence. Adding further still to Jefferson's anxiety was the reality that Mackenzie's blueprint for expansion was already a decade old. Jefferson could not be certain to what extent, if at all, the British had developed such plans. The actual nature of the highlands that gave rise to the Missouri River, and the proximity of the head of that river to the head of the Columbia River, therefore became critical information with substantial geopolitical implications.[39]

Jefferson's Message and Instructions

As the year 1802 drew to a close, then, the Mississippi River presented two challenges to the United States. On the one hand, the river drew the interests and loyalty of trans-Appalachian Americans away from the United States; on the other hand, the river drew the agents of European empires and little-known Indian groups into regular contact with the United States. Rather than offering the splendid isolation provided by the Atlantic Ocean, the Mississippi River drew America into a dangerous neighborhood. Although the Spanish had relinquished formal title to Louisiana, they remained a steady presence and active nuisance in the territory. Furthermore, they continued to control the Floridas. The French, though without significant forces in North America, now had the title to Louisiana, and this further nourished their escalating colonial aspirations. The British, who had still not withdrawn fully from the northwestern United States as prescribed by the 1783 Treaty of Paris, loomed menacingly from Canada and the Pacific slope. In order to confront the multiple challenges in the West, on January 18, 1803, Jefferson proposed to Congress a two-pronged strategy. The United States would acquire from Indians and settle new lands along the eastern bank of the Mississippi. In addition, the United States would launch an expedition beyond the Mississippi and its territorial domain, into the Missouri River country. The first element of the strategy would depend on the existing trade with familiar, domestic Indians; the second element would lay the foundation for trade with unfamiliar Indians to the west. His plan, if carried through to completion, would, more generally, reduce the liabilities of the western river boundary.

"Planting on the Missisipi itself the means of it's own safety" was an essential component of Jefferson's dual strategy. Surely, in light of the challenges presented by the Mississippi River, Congress recognized "how desireable it is to possess a respectable breadth of country on that river, from our Southern limit to the Illinois at least." As Jefferson surveyed the length of the western border of the United

States, he was concerned primarily with the strip of land adjacent to the eastern bank of the Mississippi River between the Ohio and the Yazoo rivers. He told Congress, "we possess what is below the Yazoo." Expressing confidence in the governor of the Indiana Territory, William Henry Harrison, he added, we "can probably acquire a certain breadth from the Illinois & Wabash to the Ohio." "But between the Ohio and the Yazoo," Jefferson explained, "the country all belongs to the Chickasaws." Only when the United States had acquired the land from the Chickasaws could Americans rightfully occupy that land, establish dense settlements, and subsequently organize a militia equal to its defense.[40]

On the surface, reaching a mutually agreeable arrangement between the United States and the Chickasaws for the transfer of lands might have appeared to be relatively easy. After all, "the portion of their lands which is most important for us is exactly that which they do not inhabit." Jefferson explained, "their settlements are not on the Missisipi, but in the interior of their country." Moreover, Jefferson regarded the Chickasaws as "the most friendly tribe within our limits." Even so, they were "the most decided against the alienation of lands."

While the Chickasaws may have been particularly reluctant to give up any land, Indians generally had also become increasingly resistant to the practice. Jefferson himself had observed that "the Indian tribes residing within the limits of the U. S. have for a considerable time been growing more & more uneasy at the constant diminution of the territory they occupy." Only "a very few tribes" were still willing to sell their lands; indeed, "the policy has long been gaining strength with them of refusing absolutely all further sale on any conditions." "In order peaceably to counteract this policy of theirs," Jefferson advocated two measures: encouraging Indians "to abandon hunting" in favor of farming, and "multiply[ing] the trading houses among them." If Indians were "to apply [themselves] to the raising [of] stock, to agriculture and domestic manufacture," then, Jefferson's logic purported, they would enjoy a "better . . . mode of living" that required "less land & labor." Furthermore, Jefferson explained, "plac[ing] within their reach those [material artifacts] which will contribute more to their domestic comfort than the possession of extensive, but uncultivated wilds" will finally persuade reluctant Indians to settle in compact, agricultural communities and to sell their empty land. A society's development toward agriculture, trade, and the sale of excess land was a natural progression, and one that Jefferson thought the Chickasaws were on the verge of making. Indeed, he told Congress, "they have lately shown a desire to become agricultural, and this leads to the desire of buying implements & comforts." Acquiring the targeted breadth of the Chickasaws' land between the Yazoo and the Ohio was contingent on "strengthening and gratifying these wants."

Trade, Jefferson argued to Congress, was the ideal tool by which the United States could pry still more land from the Indians residing within the territorial domain of the United States. Jefferson characteristically interpreted the transformation of the Indian economic base from hunting to agriculture and the subsequent land transactions to have positive consequences for all parties involved. He wrote, "In leading [Indians] thus to agriculture, to manufactures & civilization, in bringing together their & our settlements, & in preparing them ultimately to participate in the benefits of our government, I trust and believe we are acting for their greatest good." He was confident also that once Indians enjoyed the perspective that only "experience and refection" afford, they too would see the "wisdom of exchanging what they can spare & we want, for what we can spare & they want." The consequences for the United States and its citizens, as outlined by Jefferson, were more plausibly beneficial. By significantly underselling foreign traders, the United States trading houses could, at least theoretically, "drive them from the competition" and secure "the good will of the Indians." Such developments would, in turn, eliminate from the western section of the United States "a description of men who are constantly endeavoring to excite in the Indian mind suspicions, fears, & irritations towards us"—namely agents of the Spanish, the British, and to a lesser degree the French empires. Jefferson recognized that underselling foreign traders who were operating on domestic soil meant also underselling private American traders. His plan to increase the number of government-run trading houses throughout the trans-Appalachian United States would deprive those American traders of their livelihood. He wrote, "the extension of public commerce among the Indian tribes may deprive of that source such of our citizens as are engaged in it." Sensitive to the wavering loyalties of western Americans and to the potential for disunion, Jefferson recommended to Congress a means of assuaging those private citizens who were engaged in the domestic Indian trade. Telling the members of Congress they were responsible for the "care of individual as well as of the general interest," he suggested they "point in another direction the enterprise of these citizens." Jefferson wanted to encourage private citizens to enter the Indian trade beyond the Mississippi River.

In order to prepare the way for private Americans to operate in the Missouri River country, Jefferson proposed a reconnaissance expedition to gather useful information and to open relations with the Indians of the region. The expedition, he imagined, could be executed by "an intelligent officer with ten or twelve chosen men" who were "fit for the enterprize and willing to undertake it." He noted that "other civilized nations have encountered great expense to enlarge the boundaries of knowledge, by undertaking voyages of discovery, & for other literary purposes." Jefferson optimistically estimated that the costs for an American expedition into the Missouri River country could be held down: the men would be "taken from our posts, where they may be spared without inconvenience," and "their pay would be going on, whether here or there." The burdens of hauling supplies would further limit overhead costs: "their arms & accoutrements, some instruments of observation, & light & cheap presents for the Indians would be all the apparatus they could carry." Finally, "a soldier's portion of land on their return," one for each member of the party, would round out "the whole expense."

Jefferson may well have believed, as he claimed, that Congress bore some obligation to help the private American traders east of the Mississippi River who would be displaced by an increase in government trading houses find new opportunities. He may well have believed, as he also claimed, that the Missouri River country would eventually prove profitable for the American traders. He emphasized to Congress, though, that the business transactions of American traders west of the Mississippi River would prove more beneficial to the overall public good than they would to any private interest. He explained to Congress that "the Missouri, & the Indians inhabiting it, are not as well known as is rendered desireable by their connection with the Missisipi, and consequently with us." Jefferson recognized the powerful tendency of the Mississippi River to draw into close proximity all the nations established along its many tributary streams, and on the Missouri he saw trouble looming. "The country on [the Missouri] river," he wrote, "is inhabited by numerous tribes, who furnish great supplies of furs & peltry to the trade of another nation." Although Jefferson did not identify the other nation explicitly, presumably Congress knew he was referring to Great Britain. The majority of the British trade, he explained, was "carried on in a high latitude, through an infinite number of portages and lakes, shut up by ice through a long season." Jefferson noted that the "commerce on that line could bear no competition with that of the Missouri," which, "according to the best accounts," offered a "continu[ous] navigation from its source" and "travers[ed] a moderate climate." Moreover, Jefferson believed that only "a single portage" over what he called the "Stony Mountains" might link the Missouri to another river flowing west into the Pacific Ocean. The implications of the supposed geographic realities were clear enough to Jefferson: the British would eventually shift their operations farther south and strengthen their trading alliance with the Indians of the Missouri River country. Experience had taught Jefferson that the British had a knack for inspiring in Indians prejudice against the United States. As proxies for the British empire, he knew, the Indians of Missouri River country could become a constant drain on the nation's energies and resources or, worse yet, could draw America back into war with England. If, however, citizens of the United States were to take preemptive action by developing positive trading relationships with those Indians, and thereby securing their trust and affection, then they would likely forestall such a dire scenario. Accordingly, Jefferson requested that Congress commit "two thousand five hundred dollars" to fund a corps of soldiers who would hold "conferences with the natives on the subject of commercial intercourse, get admission among them for our traders as others are admitted, agree on convenient deposits for an interchange of articles, and return with the information acquired." Just as he had proposed to do east of the Mississippi River, Jefferson would strategically use commerce to "win the good will of the Indians" of the Missouri River country, and by extension to eliminate from that section the pernicious influence of any nation "endeavoring to excite in the Indian mind suspicions, fears and irritations toward us."

Although the "principal object" was to lay a foundation for commerce between private citizens of the United States and the Indians of the Missouri River country, the expedition would most certainly "advance the geographical knowledge of our own continent." Jefferson was somewhat ambivalent about the value of that knowledge. On one hand, he suggested the benefit was no more than an "additional gratification," the "incidental" byproduct of a mission whose purpose was altogether different. On the other, Jefferson implied that the explorers would contribute to an elevated, transnational Enlightenment project. As "other civilized nations" had underwritten "voyages of discovery" and pushed back "the boundaries of knowledge," he wrote, "our nation seems to owe to the same object . . . to explore this, the only easy line of communication across the continent." Jefferson's apparent ambivalence thinly masked his deep concern. He wanted to test Mackenzie's claims; so the party would "explore the whole line" of the Missouri, "even to the western ocean." Jefferson was anxious to know just how "easy" the "only . . . line of communication across the continent" might be. If the western mountains were a mirror of the soft Appalachian range, the British would be a threat not only from the north but also from the Pacific slope.

As of January 1803, Jefferson's plan to improve security on America's western border hinged on increasing the trade with Indians residing within the United States by building more government trading houses and on extending the trade of private citizens to Indian groups residing outside the United States. The former effort would eventually permit Americans to buy and settle strategic lands along the eastern bank of the Mississippi River, where they could organize militia and defend America as necessary. The latter would transform the dangerous Missouri River country into an American-friendly zone by winning the affection of the Indians inhabiting the region, thereby eliminating the British threat. In subsequent months, however, diplomatic developments led Jefferson to revise his plan to enhance security along the western border: the western limit of the United States itself moved.

By June 20, 1803, when Jefferson dated the final draft of his instructions for Meriwether Lewis, whom he had selected to serve as the leader of the expedition, the United States had already acquired the entire Missouri River country from France. Principal negotiators had signed the treaty for the cession of Louisiana to the United States in Paris almost two months earlier, on April 30. Although he had not yet received definitive word of the signing of the treaty, Jefferson was at least aware of its likelihood as he composed the instructions. Sensitive to the sudden and unpredictable developments characteristic of international negotiations, Jefferson took nothing for granted, and he directed Lewis as if the expedition would be departing the jurisdiction of the United States the moment it crossed the Mississippi and challenged the current of the Missouri River. Accordingly, just as he had in his message to Congress six months earlier, Jefferson emphasized that the primary concern of the expedition was to lay the foundation for positive trading relationships with the Indians of the region.[41]

Jefferson set Lewis the task of gathering as much information about the Indians of the Missouri River valley as possible. "The commerce which may be carried on with the people inhabiting the line you will pursue," he explained, "renders a knolege of those people important." Therefore, Jefferson directed Lewis, "You will . . . endeavor to make yourself acquainted, as far as a diligent pursuit of your journey shall admit, with the names of the nations & their numbers." He wanted reports on "the extent & limits of their possessions; their relations with other tribes of nations; their language, traditions, monuments; their ordinary occupations in agriculture, fishing, hunting, war, arts, & implements for these; their food, clothing, & domestic accomodations; the diseases prevalent among them, & the remedies they use; moral & physical circumstances which distinguish them from the tribes we know; peculiarities in their laws, customs & dispositions; and articles of commerce they may need or furnish, & to what extent." In short, Jefferson told Lewis he should not overlook anything that might facilitate the opening of trade between citizens of the United States and the Indians along the Missouri.[42]

In addition to learning whatever they could about the inhabitants of the Louisiana Territory, the expedition carried the corresponding responsibility of representing the United States to those inhabitants. "Make them acquainted," Jefferson told Lewis, "with the position, extent, character, peaceable & commercial dispositions of the U.S." Make clear "our wish to be neighborly, friendly & useful to them." Be sure to "allay all jealousies as to the object of your journey" and to "satisfy them of it's innocence." Let them know "of our dispositions to a commercial intercourse" and "confer with them on the points most convenient as mutual emporiums." Identify "the articles of most desireable interchange for them & us." He wrote, "In all your intercourse with the natives, treat them in the most friendly & conciliatory manner which their own conduct will admit."

So that he might better evaluate the potential threat posed by Mackenzie's grand plan for a powerful British presence in Canada and on the Pacific slope, Jefferson also devoted considerable energy to shaping the geographic knowledge—the "additional gratification" of the message to Congress—which Lewis and his party would gather. If they followed his plan, they would provide both cartographic data and an inventory of natural resources. Jefferson imagined the outbound journey as consisting of three distinct geographic sections to be studied. The first section was the Missouri River itself; the second was mountainous region dividing the Missouri and whichever river the expedition determined offered "the best communication with the Pacific ocean." The third section of the outgoing journey was that yet-to-be-determined river offering the best course to the Pacific.[43] Throughout the journey, "beginning at the mouth of the Missouri," Jefferson directed Lewis, "you will take observations of latitude & longitude, at all remarkable points" on the rivers and along the portage. He added, "your observations are to be taken with great pains and accuracy, to be entered distinctly and intelligibly for others as well as yourself." While performing their ethnographic studies and transcontinental survey, the members of the expedition were also under instruction to observe the "soil," the "animals," the "mineral productions," the "volcanic appearances," and the "climate" of the territory through which they passed.

Of the three sections into which he divided the outbound line of the western expedition, Jefferson was more interested in the first two. He stated plainly, "The object of your mission is to explore the Missouri river, & such principal stream of it" which extended farthest to the west and reached highest into the "Stony Mountains." Jefferson instructed the members of the expedition to take as wide a view as possible as they moved through the Missouri River country: "altho' your route will be along the channel of the Missouri, yet you will endeavor to inform yourself, by enquiry, of the character & extent of the country watered by it's branches, & especially on it's Southern side." He hoped to learn the nature of the territory between Missouri River and both the "Rio Bravo" and the "Rio Colorado."[44] Jefferson did have a few specific questions about the region north of the Missouri. He wrote, "if you can learn any thing certain of the most Northern source of the Missisipi, & of it's position relatively to the lake of the woods, it will be interesting to us." More to the point perhaps, Jefferson desired "some account . . . of the path of the Canadien traders from the Missispi, at the mouth of the Ouisconsing to where it strikes the Missouri." Jefferson was, in effect, attempting to assess the degree to which the Missouri River country would provide a reliable buffer between the United States and the British in North America. He wanted to know whether the geography at the limit of the Louisiana Territory would provide any natural separation between the United States and European powers on the Pacific slope and consequently offer some insulation for the trading relationships he expected to develop between U.S. citizens and Indians following the expedition. To this end, Jefferson also wanted know for certain the difficulty of the portage from the Missouri to the best waters feeding the Pacific Ocean.[45]

Although reaching the Pacific Ocean was not the principal object of the mission, Jefferson considered the possibility that the expedition would eventually make it there. Once they managed to arrive on the coast, Jefferson had two concerns. First, he wanted Lewis to determine whether the furs of the Pacific Northwest could "be collected as advantageously at the head of the Missouri as at Nootka sound, or any other point of that coast." The likelihood of such a scenario, of course, was contingent on the nature of the portage across the mountains. Jefferson was anxious to discover whether the coastal trade could be "conducted through the Missouri & U.S. more beneficially than by the circumnavigation now practised." If so, he feared the British not only might try to shift their Canadian trade southward but also might attempt to redirect their Pacific trade to the Missouri and Mississippi rivers. Jefferson's only other interest in the Pacific Ocean, should they reach it, was as a potentially safer return route.[46]

However much Lewis and his party learned about the geography and the people west of the Mississippi, Jefferson stressed the importance of returning safely. While he may well have "value[d] too much the lives of citizens to offer them to probable destruction," he emphasized the preservation of the information the expedition gathered. He advised Lewis that members of the party should use their "leisure times" to produce "several copies" of their notes and calculations. He requested further that "one of these copies be on the paper of the birch, as less liable to injury from damp than common paper." As an additional precaution, he recommended putting the documents "into the care of the most trust-worthy of your attendants" in order to "guard . . . against the accidental losses to which they will be exposed." Jefferson acknowledged, "it is impossible for us to foresee in what manner you will be received by those people, whether with hospitality or hostility," and "so is it impossible to prescribe the exact degree of perseverance with which you are to pursue your journey." In the end, Jefferson told Lewis, "To your own discretion therefore must be left the degree of danger you may risk." Jefferson cautioned him only "to err on the side of . . . safety," and "to bring back your party safe even with less information." After all, Jefferson explained, "In the loss of yourselves, we should lose also the information you will have acquired," but "by returning safely with [just some information], you may enable us to renew the essay with better calculated means."

On July 18, 1803, William Clark wrote that he would "chearfully join" Lewis and "partake of the dangers, difficulties, and fatigues" of the proposed expedition.[47] Numerous setbacks in the preparation stages prevented them from beginning their ascent of the Missouri until the following spring. Frustrating though the delays were, they coincided with significant developments in the transfer of the Louisiana Territory from France to the United States, which in turn permitted Jefferson to refine further his directions for the expedition.[48] Although, as Jefferson wrote to his son-in-law on 5 July 1803, the treaty for Louisiana "removes from us the greatest source of danger to our peace," he recognized that real danger remained along America's periphery.[49] The acquisition of the territory did not, in itself, improve the precarious situation in the West, where the British maintained a robust presence. Indeed, by removing the competing interests of France and Spain from the interior of North America, the acquisition of the Louisiana Territory had the potential to deepen the crises the United States faced across the Mississippi. Neither nature nor demography promised security. On one hand, Mackenzie's report indicated that the portage through the western mountains would be convenient or easy. On the other, Jefferson knew that United States did not have the demographic resources to populate the Missouri River country. Americans would not fully settle the lands east of the Mississippi for many years. Furthermore, to Jefferson's way of thinking, delaying American settlement was preferable. Rather than spreading the population sparsely over a large territory, Jefferson wanted to wait until "we shall be full on this side" and then advance "compactly as we multiply."[50] Without American citizens settled throughout the Louisiana Territory, however, the United States' hold on the land was tenuous.

Through the fall and winter of 1803–4, Jefferson adjusted his instructions for the expedition in two important ways. First, he narrowed the breadth of land on either side of the Missouri about which the expedition was to gather intelligence. Jefferson reported to Lewis, "I have proposed in conversation, & it seems generally to be assented to, that Congress shall appropriate [ten to twelve thousand dollars] for exploring the principal waters of the Mississippi & Missouri." The additional funding would support additional expeditions. He explained: "I should send a party up the Red river to it's head, then to cross over to the head of the Arkansas, & come down that. A 2d party for the Pani and Padouca rivers, & a 3d perhaps for the Moingona & St. Peters." No longer did the expedition need to concern itself with the character of the "dividing lands" between the Missouri and both the "Rio Bravo" and the "Rio Colorado," and of the inhabitants. Jefferson now wrote, "The object of your mission is single, the direct water communication from sea to sea formed by the bed of the Missouri & perhaps the Oregon."[51] Only once Jefferson knew the nature of that portage through the "Stony Mountains" could he fairly assess the threat posed by the British on the Pacific slope.

In January 1804, Jefferson also advised Lewis that he could now be more direct in his communications with Indians. He wrote: "N. Orleans was delivered to us on the 20th of Dec. and our garrisons & government established there. The order for the delivery of the Upper posts were to leave N. Orleans on the 28th and we presume all those posts will be occupied by our troops by the last day of the present month." Jefferson explained, "When your instructions were penned, this new position was not so authentically known as to effect the complection of your instructions." "It will now be proper," he told Lewis, that "you should inform those through whose country you shall pass, or whom you may meet, . . . that henceforward we become their fathers and friends." Moreover, having "now become sovereigns of the country . . . we are authorised to propose to them in direct terms the institution of commerce with them." No longer would the expedition merely open the way to trade with the Indians of the Missouri River country for displaced private traders of the trans-Appalachian West. Instead, the expedition became the leading edge of an official effort to secure the loyalty of the same Indians through the eventual establishment of government-sponsored trading houses.[52] Developing commercial trade and building alliances with the Indians of the Missouri River valley provided a reasonable, temporary solution. As commercial allies, Indians would serve as the trustees of the Louisiana Territory until Americans were prepared to assume direct possession.

From the outset, Lewis had understood the need to develop constructive relationships with the Indians of the Missouri River country. He wrote to Clark, "you will readily conceive the importance to the U. States of an early friendly and intimate acquaintance with the tribes that inhabit that country." They should, he explained, be "impressed with a just idea of the rising importance of the U. States." Equally well, Lewis comprehended that their loyalty to and affection for the United States would best be won through commercial interest. Accordingly, among their chief responsibilities was to inform Indians of America's intention "to become usefull to them by furnishing them . . . with such articles by way of barter as may be desired by them."[53] In an 1806 letter to a fellow American, Clark explained that "the intention of our government" was "to form trading establishments on the Missouri" in order to "secure the attachments of the nativs."[54] Of the supplies with which Lewis and Clark outfitted their expedition, the goods designated for exchange with Indians represented a significant proportion. The total on the "Summary of Purchases" was $2,160.14, and they spent $669.50 on "Indian Presents."[55]

In accordance with Jefferson's instructions, Lewis and Clark met as many of the Indian groups who lived along the Missouri River as possible. Flawed though many of their assessments may have been in the end, the explorers struggled to understand the trading network of the Missouri River valley to the best of their ability.[56] They identified the preferred trading partners of different Indian groups and the commodities each group privileged. Jefferson believed that, properly applied, such information would permit the Americans to seduce Indians away from their European trading partners, to foster peace among the Indian groups of the Missouri River valley, and to draw them into tributary relationships with the United States. Developing strong economic ties with the Indians west of the Mississippi River would provide greater protection from any European imperial power that might maintain or establish a presence along the westernmost border of the United States. In Jefferson's scheme, Indians would hold the lands between the Mississippi and the Rocky Mountains in trust until Americans were prepared to expand into the territory in compact and orderly fashion.

Jefferson and the Indians

Whenever he had the opportunity, Jefferson himself tried to sell the Indians of the Missouri country on the proposition of new trade relationships. By instructing Lewis to send willing Indian chiefs east to Washington, Jefferson, in effect, joined the expedition and worked to achieve its purposes. To Lewis he wrote, "if a few of their influential chiefs . . . wish to visit us, arrange such a visit." Jefferson instructed him to "furnish them with authority to call on our officers," and he directed that they be "conveyed to this place at the public expence."[57] Lewis made the necessary arrangements to ensure that the Indian chiefs whom he sent to St. Louis would find their way to Washington.[58] As the expedition navigated through the virtually unknown and often hostile territory of the Missouri River and repeatedly negotiated delicate encounters with large numbers of Indians, Jefferson occasionally met with several Indian chiefs in carefully choreographed ceremonies in the nation's capital. In July 1804, a group of Osage chiefs visited Washington. Jefferson assured them that although "our dwellings indeed are very far apart," they were "not too far to carry on commerce and useful intercourse." He urged his audience, "Let us employ ourselves then in mutually accomodating each other." He explained, "you have furs and peltries which we want, and we have clothes and other useful things which you want." Jefferson had sent "a beloved man, Capt. Lewis, one of my own household to learn something of the people with whom we are now united." So that "we can be useful to you," Lewis was to discover "what nations inhabited the great country called Louisiana," "what number of peltries they could furnish," "what quantities & kinds of merchandize they would require," and "where would be the deposits most convenient for them."[59]

Purchasing Louisiana authorized the United States to pursue officially commercial relationships with the Indians living in the Missouri River country. While developing economic ties would strengthen bonds between Americans and Indians and consequently improve security on America's western front, the sudden acquisition of so great an extent of land created other problems for Jefferson. The acquisition of an immense new territory challenged his conviction that there was a fundamental relationship between a nation and the land it occupies.[60] Quite simply, Americans did not live in the new territory over which they now had jurisdiction. Accordingly, in addition to sending an expedition into the Missouri River country to lay a foundation for trade, Jefferson devised other strategies to foster closer ties between American citizens and the Indians of the Missouri River valley and thus enhance national security. Jefferson pursued a tactic that incorporated inventive history and the rhetoric of family. He imagined a fantastic scheme that inserted Americans into the natural history of North America and into the bloodlines of Indians.

Meeting with Indian leaders who had traveled to Washington, Jefferson both emphasized America's strength and identified similarities between his and their peoples. To the chiefs of the Osages, Missouris, Kansas, Ottos, Panis, Ayowas, and the Sioux, Jefferson stated plainly, "we are strong." In order to support his claim, he stressed America's demographic advantage. "We are," he said, "as numerous as the leaves of the trees." So his meaning would not be lost, Jefferson offered another metaphor: "we are," he said, "as numerous as the stars in the heavens." American strength was not based merely on demography but also on potential force. Jefferson advised the chiefs that "we are all gun-men."[61] When he mentioned the expedition to the delegation, Jefferson made a veiled threat. He said to the chiefs, "I thank you for the readiness with which you have listened to [Lewis's] voice and for the favor you have showed him in his passage up the Missouri." He immediately followed up his expression of gratitude with, "I hope your countrymen will favor and protect him as far as they extend." And then Jefferson added, "on his return we shall hear what he has seen & learnt." While Jefferson made explicit that whatever information Lewis brought back would be helpful for establishing trading houses, it seems reasonable that the implicit message was that anything less than Lewis's safe return and positive report would be unacceptable.[62] Jefferson insisted that "we do not fear any nation."[63]

Although Jefferson repeatedly stressed the strength of the United States, he also often acknowledged, as he did to White-Hairs and other chiefs and warriors of the Osage Nation, that Indians were strong. "The great Spirit" had provided both peoples with such strength "not that we might hurt one another, but to do each other all the good in our power."[64] In his communications with the Indians whom Lewis and Clark sent to Washington, Jefferson usually adopted such a conciliatory tone, speaking in warm, friendly language. As he said in his preliminary remarks to the representatives of the Osage Nation on July 12, 1804, his goal was to "secure everlasting peace, friendship & commerce between the Osage nation, and the 17. United nations in whose name I speak."[65] Typically, rather than threatening to overwhelm them through demographic or military might, Jefferson rhetorically drew Indians into an alliance with Americans through inventive history and a fantastic family tree. Throughout, his goal was to increase the legitimacy of America's claim to the lands west of the Mississippi.

Although exactly "from where the aboriginal inhabitants of America came" remained a "great question" in Jefferson's day, there was little doubt that they had been in the New World for a long time. After a brief linguistic analysis in his *Notes on the State of Virginia*, Jefferson speculated that Indians had been in America for "an immense course of time; perhaps not less than many people give to the age of the earth." He was certain that Indians were at least "of greater antiquity" than the peoples of Asia.[66] Indians were so much a natural feature of the Americas that Jefferson included them in his response to Query VI of *Notes*, "Productions Mineral, Vegetable and Animal." Indians were themselves natural products of the New World, and, as such, the legitimacy of their claim to the land was virtually unassailable. Moreover, as Jefferson explained to Lewis, while the United States had become "sovereign of the [Missouri] country," there was no corresponding "diminution of the Indian rights of occupancy."[67]

The fundamental, pre-historical connection between Indians and the land on which they lived provided Jefferson with creative inspiration. As he had done a quarter century earlier in "A Summary View of the Rights of British America," he fabricated a new origin myth for Americans.[68] Jefferson downplayed the arrival of colonial Americans from Europe. Although he admitted, "we are descended from the old nations which live beyond the great water," he said that "we consider ourselves no longer as of the old nations."[69] Speaking to the Osage, he claimed it had been "so long since our forefathers came from beyond the great water, that we have lost the memory of it."[70] Washing away America's European heritage, Jefferson planted a new memory, one that suggested an elemental connection between Americans and the land they occupied. He said, "We & our fathers have been here so long that we seem like you to have grown out of this land."[71]

Jefferson had inserted Americans into the natural history of North America, and the United States suddenly possessed its territorial domain not by conquest, purchase, or labor, but in the same natural manner as Indians. If Jefferson were able to establish a family relationship between American citizens and Indians, especially those of the Missouri River valley, it would only serve to reinforce the legitimacy of the United States' title to the land. Consequently, the American Revolution, which was a "family quarrel between us and the English, who were then our brothers," was eventually followed by an effort to restore a more authentic brotherhood.[72] Born out of the same land, Americans and Indians were relatives. Jefferson repeatedly used the language of family when he spoke to and about Indians west of the Mississippi River. He told the Mandan that he considered them to be "united in one family" with Americans.[73] Jefferson often addressed Indians as "my children."[74] Significantly in a republican world without primogeniture, where brothers were equals, Jefferson also addressed them as "brothers" or "brethren."[75] Extending and emphasizing the theme of family, Jefferson informed the Osage delegation that he had specifically chosen Lewis, "a beloved man," and "one of my own household," to travel among and "learn something of the people with whom we are now united."[76] While Jefferson used the rhetoric of family to address the visiting Indian leaders in Washington, Lewis and Clark did the same as they traveled up the Missouri River.[77]

Rhetorically joining Americans and Indians together into one great North American family was not a significant sacrifice or compromise in Jefferson's mind. As early as 1785 he had made a spirited defense of Indian abilities. He affirmed "that the proofs of genius given by the Indians of North America, place them on a level with Whites in the same uncultivated state." More simply, he stated, "in body and mind," Indians were "equal to the white man."[78] Jefferson was not so much explaining a reality or demonstrating genuine affection for the Indians as he was fabricating a familial tie that would reinforce America's claim to the land. Unable to incorporate the new territory into the United States through rapid, dense settlement and the extension of American institutions, Jefferson figuratively united Indians and Americans into a single family. By way of this imaginative identification, whatever Indians owned, citizens of the United States—as members of the North American family—also owned. Unable to incorporate the lands west of the Mississippi River into the United States, Jefferson artfully incorporated Americans into the natural history of the land.

Jefferson could not deny the hostilities between the United States and the Indians east of the Mississippi River. There had been too many battles and too much bloodshed to do that, but he could exonerate both Americans and Indians. Jefferson blamed the British. Their corruption poisoned the relationship between Indians living east of the Mississippi River and citizens of the United States; the British created the "ill blood." "While we were under that government," he explained, "we were constantly kept at war with the red men our neighbors."[79] In order to strengthen their own position, the British had played one group against the other. Colonial Americans did not seek war with Indians nor did Indians seek it with colonial Americans; instead the British "kept" each at war with the other. Jefferson cast "the strangers from beyond the great water" as the common enemy of all the natives of North America.[80]

As Jefferson considered the westernmost territories of the United States, he could take comfort knowing that the hostility between Indians and Americans citizens in the east was unnatural, the result of European corruption. In the recently acquired Louisiana Territory, though, European influence remained relatively light. British and other European traders had integrated themselves into the Missouri River valley trading network. But Lewis and Clark were already at work attempting to reorient the flow of trade through the United States and to restore the authentic and harmonious— however fictitious—kinship between Indians and American citizens. Should they succeed, they would set the foundation for greater security on America's western frontier.

A Natural Boundary

Upon his return, Lewis confirmed Jefferson's fears about the British. He wrote, "The British N. West Company of Canada has for

several years, carried on a partial trade with the Minnetares Ahway-
haways and Mandans on the Missouri." He wrote that there was
"good reason for believing that [the British] intend shortly to form
an establishment near those nations with a view to engross the fur
trade of the Missouri." Lewis concluded, "if we are to regard the
trade of the Missouri as an object of importance to the United States;
the strides of this company toward the Missouri can not be too vig-
ilantly watched nor too firmly and speedily opposed by our government." Even so, Lewis had good news to offer Jefferson. He was, he
wrote, "fully convinced" that "if the government will only aid, even
in a very limited manner, the enterprize of her Citizens," that Americans would "shortly derive the benefits of a most lucrative trade"
along the Missouri River.[81] Still more pleasing would have been the
expedition's account of their activities and the geography they
encountered through the summer of 1805, the most difficult months
of their entire journey.

At the westernmost limit of the United States, the expedition
came upon a virtually impenetrable natural boundary. The mountains were "steep" and "stoney."[82] Clark called them "excessively
bad."[83] Patrick Gass thought they were "the most terrible mountains I ever beheld."[84] Approaching the headwaters of the Missouri,
Lewis had observed one particularly striking formation. He wrote,
"two curious mountains presented themselves of square figures."
The sides, which "appeared to be formed of yellow clay," rose "per-
pendicularly to the hight of 250 feet." The "tops appeared to be level
plains." Lewis commented that "these inaccessible hights appeared
like the ramparts of immence fortifications." He concluded, "I have
no doubt but with very little assistance from art they might be rendered impregnable."[85]

If the image of snow-covered mountains rising in the West appeared to Lewis as he approached them like the rock-solid, impenetrable wall of a well-built fort, the experience of passing through the
mountains led others to reach for different metaphors. The Rocky
Mountains, Gass wrote, were a "horrible mountainous desert."[86]
The trails were difficult. Lewis described, for example, one such "excessively dangerous" road. A "narrow rockey path" ran above a creek

and "generally on the side of steep precipice, from which in many places if ether man or horse were precipitated they would inevitably be dashed in pieces."[87] As they moved farther and higher into the mountains, the exploring party endured bitter cold, and heavy snows replaced driving rains. Sometimes finding any clear path proved nearly impossible. Clark wrote that "in maney places the Snow had entirely filled up the track, and obliged me to hunt Several minits for the track." He wrote, "We are continually covered with Snow." Clark commented, "I have been wet and as cold in every part as I ever was in my life, indeed I was at one time fearfull my feet would freeze in the thin mockersons which I wore."[88] Once they made it through the mountains they were tremendously relieved. Lewis felt an "inexpressible joy."[89] He wrote, "the pleasure I now felt in having tryumphed over the rocky Mountains and decending once more to a level and fertile country . . . can be more readily conceived than expressed."[90] While still in the mountains, the very sight of the plain below, approximately "60 Miles distant," was enough to provide "hope for subsistance and greately revived the sperits of the party."[91]

Gass agreed that there was "much joy and rejoicing among the corps" when they first discovered the "valley or level part of the country about 40 miles ahead." Indeed, the reaction of the Corps members as they emerged from the mountains, Gass wrote, was similar to that of "passengers at sea, who have experienced a dangerous and protracted voyage, when they first discover land on the long looked for coast."[92] The reference to the sea recalls Jefferson's first inaugural address. Jefferson had remarked that among the young nation's many natural advantages was its separation from Europe by the Atlantic Ocean.[93] The greatness of the mountains and the difficulty of crossing them seemingly stretched the distance between the mouths of the Missouri and the Columbia rivers. So immense, the mountains Lewis and Clark traversed in the summer of 1805 held promise as a natural, defensible boundary in a way that no other previously established imperial or national border in the West had. It was a boundary that did not so much limit the westward expansion of the United States as protect the underpopulated, recently acquired western territory of the young republic from penetration by a European power.

The "Stony Mountains" were themselves a great ocean and provided Americans some relief in their effort to "present as firm a front on [the western] as on our Eastern border."[94]

In his annual message to Congress, delivered just over two months after Lewis and Clark's arrival in St. Louis, Jefferson remarked that the expedition "had all the success which could have been expected." He wrote, "In the course of their journey they acquired a knoledge of numerous tribes of Indians hitherto unknown; they informed themselves of the trade which may be carried on with them, the best channels and positions for it, & they are enabled to give with accuracy the geography of the line they pursued." Jefferson's satisfaction was warranted. The "Stony Mountains" promised to be a less permeable boundary than the Mississippi River, and already there were reports of Indians in the Missouri River country who were eager to trade with Americans.[95]

Without the geographic and demographic advantages from which America benefited in the East, the western perimeter of the United States was vulnerable, particularly to colonial-minded, monarchical European empires. In order to counteract the liabilities of the Mississippi River boundary, Jefferson focused on Indian policy. Central to his design was trade with Indians, both within and outside the United States. Planned prior to the Louisiana Purchase, Jefferson intended the expedition to reduce the threat posed by foreign, particularly British, traders in the Missouri River country and surrounding areas. Executed following the Purchase, the expedition lay the foundation for a framework by which Indians would hold the territory in trust until Americans had achieved the demographic strength to settle the land themselves.[96] Jefferson sent Lewis and Clark west not to get through the interior or into the interior; rather, he sent them west *for* the interior.[97] He sent the expedition in order to make legitimate and natural—through commercial ties and fictional kinship with Indians—America's claim to the lands watered by the western tributaries of the Mississippi River, and to make more secure the western perimeter.

Acquiring the Pacific slope was never a goal of Jefferson. That the United States could expand geographically did not mean that it should. Just as he understood the dangers of a weak periphery and of a river border, Jefferson also understood the risks an empire took in overreaching.[98] Indicating his comfort with a United States of limited territory, in his January 30, 1787, letter to James Madison, Jefferson wrote, "I never had any interest Westward of the Alleghaney; and I never will have any." Although Jefferson hoped there would not be a split between eastern and western Americans, should such a division come to pass, he told his friend, it would not threaten his own vision of America.[99] Even after the Louisiana Purchase and in the midst of his planning of the exploration of the Missouri River country, Jefferson expressed similar convictions in a letter to John Breckinridge. Some Federalists, he wrote, were arguing against the Louisiana Purchase on the grounds that it would result in a separation of eastern and western Americans and the formation of a "new confederacy, embracing all the waters of the Mississippi." Jefferson asked his correspondent, "If it should become the interest of those nations to separate from us . . . why should the Atlantic states dread it?" Jefferson proceeded: "We think we see their happiness in . . . union, and we wish it. Events may prove otherwise. . . . God bless them both and keep them in union if it be for their good, but separate them, if it be better."[100] So long as republican principles took root and blossomed west of the Appalachian chain, Jefferson did not think it essential that the self-governing republics belong to a single federal entity. Republican countries, whose jurisdictions would be demarcated by permeable boundaries, would coexist peacefully and prosperously, much as the united, republican states of America already did.[101]

NOTES

1. Thomas Jefferson (hereafter TJ), First Inaugural Address, March 4, 1801, in Merrill D. Peterson, ed., *The Portable Thomas Jefferson* (New York, 1977), 290–95.

2. TJ to Secretary of Navy Robert Smith, July 13, 1804, in Donald Jackson, ed., *Letters of the Lewis and Clark Expedition with Related Documents, 1783–1854,* 2d ed., 2 vols. (Urbana, Ill., 1978) (hereafter Jackson, *Letters*), 1:199–200, note to entry 126. The literature on Jefferson and the West is extensive. The best overview of the crises in the West, the role of the Mississippi River, the Louisiana Purchase, and the uncertain control of the expanded nation is Dumas Malone, *Jefferson the President: First Term, 1801–1805* (Boston, 1970), 269–363. See also Jon Kukla, *A*

Wilderness So Immense: The Louisiana Purchase and the Destiny of America (New York, 2003); James E. Lewis Jr., *The American Union and the Problem of Neighborhood: The United States and the Collapse of the Spanish Empire, 1783–1829* (Chapel Hill, 1998), 1–40; Lawrence S. Kaplan, *Thomas Jefferson: Westward the Course of Empire* (Wilmington, 1999), 35–152; Drew McCoy, *The Elusive Republic: Political Economy in Jeffersonian America* (New York, 1980), 196–208; Peter S. Onuf, *Statehood and Union: A History of the Northwest Ordinance* (Bloomington, 1987), 1–21; Frank Lawrence Owsley Jr. and Gene A. Smith, *Filibusters and Expansionists: Jeffersonian Manifest Destiny, 1800–1821* (Tuscaloosa, 1997), 1–31; Robert W. Tucker and David C. Hendrickson, *Empire of Liberty: The Statecraft of Thomas Jefferson* (New York, 1990), 25–171; Bernard DeVoto, *The Course of Empire* (Boston, 1952, 1998), 263–432.

3. TJ, Message to Congress, Jan. 18, 1803, in Jackson, *Letters,* 1:10–13.

4. Malone, *Jefferson the President: First Term,* 260–61. Although France owned Louisiana in 1802, Spain continued to administer the district.

5. TJ, Message to Congress, Jan. 18, 1803, in Jackson, *Letters,* 1:12.

6. Thomas Hutchins, *An Historical Narrative and Topographical Description of Louisiana and West Florida* (1784; Gainesville, Fla., 1968), 23.

7. Hutchins, *Historical Narrative.* 23.

8. Kukla, *Wilderness So Immense,* 38–45.

9. Quoted ibid., 45.

10. Treaty of Paris, 1783. "The United States in Congress assembled . . ." *Documents from the Continental Congress and the Constitutional Convention, 1774–1789,* http://memory.loc.gov/cgi-bin/query/r?ammem/bdsbib:@field(NUMBER+@band (bdsdcc+08401)), American Memory, Library of Congress. For the dispute between Spain and the United States over the southern limit of the United States, see Lewis, *American Union,* 12–40; and Frederic Austin Ogg, *The Opening of the Mississippi: A Struggle for Supremacy in the American Interior* (1904; reprint, New York, 1969), 400–459.

11. Hutchins, *Historical Narrative,* 23.

12. At issue was whether the southern border of the United States just east of the Mississippi River was extended only to 32° 30′ latitude or farther south, to 31° latitude. For a fuller explanation of the disagreement, see Ogg, *Opening of the Mississippi,* 410–16.

13. Hutchins, *Historical Narrative,* 23.

14. Kukla, *Wilderness So Immense,* 59.

15. James Madison to TJ, Aug. 24, 1784, in James Morton Smith, ed., *The Republic of Letters: The Correspondence between Thomas Jefferson and James Madison, 1776–1826,* 3 vols. (New York, 1995), 1:337–38.

16. George Washington to Benjamin Harrison, Oct. 10, 1784, quoted in Ogg, *Opening of the Mississippi,* 419–20.

17. James Ronda, *Finding the West: Explorations with Lewis and Clark* (Albuquerque, 2001), 6.

18. TJ to Archibald Stuart, Jan. 25, 1786, in Julian Boyd et al., eds., *The Papers of Thomas Jefferson*, 30 vols. to date (Princeton, 1950–), 9:218.

19. TJ to James Madison, Jan. 30, 1787, ibid., 11:93. The Mississippi issue was discussed at the federal Convention later that year in Philadelphia (Max Farrand, ed., *The Records of the Federal Convention of 1787*, 4 vols. [New Haven, 1911–66], 1:585; 2:442).

20. See Kukla, *Wilderness So Immense*, 59–69.

21. David J. Weber, *The Spanish Frontier in North America* (New Haven, 1992), 279–85.

22. During the 1790s, for example, Philip Nolan ventured into Spanish Texas at least four times to trade horses and run contraband (Dan L. Flores, *Jefferson and Southwestern Exploration: The Freeman and Custis Accounts of the Red River Expedition of 1806* [Norman, 1984], 32–35).

23. December 4, 1786, in *Secret Journals of the Acts and Proceedings of Congress*, 4 vols. (Boston, 1820–21), 4:320–23. Between 1785 and 1788, John Jay and Don Diego de Gardoqui, the first Spanish envoy to the United States, attempted to negotiate a treaty. During the process, Jay did recommend to Congress that the United States give up navigation rights on the Mississippi for an extended period. In the end, though, Congress rejected the recommendation and in 1788 terminated Jay's commission to negotiate a treaty. See Whitaker, *The Spanish-American Frontier*; Ogg, *Opening of the Mississippi*, 421–441; and Lewis, *American Union*, 14–17.

24. *Secret Journals of Congress*, 4:320–23. Confirming Madison's claim to Jefferson, the anonymous author wrote, "Politicks . . . are now sounded aloud in this part of the world, and discussed by almost every person."

25. Ogg, *Opening of the Mississippi*, 451. For a fuller account of George Rogers Clark's plans to attack New Orleans, see Kukla, *A Wilderness So Immense*, 156–78. For a book-length general summary of George Rogers Clark's role in the West, see Lowell H. Harrison, *George Rogers Clark and the War in the West* (Lexington, 1976).

26. Jefferson believed that the Spanish were using the Mississippi as "bait for a defection of the Western people" (TJ to James Madison, March 29, 1789, in Smith, *Republic of Letters*, 1:607).

27. On the Treaty of San Lorenzo, see Samuel Flagg Bemis, *Pinckney's Treaty: America's Advantage from Europe's Distresses, 1783–1800*, rev. ed. (New Haven, 1960).

28. James Madison to TJ, and TJ to James Madison, March 6, 1796, in Smith, *Republic of Letters*, 2:923–24.

29. Kukla, *Wilderness So Immense*, 18–19; Alexander DeConde, *This Affair of Louisiana* (New York, 1976), 84–105; Ogg, *Opening of the Mississippi*, 460–94.

30. TJ to Robert Livingston, April 18, 1802, in Peterson, *Portable Jefferson*, 485–88.

31. For TJ on America's rivers, see TJ, "Rivers," Query II in *Notes on the State of Virginia*, ibid., 32–45. For Jefferson's understanding of how rivers may expand influence and opportunity, see Onuf, *Jefferson's Empire*, 66. Alan Taylor also describes the dual roles of rivers as "contradictory." He suggests the Niagara River was simultaneously a "place of communication, passage, and mixing"

and "a place of separation and distinction" (Taylor, "The Divided Ground: Upper Canada, New York, and the Iroquois Six Nations, 1783–1815," *Journal of the Early Republic* 22 [2002]: 56).

32. TJ, Message to Congress, Jan. 18, 1803, in Jackson, *Letters*, 1:13.

33. Historians generally agree that Jefferson's reading of Mackenzie's publication inspired him to launch the expedition.

34. Donald Jackson, *Thomas Jefferson and the Stony Mountains: Exploring the West from Monticello* (1981; Norman, 1993), 124; 158 n. 12. Jefferson purchased a second copy of Mackenzie's *Voyages from Montreal* the following summer. Most likely he gave the second copy—which was a smaller edition and therefore easier to carry—to Lewis for the expedition. See Jackson, *Letters*, 1:55–56. Alexander Mackenzie, *Voyages from Montreal, on the River St. Laurence, through the Continent of North America, to the Pacific Oceans; in the Years 1789 and 1793. With a Preliminary Account of the Rise, Progress, and Present State of the Fur Trade of that Country* (1801; reprint, Ann Arbor, 1966).

35. Mackenzie reached the Pacific Ocean at the mouth of the Bella Coola River; he was never anywhere near the Columbia River. What he assumed to be the Columbia was, in fact, eventually to be named the Fraser River, which is significantly farther north. Mackenzie had not learned of his mistake by the time he published the journal (Mackenzie, *Voyages from Montreal*, 349, 410–11). Jefferson was also unaware of Mackenzie's error, and so interpreted the data and drew conclusions accordingly—that is, based on bad geography.

36. Ibid., 397, 408, 411.

37. Ibid., 410–11; emphasis added. Also see W. K. Lam, introduction to *The Journals and Letters of Sir Alexander MacKenzie* (Cambridge, Eng., 1970), 1–53.

38. Mackenzie, *Voyages from Montreal*, 412.

39. TJ had long been concerned about the British presence in the Missouri River country. "If Gr. Britain establishes herself on our whole land-board," he wrote in 1790, "our lot will be bloody and eternal war; or indissoluble confederacy" (TJ, "Outline of Policy on the Mississippi Question," enclosed with letter to William Carmichael, Aug. 2, 1790, in Boyd et al., *Jefferson Papers*, 17:115).

40. The quotations in this and subsequent paragraphs are from TJ, Message to Congress, Jan. 18, 1803, in Jackson, *Letters*, 1:10–13.

41. TJ did not receive the official documents of the Louisiana Purchase until July 14, and the *National Intelligencer* only published reports of the enormous land transaction on July 4. For the standard account of the Louisiana Purchase, see DeConde; see also Malone, *Jefferson the President: First Term*, 284–310; and Arthur Whitaker, *Mississippi Question, 1795–1803: A Study in Trade, Politics, and Diplomacy* (New York, 1934). For a more critical view of TJ's diplomacy throughout the Louisiana crisis, see Tucker and Hendrickson, *Empire of Liberty*, 87–100.

42. The quotations in this and following paragraphs are from TJ, Instructions to Lewis, June 20, 1803, in Jackson, *Letters*, 1:61–66.

43. TJ instructed Lewis to descend "the Columbia, Oregan, Colorado, or any other

river" that proved most practical once the expedition had reached the head-waters of the Missouri River.

44. The specific information in which TJ was interested was: "Whether the dividing grounds between the Missouri & them are mountains or flat lands, what are their distance from the Missori, the character of the intermediate country, & the people inhabiting it." TJ explained that "the Northern waters of the Missouri are less to be enquired after, becaue they have been ascertained to a considerable degree, & are still in a course of ascertainment by English traders, and travellers."

45. Lewis seems to have understood that the territory of greatest concern to TJ was the Missouri River country and the Rocky Mountains. He wrote to Clark: "During the last session of Congress a law was passed in conformity to a private message of the President of the United States, inti[t]led 'An Act making an appropriation for extending the external commerce of the United States.' The object of this Act as understood by its framers was to give the sanction of the government to exploreing the interior of the continent of North America, or that part of it bordering on the Missourie & Columbia Rivers" (Lewis to Clark, June 19, 1803, in Jackson, *Letters,* 1:57).

46. The quotations in this and the next paragraph are from TJ, Instructions to Lewis, June 20, 1803, ibid., 1:61–66.

47. Clark to Lewis, July 18, 1803, ibid., 110.

48. In October 1803, TJ presented the treaty with France for the Louisiana Territory to the 8th Congress. On October 21, the treaty was proclaimed, and ten days later so too was the Louisiana Enabling Act. On December 20, the United States took formal possession of Louisiana.

49. TJ to Thomas Mann Randolph, July 5, 1803, quoted in Malone, *Jefferson the President: First Term,* 4:284. Some historians have also concluded that the Louisiana Purchase resolved the Mississippi crisis. See, for example, McCoy, *Elusive Republic,* 200–201: "in addition to resolving the Mississippi crisis, the Louisiana Purchase was important to the Jeffersonians precisely because it promised to preserve the fundamentally agricultural, and hence republican, character of American society for centuries to come."

50. TJ to John Breckinridge, Aug. 12, 1803, in Peterson, *Portable Jefferson,* 496. See also McCoy, *Elusive Republic,* 200.

51. TJ to Lewis, Nov. 16, 1803, in Jackson, *Letters,* 1:137. Historians generally point to this last sentence to argue that TJ's primary goal for the expedition was to discover an all-water route across the continent. More likely, however, is that TJ was telling Lewis to focus only on the one line across the continent. With the promise of financial support for additional expeditions along other rivers at other latitudes within the territory west of the Mississippi, gathering geographical and demographic information far north and far south of the actual course of the Missouri was significantly less important for Lewis's expedition. For the other explorations TJ proposed, see Dan L. Flores, *Jefferson and South-*

western Exploration: The Freeman and Custis Accounts of the Red River Expedition of 1806 (Norman, Okla., 1985), 3–90.

52. TJ to Lewis, June 22, 1803, in Jackson, *Letters,* 1:165–66.

53. Lewis to Clark, June 19, 1803, ibid., 57.

54. Clark to Hugh Heney, July 20, 1806, ibid., 310.

55. "Summary of Purchases," A Recapitulation of Purchases by the Purveyor for Capt. Lewis, ibid., 93–94.

56. James P. Ronda provides the most detailed account of Lewis and Clark's efforts to make sense of the trading system throughout the Missouri River valley. See Ronda, *Lewis and Clark among the Indians* (1984; Lincoln, 1988).

57. TJ, Instructions to Lewis, June 20, 1803, in Jackson, *Letters,* 1:64.

58. Lewis to Amos Stoddard, May 16, 1804, ibid., 190.

59. TJ to the Osages, 16 July 1804, ibid., 200–203.

60. Peter Onuf argues that in TJ's conception of nationhood there was "a fundamental relationship between a particular people and its territorial domain" (Peter S. Onuf, *Jefferson's Empire: The Language of Nationhood* [Charlottesville, 2000], 21).

61. TJ to the Indian Delegation, [Jan. 4, 1806], in Jackson, *Letters,* 1:282.

62. TJ to the Osages, July 16, 1804, ibid., 200–203.

63. TJ to the Indian Delegation, [Jan. 4, 1806], ibid., 281.

64. TJ to the Osages, 16 July 1804, ibid., 201.

65. TJ to the Osages, 12 July 1804, ibid., 199.

66. *Notes,* Query XI, in Peterson, *Portable Jefferson,* 143–44; "A greater number of those radical changes of language having taken place among the red men of America, proves them of greater antiquity than those of Asia."

67. TJ to Lewis, Jan. 22, 1804, in Jackson, *Letters,* 1:165.

68. TJ, "A Summary View of the Rights of British America," July 1774, in Peterson, *Portable Jefferson,* 4–5. For a relevant interpretation of the "Summary View," see Onuf, *Jefferson's Empire,* 21–23.

69. TJ to the Indian Delegation, Jan. 4, 1806, in Jackson, *Letters,* 1:281.

70. TJ to the Osages, July 16, 1804, ibid., 200.

71. TJ to the Indian Delegation, Jan. 4, 1806, ibid., 281.

72. TJ Speech to Jean Baptiste Ducoigne, [ca. 1] June 1781, quoted in Onuf, *Jefferson's Empire,* 21.

73. TJ to the Wolf and People of the Mandan Nation, Dec. 30, 1806, quoted ibid., 51.

74. TJ to the Osages, 16 July 1804, in Jackson, *Letters,* 200.

75. See for example, TJ to the Indian Delegation, Jan. 4, 1806, ibid., 1:280–83; TJ to Handsome Lake, Nov. 3, 1802, both in Peterson, *Portable Jefferson,* 305. See also Onuf, *Jefferson's Empire,* 26–27.

76. TJ to the Osages, July 16, 1804, in Jackson, *Letters,* 1:201.

77. See, for example, Lewis and Clark to the Oto Indians, Aug. 4, 1804, ibid., 203–8, and Clark's Speech for the Yellowstone Indians, undated, in Gary E. Moulton,

ed., *The Journals of the Lewis and Clark Expedition,* 13 vols. (Lincoln, Neb., 1979–2001), 8:213–15.

78. TJ to Francois Jean de Chastellux, Paris, June 7, 1785, in Peter S. Onuf, ed., *Thomas Jefferson: An Anthology* (St. James., N.Y., 1999), 102.

79. TJ to the Chiefs of the Ottawas, Chippewas, Powtowatamies, Wyandots, and Senecas of Sandusky, April 22, 1808, quoted in Onuf, *Jefferson's Empire,* 47.

80. TJ to the Osages, July 16, 1804, in Jackson, *Letters,* 1:200–203.

81. Lewis to TJ, Sept. 23, 1806, ibid., 322.

82. See, for example, Clark, Sept. 14 and 15, 1805, in Moulton, *Journals of Lewis and Clark,* 5:204–6.

83. Clark, Sept. 14, 1805, ibid., 205.

84. Gass, Sept. 19, 1805, ibid., 10:143.

85. Lewis, June 13, 1805, ibid., 4:283.

86. Gass, Sept. 19, 1805, ibid., 10:145.

87. Lewis, Sept. 19, 1805, ibid., 5:215.

88. Clark, Sept. 16, 1805, ibid., 209.

89. Lewis, Sept. 19, 1805, ibid., 215.

90. Lewis, Sept. 22, 1805, ibid., 229.

91. Lewis, Sept. 19, 1805, ibid., 215. On September 20, 1805, Gass recorded seeing "the valley ahead, but a great way off" (ibid., 10:145).

92. Gass, Sept. 19, 1805, ibid., 145.

93. TJ, First Inaugural Address, March 4, 1801, in Peterson, *Portable Jefferson,* 290–95.

94. TJ, Message to Congress, Jan. 18, 1803, in Jackson, *Letters,* 1:12.

95. TJ's Annual Message to Congress, original draft, Dec. 2, 1806, in Jackson, *Letters,* 352.

96. Once Americans reached that point, of course, the relationship between trans-Mississippi Native Americans and Americans would more nearly resemble that between those same groups east of the Mississippi River.

97. In "So Vast an Enterprise: Thoughts on the Lewis and Clark Expedition," James P. Ronda writes, "While other geographers of empire had long thought about the Northwest Passage as a way *through* North America, Jefferson also inherited ideas about the passage as a way *into* the interior" (see Ronda, ed., *Voyages of Discovery: Essays on the Lewis and Clark Expedition* [Helena, 1998], 6).

98. Onuf, *Jefferson's Empire,* 1.

99. TJ to James Madison, Jan. 30, 1787, in Smith, *Republic of Letters,* 1:461–62.

100. TJ to John Breckinridge, Aug. 12, 1803, in Peterson, *Portable Jefferson,* 495–96.

101. Well into the 1820s the tireless western booster Thomas Hart Benton believed that the Continental Divide should be the "natural and everlasting boundary of the United States" (Jack Ericson Eblen, *The First and Second United States Empires* [Pittsburgh, 1968], 4). Eblen argues that it was only between 1825 and 1848 that the "classical idea of natural limits gave way to voracious expansionism."

Thomas Jefferson's Conflicted Legacy in American Archaeology

David Hurst Thomas

THOMAS JEFFERSON HAS BEEN UNIVERsally hailed as the father of American archaeology because his innovative burial mound excavations set the standard for all subsequent archaeological explorations in the Americas. Some of us even consider Jefferson to be one of the founding fathers of American anthropology because his research on American Indians established the "four-field" agenda—archaeology, ethnology, linguistics, and physical (or biological) anthropology—that remains the hallmark of the discipline.

But in according Thomas Jefferson an iconic, "founding father" status in American archaeology and anthropology, we must likewise recognize the more complicated reality of Jefferson as both "good father" and "bad father." Jefferson's legacy to anthropology is, in fact, clouded by his protoracialist thinking and his willingness to employ science as an instrument of state power. By embedding his anthropological inquiries within a federal nexus, which led directly to the exploration and expropriation of the American West, Jefferson created tensions and long-term consequences that continue to bedevil the field of American anthropology into the twenty-first century.

This essay explores the legacy of Thomas Jefferson to the fledgling fields of American anthropology and natural history, developing three specific themes: (1) the role of science as a tool of territorial expansion; (2) the inclusion of American Indians in the study of natural history; and (3) the harnessing of anthropological theory in state-sponsored experiments in directed cultural change.[1]

Indian Imagery and the New Republic

When the Sons of Liberty hurled ninety thousand pounds of tea into the Boston harbor, they dressed up like American Indian warriors, faces painted and wrapped in tattered blankets, waving hatchets and axes. These "Mohawk" malcontents defined the terms of American independence by asserting a new symbolism for colonists disillusioned with British rule. Although grounded in the principles of self-government based on egalitarian principles, the American Revolution posed inevitable questions of identity. What does it mean to be not-British? What does it mean to be an American?

By assuming faux-Indian identities, the Boston protesters crossed the boundaries of European-style civility to attack the specific laws that vexed the colonists. They adopted the Indian as their symbol of daring, strength, individual courage, and defiance against hopeless odds. The logic of a unique Indian-style Americanism energized the Revolution and helped define a new national character. The Sons of Liberty had carved out an identity distinct from that of Mother England.

An important linguistic change took place as well. Before the Boston Tea Party, the term "American" usually meant "Indian" on both sides of the Atlantic. "Had anyone asked Captain John Smith at Jamestown or Miles Standish at Plymouth how the Americans were faring," suggests the anthropologist Robert Venables, "both would have reported on the local Indian nations. Smith and Standish were, after all, Englishmen."[2] But as they adopted Indian symbolism, the rebel colonists began naming themselves "Americans," both asserting a detachment from England and an emerging common identity with the other American—the Indians.

Who was more American than a Mohawk? The Indians and the Sons of Liberty were both American-born. Both embraced a love of independence and a certain skepticism toward authority. Because they had never experienced the feudal conditions of the Old World, Indians were viewed as somehow pure and uncontaminated—the perfect symbols of American life and liberty. "When our ancestors threw the tea overboard in Boston harbor," wrote Daniel Carter Beard, cofounder of the Boy Scouts of America, "there was a lot of junk, in the way of played-out ideas along with a monarchical form of government, which went overboard with the tea."[3]

Although Europeans of the day believed that Indians lived outside the bounds of civilization, Samuel Adams and the other American patriots increasingly gravitated toward Indian symbolism in their rejection of English-style civilization. The Indian-as-American-icon played directly into the new national narrative, reinforcing the morality and integrity of the New World and demonstrating that the New Republic possessed a distinctive history—a spirit that defined America as unique and divinely favored.

Jefferson Sticks Up for America

Still smarting from losses in the Seven Years' War and looking for a way to curtail British political ambitions, France saw the war in America as a significant drain on British manpower and resources. So the French furnished the American rebels with military supplies and equipment, clothing, blankets, and a hefty infusion of cash. As the Revolution dragged on, with the sides more evenly balanced, French and American interests became increasingly intertwined.

Eager to learn more about its new ally, the French government circulated a semi-official questionnaire among influential American leaders, requesting details about life in America. Thirty-seven-year-old Governor Thomas Jefferson of Virginia received the French inquiry during the British occupation of Virginia, one of the darkest times in his life. Immersing himself in the new assignment, Jefferson submitted his response in December 1781; the revised manuscript was eventually published as *Notes on the State of Virginia*, Jefferson's only book.[4]

Jefferson was at particular pains to disprove the then-prevalent

French thinking in natural history that disparaged the New World as inferior to the created natural order of Europe. The renowned French naturalist Georges de Buffon, in his multivolume and authoritative *Histoire Naturelle* (the first volume published in 1749), had taken the concept of a "New World" to its illogical extreme. Employing a geological perspective, Buffon described America as an immature land, still covered with an unhealthy environment of humid swamps and jungles. In Buffon's view, American flora and fauna were smaller and weaker than comparable species in the rest of the world. Since all had left the Ark approximately equal, the American species must have been degraded by their environment. This "degeneration" applied as well to the continent's native people.

Buffon's theory heavily conditioned European images of American Indians in the late eighteenth century. To be sure, Indians were children of nature, brave innocents able to withstand harsh conditions that would kill a European. But Indians were also seen as crafty and cruel, filthy and unschooled, prone to lascivious behavior, cannibalistic, and capable of inflicting great pain without remorse. Buffon—one of the first to see the Indian body as a source of scientific data—wrote that Indians had small, enfeebled organs of reproduction and that their men were prone to impotence. Because they lacked body hair and beards—time-honored European symbols of masculinity—he perceived Native American men as effeminate and lacking in "ardor for the female." They fared no better on the social level. Buffon believed that Indians lacked true families, which rendered them incapable of establishing even the rudiments of society: "their heart is frozen, their society is cold, their empire cruel."

Buffon's controversial thesis sparked a lively debate about the relative merits of the American and European continents. European images of Indians were rooted in the belief that the environment directly influenced the organism: if Indians were inferior, then they had been degraded by the American environment. In the same line of reasoning, European domesticated animals introduced into the Western Hemisphere would degenerate as well. It was just a matter of time, therefore, before transplanted Europeans also become inferior. This was why, in Buffon's view, America was so miserably lacking in the arts and letters: "America has not yet produced one good poet, one able mathematician, one man of genius in a single art or a single scientist."

Jefferson used his *Notes on Virginia* to defend America's flora, fauna, climate, geology, social institutions, and especially the American Indian. As an ardent empiricist, he had little patience for armchair arguments from Frenchmen relying on hearsay. "It does not appear that [Buffon and his colleagues] have measured, weighed, or seen those [animals] of America. It is said of some of them, by some travelers, that they are smaller than the European. But who were these travelers? Did they measure or weigh the animals they speak of? . . . Were they acquainted with the animals of their own country, with which they undertake to compare them? Have they not been so ignorant as often to mistake the species?"

The peppery attack on Buffon mingled Jefferson's deep-seated belief in scientific research with his unabashed national pride. While accepting the environmental premise, Jefferson shifted the terms of debate from theory to data. Because Americans could readily collect their own data on Indians, they could assume a position of authority. To prove his point, Jefferson prepared an exhaustive table of animal weights for the Old and New Worlds, drawing upon extensive observations, both his own and many others. He then mounted an elegant point-by-point refutation of Buffon's key assertions regarding the First Americans. Jefferson pulverized Buffon's treatise, but he did not stop there. Jefferson delivered the book to Buffon personally; he also gave his rival an immense panther skin and the carcass of a huge moose: so much for the enfeebled American wildlife!

When Jefferson defended the American Indian, he also defended America itself. But the truth is that Jefferson himself had little firsthand experience with Indian people. By the mid-eighteenth century, disease and warfare had taken a tragic toll on Virginia's native population, which survived during Jefferson's youth mostly as diminished and demoralized refugee groups. Although he had seen the occasional delegation of Indians passing through Williamsburg to negotiate with British governors, Jefferson knew remarkably few real Indians. So when he argued that Indians were fully as human as Frenchmen, Jefferson was speaking of a people he rarely saw. He was defending an imaginary Noble Red Man who lived far beyond the confines of his everyday life.

A Founding Father of American Anthropology

Notes on Virginia established Jefferson as a world-class scholar. The broad range of issues addressed demonstrated both the flexibility of Jefferson's mind and his self-described "canine appetite" for scholarship and learning. *Notes* also set out, for the first time, the rudiments of what would become the academic discipline known as American anthropology.

Since Jefferson's day, anthropologists in America have prided themselves on the breadth of their approach, classically pursuing a so-called "holistic" or "four-field" approach: archaeology, ethnology (often known as "cultural" anthropology), linguistics, and physical anthropology (today commonly termed "biological" anthropology). In his own way, Jefferson made a personal contribution to each branch of anthropology, and his intellectual legacy remains alive today.

Jefferson's Archaeology

Jefferson was born during American archaeology's "speculative period" (1492–1840), an era dominated by animated, but nonscientific conjecture about ancient America.[5] From a modern perspective, this period seems most notable for its absences. There were no full-time, professionally trained archaeologists. There was no body of accepted field methods. There were virtually no chronological controls. Although some information was available about the spectacular ruins in Middle and South America, relatively little was known about the archaeological record of North America.

Jefferson's approach to archaeology is clearly set out in *Notes on Virginia*. In his response to Query XI—which read simply, "A description of the Indians established in that state?"—Jefferson declined to employ the term "Indian monument" because the available archaeological finds did not seem to measure up, "unless indeed it be the Barrows, of which many are to be found over this country. These are of different sizes, some of them constructed of earth, and some of loose stones."[6] It was obvious to Jefferson that these were burial mounds. He was curious about how they were built. Were the mounds erected over the bodies of the fallen warriors on the battlefield? Or did the Indians collect and bury together the bones of all their dead from a certain episode? Or were they town sepulchers, erected over the bodies of those settling the town, with subsequent interments taking place incrementally? "There being one of these in my neighbourhood, I wished to satisfy myself whether any, and which of these opinions were just."

The mound (or barrow) in question was located on Jefferson's property on low-lying land near the Rivanna River, two miles above its main fork at Charlottesville, Virginia. Local Indians had abandoned this area by the time that Peter Jefferson and his colleagues settled there in the 1730s and 1740s. Jefferson had known about this mound since childhood. In *Notes,* he recorded that such mounds "are of considerable notoriety among the Indians; for a party passing, about thirty years ago, through the part of the country where this barrow is, went through the woods directly to it, without any instructions or enquiry, and having staid about it some time, with expressions which were construed to be those of sorrow they returned to the high road, which they had left about half a dozen miles to pay this visit, and pursued their journey."[7] He described the site as a "spherical form, of about 40 feet diameter at the base, and had been of about twelve feet altitude, though now reduced by the plough to seven and a half, having been under cultivation for about a dozen years." The mound was covered with trees of twelve inches in diameter (although Jefferson did not count the tree rings). Modern archaeologists have repeatedly attempted to find the site, so far without success.[8]

Jefferson apparently began exploring the mound by digging "superficially in several parts of it." He located concentrations of human bone throughout, buried at varying depths beneath the present surface. The bones occurred "in the utmost confusion, some vertical, some oblique, some horizontal, and directed to every point of the compass, entangled, and held together in clusters by the earth." Jefferson closely observed the distributions of bones as they were uncovered. They were jumbled, not preserved in their anatomical order—"small bones of the foot in the hollow of the scull, many sculls would sometimes be in contact." These field observations convinced Jefferson that the bones had been dumped "promiscuously from a bag or basket, and covered over without any attention to their order."

Jefferson also implemented a "vertical" excavation strategy, making a "perpendicular cut through the body of the barrow, that I might examine its internal structure." This strata-trench, "wide enough for a man to walk through and examine its sides," was positioned slightly off-center (a strategy commonly employed in contemporary excavations of similar sites). This well-conceived excavation plan revealed the site's stratigraphy: bones on the bottom-most level, covered by river cobbles and "stones, brought from a cliff a quarter of a mile off," then a layer of sterile fill, capped by another stratum of bones "and so on." Bones in the basal strata were more heavily weathered than those nearest the surface. The stratigraphic profile documented four distinct bone strata at one end and three at the other, "the strata in one part not ranging with those in another." This simple approach pioneered an excavation strategy that was a full century before its time. "Breath-taking" and "remarkable" wrote Lehmann-Hartleben in the 1940s: it "anticipates the fundamental approach and the methods of modern archaeology by about a full century."[9]

Jefferson's account of his explorations provides a first-rate model of archaeological reporting. He began by describing the data—location, size, method of excavation, stratigraphy, condition of the bones, artifacts—and then presented his conclusions: Why did prehistoric peoples bury their dead in mounds? He noted the absence of traumatic wounds, such as those made by bullets or arrows, and also observed the interment of children, thereby rejecting the common notion that the bones were those of soldiers who had fallen in battle. Similarly, the scattered and disjointed nature of the bones militated against the notion of a "common sepulchre of a town," in which he would have expected to find skeletons arranged in anatomical order. Jefferson surmised, quite correctly, that the burials had accumulated through repeated use and saw no reason to doubt that the mound had been constructed by the ancestors of the Native Americans encountered by the colonists.

As Jeffrey Hantman and Gary Dunham point out, Jefferson did

not excavate to clarify issues of local Indian history. He was instead attempting to determine

> the inner construction of an odd feature on the landscape, situating the mound within the cultural landscape of the Monacan people, noting that it was across the river from a Monacan town—probably Monasukapanough (one of several other late precontact/early contact villages that are known from more recent archaeological surveys in the area). In this sense, Jefferson fit his archaeology into the larger sweep of natural history; to him, digging an archaeological site was much like exploring and describing a geological or botanical oddity.[10]

Sir Mortimer Wheeler, an internationally recognized authority on the subject, declared Jefferson's to be "the first scientific excavation in the history of archaeology . . . unique not only for its age but for long afterwards."[11] Jefferson's primary legacy to archaeology, then, is the fact that he dug at all. He did not explore the burial mound to obtain curios for his mantel (although he did love to collect Indian artifacts). By excavating to answer a clearly defined question, Jefferson elevated the study of America's ancient past from a speculative armchair pastime to an inquiry built on scientific fieldwork and empirical protocols. As a well-educated gentleman of the Enlightenment and a well-schooled natural scientist, Jefferson clearly understood the importance of exposing speculation to a barrage of facts. Because the facts in this case lay buried beneath the ground, he conducted his inquiry there. In so doing, Jefferson pioneered the basics of modern archaeological method and theory: defining his hypotheses beforehand, exposing and recording his finds in meticulous detail, and ultimately publishing all for scrutiny by interested scholars. In theory at least, others could impartially test his conclusions on comparable data collected independently.

Although many textbooks (including my own) term Jefferson the "father of American archaeology," he left no immediate intellectual offspring. His praiseworthy efforts had little impact on his contemporaries, or even on the next generation of Enlightenment scholars. As Wheeler puts it, "this seed of a new scientific skill fell upon infertile soil."[12]

Beyond describing his own field explorations, Jefferson devoted little space in *Notes* to the earthworks and mounds so common in Ohio and the surrounding area. He was doubtless aware that George Washington had explored the impressive Grave Creek Mound (near Wheeling, West Virginia). The Reverend David Jones published accounts of the Scioto River (Ohio) earthworks in the mid-1770s. And a concentration of earthworks stood on land purchased by Jefferson in a real estate venture on the Great Kanawha River on the Virginia frontier.[13]

By 1797, when he assumed the presidency of the American Philosophical Society, Jefferson fully accepted the presence and significance of ancient monuments. His newly convened Committee on History, charged with investigating "the antiquity, changes, and present state" of the country, highlighted four major research objectives: (1) procuring mammoth bones and other fossils; (2) learning more about the archaeology of ancient monuments; (3) continuing geological and geographic research; and (4) investigating the "Customs, Manners, Languages and Character" of Native Americans, both ancient and modern. Specifically with respect to the monuments and earthworks, Jefferson and the other members of the Committee on History requested detailed maps and measurements of these ruins. Jefferson pulled together a questionnaire soliciting "accurate plans, drawings and descriptions of whatever is interesting . . . especially of ancient Fortifications, Tumuli, and other Indian works of art; ascertaining the materials composing them, their contents, the purposes for which they were probably designed, etc."[14] The circular requested that "cuts" be made in various directions through the mounds and earthworks, to determine structure and composition. Seeking to improve on the methods of his own Virginia excavation, he specifically asked investigators to count rings on the largest trees growing from the mounds (to determine a minimum age of construction) and to describe the nature of masonry and stone constructions. Jefferson himself soon was immersed in his duties as president of the United States, and the direct results of his circular were minimal. But simply by posing these specific questions and suggesting appropriate field methods for providing their answers, Jefferson fully anticipated the next major stage in American archeology—the so-called "classificatory-descriptive period," which lasted from 1840 to 1914.[15]

Jefferson's call for more accurate information was answered in part when publisher Isaiah Thomas founded the Massachusetts-based American Antiquarian Society. Established in 1812, the society attracted a stellar membership that included Thomas Hart Benton, DeWitt Clinton, and Daniel Webster. Although Thomas's artifact-oriented objective was "the collection and presentation of the antiquities in our country," the society also encouraged preparing the maps, plans, and descriptions of earthworks. Their first publication was Caleb Atwater's *Description of the Antiquities Discovered in the State of Ohio and Other Western States* (1820)—a benchmark compilation that presented precisely the kind of data that Jefferson had called for two decades earlier.

Jefferson and Biological Anthropology

Only brief comment is required here about Jefferson's early contribution to physical anthropology (although I will return to this controversial subject). During his "superficial" mound excavations, Jefferson encountered numerous disarticulated skeletons. He estimated that the mound contained perhaps one thousand individuals, and by closely observing the distribution of human bones, he concluded that the remains had been dumped "promiscuously" rather than buried individually.

Jefferson also paid close attention to the composition and preservation of the bone assemblage, noting that the more robust elements (mandibles, isolated teeth, long bones, and bones of the foot and hands) vastly outnumbered the more fragile ribs and vertebra. Skulls were particularly fragile to the touch, as were the bones of infants and adolescents. This was an important point, since Jefferson could document the burial of children, despite the fact that their bones were badly decayed and difficult to recover. He also made several observations on the bones and teeth, comparing the lengths of various specimens to determine approximate age at death.

Jefferson's meticulous observations on the human bones fully anticipated the "in-the-ground-autopsy" approach followed by modern biological anthropologists. In effect, Jefferson approached his mound excavation the way a detective conducts a crime-scene investigation—observing both condition and contexts of the remains, attempting to identify the individuals involved and to reconstruct the events that took place there. As with his archaeological technique, Jefferson was decades ahead of his time.

Jefferson's Linguistics

Despite his fascination with archaeology, Jefferson believed that the study of Native American languages provided the most reliable way to document the origins of American Indian populations. "It is to be lamented then, very much to be lamented," he wrote in *Notes,* that so many Indian languages had already passed into extinction without even the rudiments being recorded adequately.[16] Jefferson pursued an ambitious program of comparative American Indian linguistics, issuing a call for detailed recording of surviving languages and emphasizing the importance of collecting standardized word lists.

During his stay in France (1784–89), Jefferson came into contact with others pursuing linguistic studies in Asia. He secured published records of more than two hundred Asian word lists and may have learned of Empress Catherine's program of recording the exotic languages spoken throughout the Russian empire. After returning to the United States, Jefferson prepared his own standardized list of 250 words. Although collecting only one or two such vocabularies personally, Jefferson relied on an extensive network of missionaries, Indian agents, and travelers to record the rapidly vanishing American Indian dialects. By 1803, Jefferson had acquired twenty-two such vocabularies, which he systematically synthesized into detailed comparative tables. The Louisiana Purchase provided Jefferson fertile new ground for adding to this store of linguistic data, and Meriwether Lewis collected perhaps a dozen additional vocabularies.

Jefferson's initial assessment of the linguistic evidence suggested an Asian origin for the American Indian—either across the (yet to be discovered) Bering Strait, or perhaps across the North Atlantic, with stops at Iceland and Greenland. Even before he prepared his linguistic overview for *Notes,* however, he was convinced that the extreme diversity of American Indian languages and dialects pointed to an Asian connection. Jefferson speculated that "if the two continents of Asia and America be separated at all, it is only by a narrow streight.

So that from this side also, inhabitants may have passed into America; and the resemblance between Indians of America and the Eastern inhabitants of Asia, would induce us to conjecture, that the former are the descendants of the latter."[17] In later decades, Jefferson was even less certain about American origins and, typically, sounded the call for additional high-quality data.

Jefferson's thirty-year linguistic project came to a sorry end. When leaving Washington in 1809, the ex-president packed up his preliminary compilation of fifty vocabularies, plus all of Lewis's still-unanalyzed word lists, into a trunk of stationery, which he sent in a shipment of thirty crates of personal effects. While ascending the James River, the packet containing the linguistic manuscript was stolen, and when the disappointed thieves found only apparently worthless list of foreign words, they tossed the papers into the river. A devastated Jefferson wrote that some of his notes "floated shore & were found in the mud; but these were very few, & so defaced by the mud & water that no general use can ever be made of them. . . . Perhaps I may make another attempt to collect, altho' I am too old to expect to make much progress in it."[18]

Jefferson's Ethnology

In *Notes,* Jefferson displayed his strongly historical bent toward Native American ethnology. He emphasized that Indians were well established in Virginia long before Europeans got there, relying heavily on John Smith's account of aboriginal people living in the Jamestown area. He documented the current distribution of Indians in Virginia, noting that most had already moved on. "So few Native Americans still remained [in Virginia]," writes Anthony Wallace, "that his account of them amounted to little more than a recital of the names of the extinct tribes and confederacies."[19]

Although making a few cursory comments about aboriginal mining, ethnobotany, and hunting practices, Jefferson betrayed little interest in Native American "culture," as the term is used today—ignoring topics such as division of labor, specialization, marriage practices, rules of kinship and descent, leadership, social stratification, gender ideologies, and so forth. Jefferson instead painted a generally favorable, but extremely generalized, picture of "savages" who once lived in Virginia.

But Jefferson was well aware of the importance of tribal-level ethnographic detail, and he called for a "natural history" approach to the American Indian. Working with others in the American Philosophical Society, Jefferson urged that all exploring expeditions to the American West should augment their biological and geological objectives with solid ethnographic inquiry about the aboriginal people living there. As noted earlier, Jefferson's Committee on History at the American Philosophical Society realized his earlier program outlined in *Notes on Virginia* by calling for detailed investigation into "the Customs, Manners, Languages and Character of the Indian nations, ancient and modern, and their migrations." "If sufficient materials could be assembled," comments Wallace, "it could have led to an up-to-date *Notes on the United States of America*. But such a document was not to be."[20] A few years later, the Louisiana Purchase rendered Jefferson's "Committee on History" an important preliminary for the ambitious expedition headed by Meriwether Lewis and William Clark.

Science in the Service of Territorial Expansion: The Legacy

The Thomas Jefferson who elevated the study of the American Indian to a proto-anthropological approach remains recognizable in the discipline today. But he was more than an aspiring intellectual. As a founder and administrator of the new republic, Jefferson found a way to dovetail his love of natural history with his responsibilities to provide for national security and economic well-being.

A man of profound contradictions, Thomas Jefferson saw America's future as a medium-size agrarian republic, with few ambitions for world power. Yet with a single stroke of his pen, Jefferson's Louisiana Purchase doubled the size of the United States—the new republic was now as big as Europe. Although unsure of the constitutionality of his acquisition, Jefferson clearly understood that "the *idea* of America always existed beyond the boundaries of the moment."[21] Purchasing the western lands was only part of the issue: expanding America into the remote hinterland required more than military force and political negotiation. It required that the new territory be annexed into the American psyche. But in pursuing his expansionist agenda, Jefferson joined the lengthy procession of Euro-American leaders and explorers attempting to control the American continents. And like his predecessors, Jefferson faced the dilemma of what to do with those already living there.

Some Columbian Consequences

America's national narrative began with the initial encounter between Christopher Columbus and the native people living on a small Caribbean island they called Guanahani. In October 1492, Columbus followed the international protocols of finders-keepers, taking possession of the land (and its people) for the Spanish Crown and renaming the island "San Salvador."

The Arawak-speaking people who lived on "San Salvador" did not ask Columbus to rename their island. They had called their home Guanahani since first arriving there centuries before. As they watched the three ships make their way toward the shore, they must have wondered about the voyagers' origins. They must have applied their own names to these curious bearded strangers. But these names and musings are forever lost because within a decade after the encounter, the Arawak-speakers on Guanahani had all died.

For the three months following his first landfall, Columbus piloted his three ships through a maze of islands, "discovering" and naming each one. After San Salvador came "Santa María de la Concepción," and then, on October 16, "Fernandina," named after King Ferdinand. As he proceeded southward, still seeking the Asian mainland, Columbus soon encountered the island he named "Isabela." A Haitian harbor became "San Nicholás" (because he entered it on December 6, the feast day of that saint). The nearby headland was "Cabo del Estrella," named for the Southern Cross in the sky immediately above. "Thus I named them all," Columbus wrote in his diary.

In the letter announcing his feats to the world, Columbus coined another name when he called the people he found "los Indios," broadening the geographical "India" to denote all of Asia east of the Indus River. Even after Europeans discovered Columbus's navigational error (a pair of intervening continents), his term "Indios" was retained and translated into the other languages of conquest—the French "Indien" and the English "Indian." Thus the invented word "Indian," which originated in a navigational misnomer, would carry enduring colonial connotations. It would mask the enormous complexities and variability of Native American people by grouping them together into a vastly oversimplified pantribal construct.

These names helped establish an agenda under which the rest of the encounter would be played out. After discovering a patch of "unclaimed" land, the conqueror waded ashore and planted his royal banner. He proclaimed that these newly discovered lands were now his patron's domain and laid claim to the newfound riches, the natural resources, and the things living and inanimate—all of which was simply wilderness before being "discovered" and defined by Europeans. During the golden age of discovery, European colonial powers competed in a high-stakes game of finders-keepers. The power to name reflected an underlying power to control the land, its indigenous people, and its history.

During the five centuries following the Columbian encounter, as wars were fought and new governments born, the New World was carved up into dozens of new states, some of which became world powers, the process being the logical consequence of political power struggles that began in 1492. As David Goldberg writes in *Racial Subjects,* minorities throughout the world are now learning that "to pry loose the hold over naming . . . is the first step toward (self) representation. This is the first step toward self-determination, for it enables one to assert power over self-definition."[22] The names "Indian" and "San Salvador" persist today because they were created and retained by the conquerors of this "New World." As usual, the winners got to write the history books.

The Corps of Discovery

Three centuries after Columbus, Thomas Jefferson recast the time-honored ritual of exploration, this time following the protocols of science rather than the church. But the same basic rules of finders-keepers still applied.

To implement this plan, the president convinced Congress to authorize a secret expedition westward, and in 1804–6, Jefferson sent his hand-picked representatives to the Missouri valley and far beyond. He asked Meriwether Lewis and William Clark to find an all-water route to Cathay, directly across the American continent. This was, of course, precisely the same task assigned young Columbus by Ferdinand and Isabela.

Although Jefferson downplayed the role of the state in the new nation's development, he believed in the vigorous exercise of state power, "whether in securing an enslaved laboring population or in expropriating Indian lands."[23] Knowing that Congress would not fund a strictly scientific expedition and aware that a purely commercial venture would alarm Spanish and British officials, Jefferson had cleverly situated his Corps of Discovery as a jointly scientific and commercial enterprise. Science provided the Lewis and Clark expedition with the perfect cover for the construction of Jefferson's Pacific empire.

Taking Captain Lewis under his wing, Jefferson personally instructed his protégé in surveying, map reading, and describing flora, fauna, rivers, mountains—and people. The president trained Lewis in the basics of the Linnaean classification, drilling him on how to use this system of binomial Latin names in his biological fieldwork. As Lewis attended to the logistics of the undertaking, Jefferson labored over his instructions to the Corps of Discovery. The West was vast and largely unknown—and Jefferson wanted to know everything. He instructed his captains to make detailed accounts of the natural history they encountered on the way, including the conditions of the Indians and any "monuments" they might find. He also warned them to look out for live mammoths—for which, he recounted in *Notes on Virginia,* there is "traditionary testimony of the Indians that this animal still exists in the northern and western parts of America. . . . [H]e may as well exist there now."[24]

The instructions grew into a long, complex document, which the president circulated among his cabinet and qualified scholars for comment. As noted by historian Donald Jackson, Jefferson's instruction to Lewis and Clark "embrace years of study and wonder, the collected wisdom of his government colleagues and his Philadelphia friends; they barely conceal his excitement at realizing that at last he would have the facts, not vague guesses, about the Stony Mountains, the river courses, the wild Indian tribes, the flora and fauna of untrodden places."[25]

Jefferson ultimately charged Lewis and Clark to undertake nearly one hundred potential lines of inquiry into American Indian life, distilled into ten major categories: Physical History and Medicine, Morals, Religion, Traditions or Natural History, Agriculture and Domestic Economy, Fishing and Hunting, War, Amusement, Clothing and Ornaments, Customs and Manners Generally—a list that pretty well defines the reach of what most modern ethnographers would call "culture." Kinship and social organization seem to be the most obvious omissions.[26] President Jefferson urged captains Lewis and Clark, as men of the Enlightenment, to make the most accurate observations and measurements, to contribute to the store of human knowledge. Always the empiricist, Jefferson urged "that persons who go thither . . . make very exact descriptions of what they see . . . without forming any theories. The moment a person forms a theory, his imagination sees in every object only the facts which favor that theory."[27]

Ordering America: Finders-Keepers

After an exhausting twenty-nine months afield, Meriwether Lewis began composing his good news/bad news report to the president on September 23, 1806, as his canoe descended the last miles of the Missouri River to St. Louis. His second sentence dispensed with the unwelcome news: sorry to say, there is no all-water route linking the Atlantic and Pacific oceans. Whereas navigation of the Missouri is "safe and good," and the Columbia is passable from its source, passage between the two great waterways required a 340-mile portage, one-third of which was nearly impassable. So much for the Northwest Passage.

Lewis was well aware of the political impact of this news. Here was powerful ammunition for Jefferson's enemies, the Federalists seeking any excuse to attack his purchase of Louisiana as foolhardy. So, during subsequent months, Lewis and Jefferson emphasized the key scientific finds—the extraordinarily good news from the Corps of Discovery.

The Lewis and Clark expedition, perhaps the world's most successful and exhaustive geographical adventure, garnered a wealth of botanical, mineralogical, and ethnographic specimens. Members of the expedition had described the natural history and collected specimens across nearly two-thirds of the North American continent. As instructed, they assigned names to their discoveries, defining the identity and the very existence of the new American territory. In naming (and renaming) the rivers, mountains, and valleys, Lewis and Clark took symbolic possession of the new American West.

In the early stages of the trip, as they moved up the Missouri, the explorers found that most creeks, islands, and prominent landforms already had names (mostly French). But as they moved farther upstream, the European-style names dropped off, and the Corps of Discovery began assigning its own names. Lewis and Clark generally shared naming responsibilities: the first captain to spot a river earned the right to name it.

Lewis and Clark usually respected previous European designations, but they commonly overlooked Native American names. When the Hidatsas, for instance, told Lewis about a river they called "The River Which Scolds at All Others" in today's Glacier National Park, he renamed it "Milk River" (because of the glacial color of the water), and the name remains today. This naming protocol reflected the expedition's general attitude toward the Indians encountered; throughout his journal, Lewis downplayed Native American contributions to his success, even neglecting to thank Sacagawea for her pivotal role (although he did name a stream after her).

Early in the expedition, Lewis and Clark tended to assign names that honored their men and relatives, although sometimes they commemorated unusual features or incidents of travel. The captains bestowed their first name ("Cupboard Creek") on July 3, 1804. The next day, when Private Joseph Field was bitten by a snake, Lewis was forced to pull over. He asked the local French voyagers if the creek had a name. No, he was told, it was unnamed—so the captains called it "Independence Creek." Further upstream, when Sergeant Charles Floyd died, the expedition named "Floyd's River" and "Floyd's Bluff" to honor their fallen comrade. "Corvus Creek" was named for a bird collected nearby. Then came "Bad Humored Island" and "Porcupine River" (today's Poplar River, a tributary of the upper Missouri), named after the large number of porcupines spotted there. Farther upstream, Clark named its first tributary "2,000 mile creek" (today's Red Water), commemorating the fact that the expedition was now two thousand miles above the mouth of the Missouri. Because of the lengthy delay in publishing the Lewis and Clark journals, some of these names did not stick, as subsequent trappers and miners gave their own names to these waters. "Slaughter Creek" (today's Arrow Creek) was a place where numerous buffalo had drowned and wolves were feasting on the rotten meat. Clark named "Judith's River" for his cousin Julia Hancock, and Lewis followed suit, naming "Maria's River" after his cousin Maria Wood.

About the third week of July 1805, after passing the Great Falls of the Missouri, Lewis and Clark changed their pattern. "It was as if they suddenly recalled," writes Stephen Ambrose, "that they had some political responsibility here, that no politician can ever be flattered too much or too brazenly, and that nothing matches having a river named after you." So it was that "Smith's River" was named for Jefferson's secretary of the navy, Robert Smith, and nearby was "Dearborn's River," for Henry Dearborn, the secretary of war.[28]

When the party arrived at Three Forks of the Missouri, the explorers broke protocol entirely. Clark was the first to see the rivers as they merged to form the Missouri, but Lewis got to assign the names: the southeastern fork became "Gallatin's River" (after Albert Gallatin, secretary of the treasury); the middle fork was named "Madison's River" (for Secretary of State James Madison); and the southwestern fork became "Jefferson's River" (named of course, for the great patron of exploration).[29] The next day, Lewis discussed this breach with Clark, who agreed that neither should assert the right of place and concurred that the names Gallatin, Madison, and Jefferson were indeed appropriate.

As a Royal Arch Mason, Lewis then turned to Masonic ritual for names to tributaries of the Jefferson. Lewis "called the bold rapid an clear stream *Wisdom* [today's Big Hole River] and the more mild and placid one *Philanthropy* [the modern Ruby River], in commemoration of two of those cardinal virtues, which have so eminently marked that deservedly selibrated character [Jefferson] through life."[30]

Lewis and Clark knew that the Columbia River had already been named by American sea captain Robert Gray, who sailed his ship *Columbia* into the estuary of that river on May 11, 1792. During the triumphal return of the transcontinental heroes to Washington, poet Joel Barlow spearheaded a movement to rename the mighty Columbia River in honor of Lewis—a suggestion that Jefferson wisely chose to ignore: the name of the Admiral of the Ocean Sea remained on the great river of the American West.[31]

Ever mindful of Jefferson's explicit marching orders, Lewis and Clark reprised the Columbus's finder-keepers strategy of some three hundred years earlier. When Columbus renamed the land and people of the Caribbean, he employed a religious idiom, reenacting a well-known biblical scenario, as recounted in Genesis: "And out of the ground the Lord God formed every beast of the field, and every fowl of the air; and brought them unto Adam to see what he would call them: and whatsoever Adam called every living creature, that was the name thereof. And Adam gave names to all cattle, and to the fowl of the air, and to every beast of the field." Whereas Columbus had claimed the Caribbean islands and people for Christianity, Lewis and Clark were military naturalists, taking symbolic possession of Jefferson's new American West. But whether marching beneath the banner of God or science, the basic rules of the name game still applied.

Curtis Hinsley has termed the process a "discourse of domination through ordering," imposing a Euro-American order on the new territory: choosing and selecting, naming, and categorizing. Collecting and removing the territorial resources—botanical, mineralogical, and ethnographic—Lewis and Clark returned home, argues Hinsley, with the "proofs of conquest, proprietorship and ultimate incorporation."[32] In this way, Jefferson cleverly situated his Louisiana Purchase into the national imagination, affirming a conquest and proprietorship over the distinctive natural resources of the American West—including its aboriginal inhabitants.

Under Jefferson's firm hand, the study of natural history became a tool for establishing the agenda of American expansion westward. In this way, he fully anticipated—and to some degree invented—the natural history mentality that would establish nineteenth-century anthropology's approach to Indians as scientific specimens, as objects for study not terribly unlike mastodons and glaciers.

The legacy endures. In 1996, when a nearly complete 9,400-year-old skeleton washed out of a Washington riverbank near the town of Kennewick, archaeologist James Chatters named him "Kennewick Man." Although scientific protocol says the bones were Chatters's to name, something of a local skirmish broke out when civic boosters of two other nearby cities proposed, apparently with straight faces, that the skeleton be renamed "Kennewick-Pasco-Richland Man." It is hardly surprising that the Umatilla tribe, claiming the skeleton as their own, rejected the scientist's name, preferring to call it *"Oyt.pa.ma.na.tit.tite,"* or "the Ancient One." Apparently the Umatilla people resented being named and classified as part of America's natural history.[33]

Indians as Natural History: The Legacy

In the imposing entrance hall of Monticello, Thomas Jefferson proudly displayed his collection of natural history specimens, many of them collected personally by Lewis and Clark. Mastodon bones and other fossils are along one wall, a mix of prized Indian relics against the other. His estate at Poplar Forest continued the theme, displaying a Cree deerskin dress collected by Lewis and Clark at Fort Mandan, painted buffalo robes from the Plains, a Chinook woman's skirt of cedar bark, an Omaha tobacco pouch, and a Crow Indian cradleboard.

When Jefferson died, his Indian artifact collection was dispersed. A number of his most valued Indian artifacts were later lost to fire. Some were simply discarded by those who did not share Jefferson's enthusiasm for things Indian. Some today are curated in Harvard's Peabody Museum. A few have found their way back to Virginia and are installed in a reconstruction of Jefferson's Monticello entrance hall, which historian Roger Kennedy calls "the nation's first museum of the American Indian."[34]

American anthropology arose when eighteenth- and nineteenth-century intellectuals decided it was important to gather facts and artifacts before Indians vanished completely. Anthropologists tried to transcend narrative history and Indian imagery, emphasizing instead what mainstream historians have commonly regarded as trivial and inconsequential—family structure, economics, technology, religion, political organization, and ideology.

America's Golden Age of Natural History

Thomas Jefferson believed that American Indians could—and should—be studied as part of the rest of nature. Jefferson defined American Indians as specimens, like mammoth bones and the fruit trees in his own garden, to be empirically investigated and objectively understood. And through his involvement with Peale's Museum, the American Philosophical Society, and the Corps of Discovery, Thomas Jefferson spearheaded the development of natural history museums in America.

It was not an overnight process. When the famed Swiss naturalist Louis Agassiz first visited the United States in the 1840s, he was shocked at the public apathy toward the study of natural history. Agassiz shared Jefferson's belief that the most important scientific task at hand was to collect, describe, and classify the species of the natural world—including man. The small size and poor quality of the natural history collections in the United States appalled him. The few amateur natural history societies that had sprung up lacked any public support and members had to store their collections in homes or barns, where they were vulnerable to theft and fire. On accepting a professorship at Harvard in 1847, Agassiz lobbied his adopted country to establish world-class institutions to curate and analyze systematic natural history collections.

Agassiz's extraordinary personality and enthusiasm for science attracted a number of wealthy patrons anxious to see America take its rightful place in the global community. After raising sufficient funds to establish Harvard's Museum of Comparative Zoology in 1856, Agassiz urged the creation of large public museums, along the lines of the famed British Museum and the Musée National d'Histoire Naturelle in Paris. The United States government had already in 1840 received a half-million-dollar gift (in gold) from an Englishman who never set foot on New World soil. James Smithson's wishes were simple enough: to establish an institution "for the increase and diffusion of knowledge among men." After wrestling with several alternatives, including a library, observatory, agricultural experiment station, and university, Congress finally established, in 1846, a new national museum to be called the Smithsonian Institution. Building the Smithsonian collection began in earnest when zoologist Spencer Baird joined the staff as assistant secretary in 1850 and brought along his personal collection, part of which had been given to him by John Audubon. Two years after the 1876 centennial, Baird became secretary, and the Smithsonian Institution's collecting binge intensified.

Fearing that the Smithsonian might grab up all the best collections, wealthy private donors founded rival institutions. George Peabody donated part of his huge personal fortune to Yale and Harvard universities so that each could establish a "Peabody Museum" devoted to the study of natural history, including archaeology and ethnology. He also funded the Peabody Academy of Sciences in Salem, Massachusetts. Albert Bickmore, an Agassiz student at Harvard, sold his idea of a New York–based natural history museum to that city's social and economic elite, which included J. Pierpont Morgan, Joseph Choat, and Theodore Roosevelt Sr. The considerable political clout of then State Senator (later Mayor) William "Boss" Tweed helped establish the American Museum of Natural History in 1869. Located across the street from Frederick Law Olmsted's Central Park (begun in 1857) and soon joined by the Metropolitan Museum of Art (founded in 1874), the American Museum helped create an urban oasis of culture, education, and amusement. In Philadelphia, the long-standing Academy of Natural Sciences (1812) was joined by the University Museum of Archaeology and Paleontology, established at the University of Pennsylvania in 1887. Chicago's Field Museum was incorporated in 1893, and the Museum of Anthropology at the University of California was founded in 1899. Beyond these major players in the museum world, hundreds of smaller, local museums and historical societies sprang up across America.

Each of these museums began buying up existing natural history collections. The American Museum purchased a huge trove collected by the late German naturalist Prince Maximilian Alexander Philipp of Wied—more than four thousand mounted birds, six hundred mounted mammals, and two thousand fish and reptiles preserved in alcohol. In 1874, the same trustees bought, for $64,000, a collection of tens of thousands of fossils representing more than seven thousand species. Agassiz himself had bid unsuccessfully for it, arguing that "whoever gets this collection gets the geological museum of America."[35]

But such expensive, ready-made collections severely stretched the museums' limited budgets. The trustees of America's natural history museums were mostly businessmen, and the high cost of purchasing collections went against their best business sense. Wouldn't it be more cost-effective, some asked, to return to Jeffersonian-style sponsorship of scientific expeditions: what if we eliminated the middleman and made our own collections? As practicing natural scientists, museum curators jumped at the chance to launch their own collecting expeditions; scientifically collected specimens could form the basis of understanding the origin of life and our place in it. Following on the heels of Lewis and Clark, the subsequent collecting expeditions brought prestige and celebrity to the scientists, museums, and benefactors who showed the foresight to grab the lead in America's golden age of natural history—a direct legacy of Jefferson's fascination with natural history.

Constructing Race in the New Republic

Jefferson, of course, was profoundly conflicted on the subject of race. And in his role of anthropological forebear, he left a uniquely ambiguous legacy in this regard. Whereas the birthing of American anthropology was inextricably linked to encounters with Indians, the racial precepts that came to dominate nineteenth-century anthropology derived largely from considerations of African and African American people. Ironically enough, Jefferson paved the way for nineteenth-century racial determinism, but almost in spite of himself.

The natural philosophy of Jefferson's day was heavily influenced, as was Jefferson himself, by the humanitarian and egalitarian principles of the French Enlightenment. Most scholars of that era, Jefferson included, looked to the environment as the key to understanding the world around them. Human beings, like all animals, changed in response to changes in this environment; it was climate, diet, living conditions, social organization, and so forth that determined one's physical appearance and a society's level of civilization.

This pervading environmentalism allowed Jefferson to visualize American Indians as a product of their setting. Left to themselves, the Indians would progress very slowly. But by improving their immediate environment—by, say, turning them into farmers—these Native Americans could proceed more rapidly toward civilized life. This Noble Savage imagery, arising as it did from the egalitarianism of the Enlightenment, carried with it an implicit assumption of a single biblical Creation. So-called primitive cultures could be visualized as having equal capacities, like proto-Europeans before exposure to civilization. Because humanity was seen as unified and fundamentally good, the pristine savage was imagined as a childlike innocent—irresponsible and incapable of self-government or owning land. European civilization became the ultimate blessing to be bestowed upon the "other."

For a time, Jefferson attempted to extend this argument to enslaved Africans in America. Framing the debate in philosophical terms, he suggested initially that perhaps economic and political forces—rather than inherent racial inferiority—were sufficient to account for the degraded conditions of Virginia's slave populations. Maybe the enslaved blacks were merely a powerless people, for whom "captivity defined their national identity."[36] But Jefferson's racialist bias ultimately won out, and in *Notes on Virginia* (Query XIV), he admitted his suspicion that blacks "are inferior to the whites in the endowments both of body and mind." But even in this supposition, Jefferson remained both "tentative and circumspect," hinting that he wished these purely philosophical speculations were perhaps mistaken.[37]

Hence the much-bruited Jeffersonian dilemma: in the Declaration of Independence, Jefferson's initial narrative on race, he implied not only legal and social equality but also equality in a God-given biological sense. Slavery stood in direct conflict with such beliefs, raising the question of whether or not African populations were really the product of the same Creation that begat those "men" addressed in the Declaration. "This is why his commentary concludes so weakly," concludes Peter Onuf, "with 'a suspicion only, that the blacks, whether originally a distinct race, or made distinct by time and circumstances, are inferior to the whites in endowments both of body and mind.'"[38]

Despite his philosophical uncertainties, Jefferson-the-politician went on to deny political equality to blacks due to the suspected "real distinction that nature has made" between the races. This basic, observable racial difference—"fixed in nature" as it was— overwhelmed environmental determinants and doomed the black populace to political inferiority. Noting that white slaves held by the classic Romans still made notable achievements in science, art, and literature—because "they were the race of whites"—Jefferson concluded that America's enslaved blacks would never make similar contributions because they were not white.[39]

This, then, was Jefferson's conflicted construction of race in America. In the end, he abrogated responsibility for clarifying the racial situation, calling for additional empirical investigation and scientific analysis—a near-universal panacea in the early nineteenth century. With Jefferson's passing, the grand and unifying themes of the Enlightenment fell from favor. Although Albert Gallatin and a few others held onto environmentalism, most proto-anthropologists and natural historians emphasized the role of race as the key determining factor. Anthropologist Marvin Harris has termed this shift a "biologization" of human history.[40]

By the mid-nineteenth century, most anthropologists (picking up on Jefferson's racial "suspicions") assumed a direct correlation between heredity and behavior, attributing cultural differences to deep-seated inherited drives. Asked why Plains Indians so readily fit European horses into their lifestyle, the nineteenth-century natural historian might have responded that horsemanship was "in their blood." This was hardly the figurative expression it is today; before anything was known of Mendelian genetics or DNA, blood was literally thought to be the medium through which racial traits were passed from generation to generation. The so-called American school of anthropology argued for polygenism (multiple creations of the races) and stressed the deep, intrinsic causes of human variability. Noble Savage imagery gave way to an increased impatience, even repugnance, toward primitives. This calcification of racialist think-ing set the stage for mixing scientific findings with social, religious, and political priorities.

This is why nineteenth-century anthropology-as-natural-history came to focus on the human skull as a means for defining the races scientifically. By conflating cultural differences with disparities in human intelligence, scientific racism created a global cultural hier-archy, with studies of human racial variability providing the scien-tific evidence necessary to document the inequality of the races. The proto-anthropology of Louis Agassiz, among others, generated the scientific, biological "facts" necessary to justify slavery. Scientifi-cally sanctioned racism also informed federal Indian policies that enabled Euro-Americans to seize Indian lands and justified the dis-graceful Indian wars. At a time when the American melting pot seemed increasingly unworkable and the "civilization" of Indians unlikely, these theories of race suggested that an innate cultural infe-riority of the Native Americans doomed them to extinction.

"The Dead Have No Rights"?

Modern natural history museums resemble the entrance hall at Monticello, only on a larger, more evolved scale. Visitors come to see the dinosaur bones, gems and meteorites, and dioramas of exotic wildlife and faraway culture. Little more than a decade ago, few museumgoers were aware of the formidable research collections stored behind the scenes, of the tens of thousands of Indian skulls and skeletons in the research collections. Although these skeletal libraries have never been a secret, many expressed surprise when told of them. "When I was first made aware of the thousands of Native American human remains housed in the Smithsonian Institution and other great museums and scientific institutions," wrote Senator Daniel Inouye, "I was shocked and appalled."[41] Where did all these skeletons come from? And why were they collected by America's nat-ural history museums? Yet another Jeffersonian legacy?

The answer is yes and no. Historian Richard Drinnon has cited Jefferson's colorful phrase "the dead have no rights" to accuse Thomas Jefferson of a callous, even ghoulish attitude toward the American Indian and their remains.[42] But when one examines the fuller contexts of this statement, it becomes clear that Drinnon has twisted the ex-president's words to create a straw man. In fact, when Jefferson used the expression "the dead have no rights," he was not even remotely considering human skeletal remains.[43]

Jefferson cared very little about human remains at all. When he conducted his pioneering excavation in his Virginia burial mound, Jefferson expressed no particular desire to collect human skeletons; he simply described what he found. His subsequent collecting guidelines, promulgated by the American Philosophical Society in 1797, likewise reflect only a passive interest in human bones. When he called for "accurate plans, drawings and descriptions of . . . ancient Fortifications, Tumuli, and other Indian works of art," his concern was largely with finding out how they were made and why they were constructed. Human bones were, without question, included in most of the tumuli. But to Jefferson, the bones were relevant mostly for what they indicated about the construction, structure, and composition of the earthworks. And to the best of our knowledge, Jefferson did not instruct Lewis and Clark to collect human bones either. Because he believed so strongly in environmental (rather than racial) determination, Jefferson saw little research potential in the human body as such.

That said, Jefferson showed little hesitation when it came to digging up American Indian bones, even when he knew that living Indians still considered the burial mound to be sacred ground. While white cemeteries were viewed as sanctuaries for departed friends and relatives, Indian burial mounds fell under the aegis of natural history, meaning that the dead buried there were fair game. Since the days of Jefferson, American Indian graves have been excavated by the thousands in the name of science. But when was the last time that an American archaeologist—regardless of the research potential—received permission to excavate graves at, say, Arlington National Cemetery? Or the tomb of Thomas Jefferson? While the dead may have no rights, clearly some have enjoyed more rights than others.

Harvesting human skulls was, to be sure, more dangerous than netting butterflies or digging up dinosaur fossils, but skull collecting during the early nineteenth century became, in the words of one critic, "a cottage industry on the frontier."[44] Reliable documentation, including the individual's tribe or band, cause of death, level of intelligence, and personality traits, could inflate a skull's market value, sometimes dramatically, because these data helped skull scientists correlate personality and intelligence with cranial attributes.

Faced with the difficulties of financing his new museum at Harvard, Agassiz came up with a novel way to enlarge America's growing natural history collections. In 1865, he wrote to Secretary of War Edwin Stanton with a simple request: "let me have the bodies of some Indians. . . . All that would be necessary . . . would be to forward the body express in a box. . . . In case the weather was not very cold . . . direct the surgeon in charge to inject through the carotids a solution of arsenate of soda. . . . I should like one or two handsome fellows entire and the heads of two or three more." U.S. Surgeon General William A. Hammond played along, issuing orders to all medical officers "diligently to collect, and to forward to the office of the Surgeon General, all specimens of morbid anatomy, surgical or medical, which may be regarded as valuable. . . . These objects should be accompanied by short explanatory notes. . . . Each specimen in the collection will have appended the name of the medical officer by whom it was prepared." Hammond's policy succeeded as hoped. As Indian tribes were being confined to reservations or hunted down, the bones of their dead were systematically gathered up and shipped to the newly founded Army Medical Museum.[45]

Nineteenth-century anthropologists, guided by their belief in biological determinism, turned to Native American graves—fresh and ancient—as new sources of data. Indian corpses were beheaded on the battlefield to feed the demand for skulls for America's new natural history museums. Live Indians became "living fossils" in the "ethnographic zoos" sponsored at several World Fairs; some even moved in to live in natural history museums. Sometimes, when these Indians died, their bodies were not buried at all but rendered into bones, numbered, and stored away as part of America's greater heritage.

By the early twentieth century, literally thousands of Indian skeletons were curated in America's natural history museums, virtually all of them collected without consent of their Native American descendants. Indian people were horrified when they learned the scale of the museum holdings and the sometimes shocking circumstances under which the skeletons were acquired. "To many Native Americans," wrote Douglas Preston in a 1989 *Harper's Magazine* article, "the collecting of their ancestor's bones and bodies by museums is a source of pain and humiliation—the last stage of a conquest that already had robbed them of their lands and destroyed their way of life."[46]

Some see a lingering racism in the conflation of American Indians with the rest of America's natural history. W. Richard West Jr., director of the National Museum of the American Indian (himself a Cheyenne), tells of how he once asked a clerk in a bookstore for help in finding a book about American Indians. "Believe it or not," West writes, "she referred me to the *Nature* section! It's as if we Native Americans were considered to be something less than human—something apart from the family of man. By the same token, it was not unusual when I was a child to walk into a museum and find Indians displayed next to dinosaurs and mammoths—as if we too were extinct."[47]

Although federal legislation today mandates the return of "culturally affiliated" remains to tribes, the very existence of these enormous skeletal libraries has driven a wedge between anthropologists and the Indian people they wish to study. From a modern perspective, the callous disregard demonstrated by anthropologists during the nineteenth and twentieth centuries strikes many as racist, elitist, and disrespectful of the dead. Throughout Indian Country, native people still resent what they see as an academic arrogance that permitted anthropology museums to collect the skeletons of dead Indians for the good of science.

Modern attitudes in anthropology are very different. Few modern anthropologists are racists, and none, to my knowledge, engages in the kind of out-of-control grave robbing that was common a century ago. Still, anthropology's long romance with scientific racism, traceable to Jefferson's musings on enslaved Africans, has left an undeniable legacy. Thousands of Indian skulls are still curated in America's museums, and the reasons they were brought there reflect archaeology's roots in the crass racial determinism of the nineteenth century. It is small wonder that many Indian people still associate Thomas Jefferson's archaeology with grave robbing.

Applying Anthropological Theory: The Legacy

The new republic began as an amalgam—*E pluribus unum*—an experiment in nation building that asked its citizens to leave behind former loyalties and band together to share a new life. George Washington warned newcomers against retaining the "language, habits and principles (good or bad) which they bring with them." Let them come as individuals, Washington said, ready to be "assimilated to our customs, measures and laws: in a word, soon become *one people.*" According to historian Arthur Schlesinger Jr., "the point of America was not to preserve old cultures, but to forge a new American culture." During the early twentieth century, the metaphor of a melting pot arose to denote the process by which immigrants were to become real Americans.[48]

But what to do with the Indian? Though useful as a symbol, the flesh-and-blood American Indian was not welcome in the new republic. Jefferson mentioned American Indians only once in the Declaration of Independence, as "merciless Indian Savages." As western expansion drove Indians off their lands, President Washington encouraged the country to undertake "rational experiments . . . as may time to time suit their condition" with the aim of preparing the Indian for eventual assimilation—just as so many other groups were being drawn into mainstream American life. To be sure, Indians must give up their traditional hunting grounds—huge forested tracts that would doubtless be overrun by white settlers. But if they were to become farmers, they could retain their most fertile lands forever. That is, the Indian must either whiten himself to join civilized America or be exterminated. Washington's plans never materialized, and at the dawn of the nineteenth century, the "Indian problem" was left for Thomas Jefferson to solve.

True to his long-standing belief in the capacity of environment to shape humanity, Jefferson and his supporters hoped to "free" the native from his savage background so that he could partake more fully of the national prosperity. Unlike the Negro, Jefferson asserted, the red man is "in body and mind, equal to the white man." In the view of historian Winthrop Jordan, Jefferson transformed the Indian "into a degraded noble brand of white man. . . . Amalgamation and identification, welcomed with the Indian, were precisely what Jefferson most abhorred with the Negro. The Indian was a brother, the Negro a leper."[49]

Jeffersonian philanthropy required that the Indian abandon his hunter-warrior culture, his tribal order, his pagan superstitions, and his communal ownership of land. In 1808, President Jefferson invited the Indian people to "unite yourselves with us, and join in our great councils and form one people with us and we shall all be Americans" and throughout his presidency, Jefferson welcomed numerous delegations of his "brothers" to Washington. As he told a group of Miami, Potawatomi, and Wea leaders, Americans were "made by the same Great Spirit, and living in the same land with our brothers, the red men, . . . consider ourselves as of the same family; we wish to live as one people and to cherish their interests as our own." To delegation after delegation of Indians, Jefferson repeated his version of Washington's master plan. Addressing Indian leaders of the Northwestern Territory in 1802, Jefferson said it again: "we shall with great pleasure see your people become disposed to cultivate the earth, to raise herds of useful animals and to spin and weave, for their food and clothing. These resources are certain, and they will never disappoint you, while those of hunting may fail, and expose your women and children to the miseries of hunger and cold."[50]

But Jefferson's policy of easy assimilation quickly bogged down. Because he viewed Native Americans in the abstract, drawing upon both noble and violent imagery, his Indian policy was doomed to failure. "The Indian could not hope to equal the level of virtue attributed to him," argues historian Bernard Sheehan, "because the primitivist formulations drew on a set of presuppositions wholly different from those within the reach of real men."[51] As Christian Keller has demonstrated, in 1803 a frustrated Thomas Jefferson "changed his mind" about the Indians, abandoning his philanthropic idea of acculturation. Jefferson's "bottomless pool of optimism" had dried up because, despite all that his administration had done to help them, Indians still clung to their old ways. In their zeal to promote an agrarian way of life, the Jeffersonians had seriously underestimated the Indian devotion to their own lifeways. Although altruistic whites had tried their best to uplift the Indian, the Native Americans preferred tribalism to progress, thereby proving themselves unworthy of the faith Jefferson had placed in them.[52]

Here, then, is Jefferson's fundamental ambivalence toward Indian people—a compassionate altruism tempered by a desire to maintain absolute control. With his memorable invocation of "self-evident . . . truths," Jefferson had set the cornerstone of white American liberalism. But, with respect to Indians, he cast himself in the role of Great White Father. When native people resisted, they mocked their father, and like spoiled children, perhaps they deserved a good spanking.

Discouraged by the failure of his Indian policy, Jefferson backed a brutal war against recalcitrant Indians and took strong measures to usurp their tribal lands. President Jefferson even articulated a policy of running influential Indian chiefs into debt to government trading houses, then forcing them to pay off their debts by ceding tribal lands. With the apparent failure of melting pot democracy, the United States stepped up its wars of territorial consolidation against Indian people. Although the Indian wars saw inexcusable acts on both sides, the United States never formally declared a policy to exterminate Native Americans. The unspoken premise was that Indians would continue to die out through undeclared warfare, disease, and the "natural" process of one race supplanting another. By the late nineteenth century, mainstream Americans believed that all Indian cultures and lifeways were destined to disappear. But many opposed needless cruelty toward the victims, seeking instead to revive Jefferson's long-abandoned assimilationist program to elevate Indians to civilization as rapidly as possible. Beginning in 1883, the so-called "Friends of the Indian" sponsored annual get-togethers at New York's Lake Mohonk, attracting a broad range of supporters, including some of the most influential anthropologists of the day. Although the Lake Mohonk reformers assigned blame to failed federal Indian policies, they decided that the main force of oppression in Indian life was tribalism—the ingrained Indian-ness that kept native people from participating more fully in the American dream.

Anthropologists who invoked the then-popular "ladder of social evolution" explained the "Indian problem" in scientific terms, in effect shifting the blame to the natives themselves. As the final Indian wars played out—as the Lakotas and Comanches, Cheyennes, and Apaches fought to retain their lands—cutting-edge anthropological theory affirmed that, unless these Indian diehards could be convinced to give up their tribal ways and join civilized America once and for all, they were doomed by their own cultural and biological inferiority. The mission of the Smithsonian's Bureau of American Ethnology became to translate this scientific perspective into effective government policy.

Alice Fletcher and other prominent anthropologists spearheaded the powerful reform movement that reached across American society toward the end of the nineteenth century. Fletcher and the Lake Mohonk liberals followed the Jeffersonian precept that a white American was trapped inside every Indian, ready to own property, become a farmer, and assume the mantle of U.S. citizenship. American Indians, the thinking went, were being held back in their natural evolutionary progression by a corrupt reservation system, which perpetuated a retrograde sense of tribalism by emphasizing communal ties to traditional territories. Anthropological theory, especially that drawn from Lewis Henry Morgan's influential *Ancient Society*, stressed the importance of private property, which had historically stimulated the development of civilized behavior throughout the world and would do so in the future. Not a single responsible scientist in the 1880s questioned Morgan's evolutionary scheme that arrayed human cultural history as a stepwise progression from savagery to barbarism to civilization.

If the Indian people of North America were truly trapped in "upper savagery" and "lower/middle barbarism," then a means must be found to elevate them to civilization as rapidly as possible. To nudge Indian tribes toward the threshold of civilization, they must move from reservation life to individually owned, self-sufficient farmsteads. Anthropological theory soon translated into federal law when, in 1887, Congress passed the Dawes Severalty Act, which was eventually amended to include nearly every tribe in the United States. With the passage of the Dawes Act, surveying parties divided Indian

Country into 160-acre parcels (the average for a single Indian family). At the time, the Dawes Act was widely hailed as the "Indians' Magna Carta," reifying total assimilation as an American ideal. Indians were to become farmers, participants in government, and, above all, "civilized." Teddy Roosevelt hailed the Dawes Act as "a mighty pulverizing engine to break up the tribal mass."[53]

As it turned out, the anthropological theory that was the backbone of the Dawes Act was fatally flawed. In the early twentieth century, the anthropological tide turned against the ethnocentric (and unmistakably racial) notion of progress. Franz Boas led a successful rebellion against cultural evolutionary theory, and only two decades after the Dawes Act became law, Morgan's theory of social evolution was thoroughly discredited.

The Dawes Act was a monumental disaster for the American Indian. Farming did not work well for many, and the land often was leased immediately to non-Indians who had flocked onto the former reservation lands. Reservations were overrun by land sharks eager to snatch up Indian land by whatever means available. By 1934, Indian people had lost two-thirds of the allotted land to non-Indian outsiders. Anthropologist Peter Nabokov believes that the Dawes Act, passed just two years before the slaughter at Wounded Knee Creek, "probably created more widespread Indian suffering and left a more destructive legacy for Indians in the future than that infamous massacre." The Dawes Act fiasco, which flowed directly from Jeffersonian assimilation policy, prompted Franz Boas to issue a stern warning to future generations of anthropologists: avoid contemporary politics and abstain from applying their untested theories to actual Indian issues.

Despite this lesson learned, President Theodore Roosevelt continued to promote a Jeffersonian program of state-sponsored anthropology. In the early twentieth century, Indians no longer posed a physical threat and were routinely written out of mainstream American history. But an element of Indian imagery was still required to make the concept of America actually work. "The westward experience," writes Alan Trachtenberg, "seemed for Roosevelt . . . a foreclosing event, an inevitable advance from low to high, from simple to complex, and in more senses than one, from 'Indian' to 'American.' . . . In this 'progress,' this proof of 'America,' the profoundest role was reserved not for the abundance of land but for the fatal presence of the Indian. . . . 'Civilization' required a 'savagery' against which to distinguish itself."[54]

For Roosevelt's generation, archaeology became a way to document the course of American culture from one evolutionary stage to the next—from "Indian" to "American"—in the process validating the doctrines of progress and Manifest Destiny. Archaeologists and historians usually obliged, suggests historian Frederick Hoxie, providing the American public "with an image of Indian people and Indian history that conformed to the power relationships of their day."[55] In effect, the Roosevelt administration challenged America's archaeologists to help write the national narrative.

But it was clear that just as Indians were vanishing, so were the archaeological traces of their history. The House of Representatives' Committee on Public Lands recognized the threat of uncontrolled excavation of archaeological sites and, in 1906, pointed out that "practically every civilized government in the world has enacted laws for the preservation of the remains of the historic past, and has provided that excavations and explorations shall be conducted in some systematic and practical way so as not to needlessly destroy buildings and other objects of interest." Effectively prodded, Congress enacted the Antiquities Act of 1906, reflecting Roosevelt's passion for conserving and studying natural history, protecting America's remote past, and ensuring continued access for a fast-growing scientific community.

The Antiquities Act fixed in law what had been an American reality since Jefferson, with white intellectuals looking to archaeology for answers about American Indian origins. "Archaeologists" throughout most of the nineteenth century were well-educated hobbyists, who drew upon their general educational background to make sense of what they found. After a century of give-and-take, scientific authority came to rest with those scholars affiliated with one (or more) of America's rapidly growing natural history museums.

The 1906 Antiquities Act formalized scientific investigation as an arm of the federal government and recognized a new archaeological establishment by permitting only professionally sanctioned archaeologists to remove antiquities from federal lands. The legislation specifically charged the Smithsonian Institution to administer the new permitting process. The bill also empowered the president to designate key archaeological sites as national monuments and anointed the Smithsonian as the official repository for duplicate copies of field notes, photographs, and any collections made without regulatory compliance. Indians, who almost universally lacked the requisite training, were, by definition, amateurs, and by criminalizing unauthorized artifact collecting on federal lands, the 1906 law effectively quashed nonprofessional access to the American past. A series of antiquities-related acts followed over the next half-century or so: establishment of the National Park Service in 1916, the National Environmental Policy Act (NEPA) of 1969, the Archeological Resources Protection Act of 1979, and so forth.

These congressional acts professionalized American archaeology and doubtless preserved many archaeological sites for future generations. But they also ensured that generations of professional archaeologists came to view the archaeological record of America as their exclusive intellectual property. By law, it essentially was.

Congressionally sanctioned scientific authority conferred a power over the past. American archaeologists came to perceive themselves as sole proprietors of and reigning authorities on the remote Indian past. When archaeologists appeared as expert witnesses in court cases, their testimony carried more weight than that of tribal elders. Archaeologists wrote the books about First Americans, gave the public lectures, and taught the classes. Archaeologists generally controlled access to museum collections of Native American objects from that very distant past. One archaeologist has recently stated, "all origin myths are equally absurd, but some are more politically correct than others." Another expressed a similar viewpoint in a particularly vivid oxymoron: "I don't think that . . . oral traditions are worth the paper they're written on."[56]

This is why American Indians did not figure into American archaeology for most of the twentieth century. Although archaeology in North America consisted almost entirely of Indian artifacts and sites—with only a recent veneer of Euro-American material culture—there was no recognition, in 1906 (or for decades after), that

Indian people might have religious, spiritual, or historical connections to the material record of their own past. That past belonged
with "natural history" rather than American history. With the Antiquities Act, Congress had legally defined the American Indian past as
part of the greater public trust, like Yellowstone and the passenger
pigeon.

American Indians, of course, refused to vanish. Their numbers
bottomed out in the 1890s and have dramatically increased ever since.
Twentieth-century Indian people survived their predicted extinction
and began exploring non-Indian America on their own, applying their
"ancient ways" to fresh pursuits, including art, politics, medicine and
the law, sports, and even anthropology. Indians began creating their
own reality, defining pathways distinct from those that had nearly
destroyed them

With the rise of the American civil rights movement, the protests against the Vietnam War, the successes of the United Farm
Workers, and the growth of feminism, history became a weapon for
redressing the imbalances inherent in the top-dog perspective. Academics in the humanities, arts, and social sciences began including
gender, race, ethnicity, and class as justifiable areas of inquiry. Indian
Red Power activism is one facet of this movement. The echoes of
underdog history carried far beyond the ivory towers, permeating
popular culture and, in the process, threatening archaeology's foot-
hold in mainstream American history. Particularly since the 1960s,
Indian people stepped up their fight to reclaim and reinforce their
treaty-guaranteed sovereignty, borrowing strategies and guidelines
from the world of international law. American Indian activists joined
up with the so-called Fourth World—the descendants of a nation's
original inhabitants who find themselves marginalized and deprived
of their traditional territory and its riches.

Courts had long given preference to the testimony of non-Indian
historians and anthropologists over the authority of tribal elders.
Legal authorities have long discounted tribal perspectives; yet they
commonly accept at face value the firsthand written observations of
European colonists. Mainstream historical perspectives put the onus
on indigenous societies to justify their aboriginal claims according
to colonial rules. Tribal leaders and Indian scholars, attacking what

they see as myths maintained by historians and politicians, have attempted to revitalize their indigenous identities demolished by war and trampled by dominant culture politics.

Such indigenous ideologies assert an essential native subjectivity, promoting themes of self-worth and cultural preservation and suggesting that Indian culture could help correct some problems of modern mainstream culture. At the same time, these once powerless groups were defining ways to navigate a cultural tide that had long run against them. Since the 1960s, the emerging Indian identity—what Vine Deloria Jr. calls a "retribalization"—has severely threatened the long-standing balance between mainstream and underdog histories. "Until the majority of Americans have concurred, both formally and informally, that American Indians are equal and autonomous entities, entitled to every freedom and course of redress that pertains to its Christian majority," argues Scott Vickers, "then that majority will have failed itself, its own religion, and its historical trajectory toward 'freedom for all.'" [57]

Achieving power over their own history has tangible payoffs in the everyday life of Indian people who are neither fully sovereign nor wards of the state and who remain subject to the vagaries and contradictions of federal policy. Economic development in Indian Country remains integrally connected to politics, intertwined with issues of sovereignty, tribal identity, access to resources, cultural issues, and ideology. By taking hold of the imagery that still frames negotiations with state and federal governments, they seek to translate historical and cultural identities into tangible political power.

The bottom line is defining which history gets taught and who gets to teach it. In seeking identities independent of non-Indian historians and anthropologists, many Native Americans have come to resent the appropriation of their ancient artifacts and ancestral bones by "experts" claiming an authority denied to the Indians themselves. As native people across the land try to recapture their own language, culture, and history, they are increasingly concerned with recovering and taking control of tribal heirlooms and human remains. Troy Johnson spoke for many when he suggested that "perhaps no more insulting and insensitive scene can be imagined than the desecration of Native American burial sites by researchers or grave robbers who disregard the law and cultural sensitivities of the Native American Indian people."[58] In 1975, the widely distributed Indian newspaper *Wassaja* defined anthropology as a "vulture culture."

Congress responded to these concerns in 1990 by passing the Native American Graves Protection and Repatriation Act (NAGPRA). NAGPRA protects newly discovered Indian graves, but it also mandates that America's universities and museums audit their Indian collections and return certain cultural items to tribal representatives. This legislation marked a significant shift in the federal stance toward the rights of Indian people and a sea change in the perception and practice of American archaeology. The 1990 law explicitly acknowledged that Indian pasts are relevant to the American present. This public and visible benchmark reflected a deep-seated shift in thinking, emphasizing America's self-perception as a multifaceted, pluralistic society. The American creed shifted away from the melting pot to recognition of the merits of a multicultural society.

Such an interpretation of the American character was unimaginable in Jefferson's day. For the first time, native people were empowered to question mainstream American ownership of the Indian past, both literally and metaphorically. No longer were Indian bones found on public lands automatically defined as natural resources, as federal property to be safeguarded in scientific custody. No longer did science have a monopoly on defining the meaning of archaeology; instead, native groups were invited to assign their own spiritual and historical meanings to archaeological sites and their contents.

Not surprisingly, some Americans are alarmed by Indian "retribalization" and the recognition by Congress of indigenous ideologies. Census Bureau numbers suggest a skyrocketing American Indian population, and some question the authenticity of these self-proclaimed Indians. Many mainstream Americans would agree with Jefferson that "real, authentic" Indians did indeed vanish a century ago. Some accuse Indians of learning their "traditions" from old anthropology books, and others see twenty-first-century "Indian-ness" as just another New Age fad. Skeptics suggest that NAGPRA and related legislation smacks of public relations, exploiting the Noble Red Man imagery at the expense of historical accuracy. Some anthropologists accuse Indians of inventing instant traditions for current political purposes. Some professional historians see a self-serving, second-rate scholarship making shoddy use of historical and ethnographic documents.

In *The Disuniting of America*, historian Arthur Schlesinger writes of a "tribalization of American life [that] . . . reverses the historic theory of America as one people—the theory that has thus far managed to keep American society whole."[58] From Yugoslavia to Canada, from the former Soviet Union to much of Africa, post–Cold War Balkanization has torn apart one nation after another. Is America in danger of being torn apart into ethnic and racial tribes? Is Schlesinger correct that tribal identity has become "the AIDS of international politics—lying dormant for years, then flaring up to destroy countries"? With the metaphor of the great American melting pot under attack, Schlesinger sees an America "giving ground to the celebration of ethnicity. . . . The multiethnic dogma abandons historic purposes, replacing assimilation by fragmentation, integration by separatism. It belittles *unum* and glorifies *pluribus*."[59]

Some go even further, asserting that American values simply cannot be negotiated and remade at will. For them, the American family—a natural institution blessed by God—carries with it critical core values and social attitudes that have raised America above other countries. Was President Ronald Reagan thinking of Jefferson when he wondered aloud if "we made a mistake in trying to maintain Indian cultures. Maybe we should not have humored them in wanting to stay in that kind of primitive lifestyle."[60]

Thomas Jefferson: Good Father, Bad Father, and Great White Father

This essay has explored Thomas Jefferson's iconic "founding father" status in American archaeology and anthropology. His innovative burial mound excavations—particularly his keen sense of purpose, his discerning evaluation of the evidence, and his articulate description of his findings—established the gold standard for all subsequent fieldworkers. By excavating to answer a question rather than simply to recover antiquities, Jefferson defined the dictum that guides modern archaeology: It's not what you find, it's what you find out.

Jefferson likewise receives high marks for helping to establish the holistic "four-field approach"—archaeology, ethnology, linguistics, and biological anthropology—that became the hallmark of anthropology in the twentieth century. Beyond his contributions to archaeology, Jefferson's ambitious thirty-year program furthered the study of comparative American Indian linguistics by developing standardized word lists and emphasizing languages in danger of extinction. His ethnological writings tended to be largely historical, with little personal concern for "culture" as the word is used today. But Jefferson's meticulously framed instructions for others encouraged a natural historical perspective that generated broad-based ethnographic data fully comparable to the biological and geological investigations of the day.

Although his self-described "canine appetite" for scholarship ranged far beyond national boundaries, Jefferson's fascination with the American Indian dominated all of his anthropological efforts. His feisty attack on the prominent French naturalist Buffon combined Jefferson's undisguised national pride with his own knowledge of Indian people. In the celebrated *Notes on Virginia*, Jefferson's sentimentality transformed American Indians into "natural republicans" who lived a blissful, childlike existence in an Edenic American world, free of the state's coercive power.

But any consideration of Jefferson as the patriarch of American anthropology must be tempered—and to some degree even compromised—by his heavy-handed treatment of the American Indian. In truth, Jefferson was both "good" and "bad" father, creating tensions that continue to complicate relations between anthropologists and the American Indians they wish to study, particularly with his views on acculturation, racial equality, and the involvement of the state in the pursuit of scientific research.

Jefferson saw no useful role for American Indians in his new republic. The Indian must either join mainstream America as civilized (non-Indian) participants, or they must be exterminated altogether. Jefferson took it upon himself to engineer the transition to civilization by providing the tools and education necessary to nudge the Indian from the primitive stage of hunting to more civilized behavior based on agriculture and private property. But because he lacked firsthand experience with real Indian people, Jefferson naïvely expected that the civilizing process could take place within a short time. When it did not, he was bitterly disappointed and perfectly willing to pursue more aggressive military programs to remove the Indians westward. "Jefferson's philanthropy was as real as Jeffersonian animosity," argues the historian Richard White, "but both in different ways envisioned the disappearance of the Indian."[61]

Jefferson's spirited defense of American Indian virtues flowed directly from Enlightenment environmentalism. But if he saw the American Indian as potentially equal to the white man, enslaved Africans were probably "inferior to the whites in the endowments both of body and mind."[62] Jefferson's ambivalence on the question of racial equality paved the way for the full-blown racial determinism—the "biologization" of human history—that came to dominate anthropological thinking during the nineteenth century.

By the 1960s, black activists had become increasingly disillusioned with white liberals who, like their hero Jefferson, seemed to say one thing, yet do another. "Where Martin Luther King, Jr. and other civil rights leaders portrayed Jefferson as a well-meaning white man caught on the horns of a moral dilemma, Malcolm X saw only a white slaveholder caught in a web of deceit."[63] About the same time, the American Indian community was voicing similar sentiments about Jefferson's well-meaning anthropological descendants: "perhaps we should suspect the real motives of the academic community" wrote the Dakota Indian activist, Vine Deloria Jr. "They have the Indian field well defined and under control. Their concern is not the ultimate policy that will affect the Indian people, but merely the creation of new slogans and doctrines by which they can climb the university totem pole."[64]

When Lewis and Clark returned home with their proofs of conquest, they affirmed American proprietorship over the distinctive natural resources of the West—including those aboriginal inhabitants still living there. The intellectual study of natural history had become an instrument for the power of the federal state, which would ultimately have a catastrophic effect on Indian Country. And the natural historians who followed in Jefferson's wake excavated Indian graves by the thousands. At one point, the U.S. surgeon general even ordered his medics to send dead Indians from the battlefields to natural history museums back East—all in the name of state-sanctioned science. Although attitudes in anthropology now differ greatly from the biological determinism that Jefferson helped foster, it is hardly surprising that many native people still associate archaeology with robbing the graves of their ancestors.

In a curious sense, then, Jefferson's complex image as American anthropology's "good" and "bad" father echoes his conflicted status in American history writ large. With the ringing words of the Declaration of Independence, "all men are created equal," the slave-owning Jefferson established the agenda of white liberalism. Yet that same enlightened liberalism translated anthropological theory into federal law—ultimately mobilizing Jefferson's agrarian dream into the Dawes Act—and the results were disastrous for the American Indian. Whereas the Antiquities Act of 1906 professionalized the practice of American archaeology and saved countless sites from looting, the same act reinforced the Jeffersonian conception of the Indian past as "natural history" rather than true "American history."

NOTES

The author especially wishes to thank the participants in the Thomas Jefferson Foundation Distinguished Lecture Series, held at the University of Virginia in October 2001. I am especially grateful to Peter Onuf and Jeffrey Hantman for their comments, which were invaluable in revising an earlier draft of this paper.

1. Some of the topics in this paper are developed in more detail in David Hurst Thomas, *Skull Wars: Kennewick Man, Archaeology, and the Battle for Native American Identity* (New York, 2000).

2. Venables quoted in Chief Oren Lyons and John Mohawk, *Exiled in the Land of the Free: Democracy, Indian Nations, and the U. S. Constitution* (Santa Fe, 1992), 75.

3. Beard quoted in Philip J. Deloria, *Playing Indian* (New Haven, 1998), 224.

4. Over the next couple of years, Jefferson (hereafter TJ) circulated the manuscript to friends and colleagues for comment. The revised version was printed in Paris, without the author's name and destined for private distribution only, in 1785. John Stockdale finally printed an English version of *Notes on the State of Virginia*, ed. William Peden (Chapel Hill, 1954), xiv–xx.

5. Gordon R. Willey and Jeremy A. Sabloff, *A History of American Archaeology*, 3d ed. (New York, 1993).

6. TJ, *Notes on Virginia*, 99.

7. Ibid., 100.

8. Jeffrey L. Hantman and Gary Dunham, "The Enlightened Archaeologist," *Archaeology* (May/June 1993): 44–49.

9. Karl Lehmann-Hartleben, "Thomas Jefferson, Archaeologist," *American Journal of Archaeology* 67 (1943): 161–63, quotation on 163.

10. Hantman and Dunham, "The Enlightened Archaeologist," 48.

11. Mortimer Wheeler, *Archaeology from the Earth* (Oxford, 1954), 6. Other archaeologists have questioned whether Jefferson was really America's first "scientific" archaeologist. Alice Beck Kehoe (*The Land of Prehistory: A Critical History of American Archaeology* [New York, 1998], xii) suggests that the 1675 work of Carlos de Siguenza y Gongora at Teotihuacán had real scientific value. Donald Blakeslee ("John Rowzee Peyton and the Myth of the Moundbuilders," *American Antiquity*, 5 [1987]: 784–92) speculates that John Rowzee Peyton, who dug a Kansas burial mound in 1774, may be responsible for starting the Mound Builder controversy, a topic that dominated archaeological inquiry in American for a century.

12. David Hurst Thomas, *Archaeology*, 3d ed. (Fort Worth, 1998); Willey and Sabloff, *History of American Archaeology*, 33; Wheeler, *Archaeology from the Earth*, 43.

13. Anthony F. C. Wallace, *Jefferson and the Indians: The Tragic Fate of the First Americans* (Cambridge, Mass., 1999), 13.

14. Quoted in Willey and Sabloff, *History of American Archaeology*, 32.

15. Ibid.

16. Wallace, *Jefferson and the Indians*, 145.

17. TJ, *Notes on Virginia*, 101.

18. Quoted in Wallace, *Jefferson and the Indians*, 152.

19. Ibid., 91–92.

20. Ibid., 157.

21. Curtis M. Hinsley, "Collecting Cultures and Cultures of Collecting: The Lure of the American Southwest, 1880–1915," *Museum Anthropology* 16 (1992): 12–20, quotation on 12.

22. David Theo Goldberg, *Racial Subjects: Writing on Race in America* (New York, 1997), 22.

23. Peter S. Onuf and Leonard J. Sadosky, *Jeffersonian America* (Oxford, 2002), 161.

24. TJ, *Notes on Virginia*, 54.

25. Donald Jackson, *Thomas Jefferson and the Stony Mountains: Exploring the West from Monticello* (Urbana, Ill., 1981), 139.

26. Wallace, *Jefferson and the Indians*, 99–100.

27. Quoted in Roger G. Kennedy, *Hidden Cities: The Discovery and Loss of Ancient North American Civilization* (New York, 1994), 136.

28. Stephen E. Ambrose, *Undaunted Courage: Meriwether Lewis, Thomas Jefferson, and the Opening of the American West* (New York, 1996), 252–54. The modern traveler working upstream on the Dearborn will also encounter Lewis and Clark Pass

(that leads directly into Missoula, Montana) and the Clark Fork River (that flows into the Columbia). Both names were added later to honor the expedition leaders.

29. Ironically, the name "Jefferson" did not stick. The river is known today as the Beaverhead.

30. Lewis quoted in Ambrose, *Undaunted Courage,* 260.

31. Ibid., 422–23.

32. Hinsley, "Collecting Cultures and Cultures of Collecting," 127.

33. Disputes over the naming process remain part of modern America's "skull wars," as discussed in Thomas, *Skull Wars.*

34. Kennedy, *Hidden Cities,* 219.

35. Agassiz quoted in Douglas J. Preston, *Dinosaurs in the Attic: An Excursion into the American Museum of Natural History* (New York, 1986), 21.

36. Peter S. Onuf, *Jefferson's Empire: The Language of American Nationhood* (Charlottesville, 2000), 160, 168.

37. Ibid., 147.

38. Ibid., 169.

39. Paul Finkelman, "Jefferson and Slavery: 'Treason against the Hopes of the World,'" in *Jeffersonian Legacies,* ed. Peter S. Onuf (Charlottesville, 1993), 181–224, quotation on 184.

40. Marvin Harris, *The Rise of Anthropological Theory* (New York, 1968), 80–81.

41. Inouye quoted in Roger C. Echo-Hawk and Walter R. Echo-Hawk, *Battlefields and Burial Grounds* (Minneapolis, 1994), 1.

42. For example, Richard Drinnon, *Facing West: The Metaphysics of Indian-Hating and Empire Building* (1980; Norman, Okla., 1997), 92–93.

43. The phrase "the dead have no rights" appears in a letter written by Jefferson on July 12, 1816, to Samuel Kercheval (in Andrew A. Lipscomb and Albert Ellery Bergh, eds., *The Writings of Thomas Jefferson,* 20 vols. [Washington, D.C., 1903–4], 15:43), in which the former president responded to an inquiry regarding the propriety of constitutional revision. Jefferson noted that perhaps "two-thirds of the adults . . . living" when the Virginia Constitution of 1776 was drafted "are now dead." Jefferson asked whether the now-deceased majority still had the right to expect their laws to be maintained without change. Jefferson thought not: only those in the present generation "have a right to direct what is the concern of themselves, alone, and to declare the law of that direction. . . . the majority, then, has a right to depute representatives to a convention, and to make the Constitution what they think it will be the best for themselves." That is, the living electorate must always control the law and amend it as appropriate. What, then, about the other two-thirds, those law-makers who had passed away? "The dead?" Jefferson asked, "But the dead have no rights. They are nothing; and nothing cannot own something. Where there is no substance, there can be no substance. This corporeal globe, and everything upon it, belong to its present corporeal inhabitants, during their generation."

44. Robert E. Bieder, *Science Encounters the Indian, 1820–1880* (Norman, Okla., 1986), 67.

45. Agassiz quoted in Andrew Guilliford, "Bones of Contention: The Repatriation of Native American Human Remains, in "Representing Native American History," ed. Clara Sue Kidwell and Ann Marie Plane, special issue, *Public Historian* 18 (1996): 119–43, quotation on 124.

46. Douglas J. Preston, "Skeletons in the Closet," *Harper's Magazine* 278 (1989): 66–75, quotation on 67.

47. W. Richard West Jr., in a promotional appeal produced by the National Campaign committee office, National Museum of the American Indian, Smithsonian Institution (Nov. 1, 1992).

48. Arthur M. Schlesinger Jr., *The Disuniting of America: Reflections on a Multicultural Society* (New York, 1992), 13.

49. Jordan quoted in Drinnon, *Facing West*, 83.

50. TJ quoted in Fergus M. Bordewich, *Killing the White Man's Indian* (New York, 1996), 38.

51. Bernard Sheehan, *Seeds of Extinction: Jeffersonian Philanthropy and the American Indian* (New York, 1973), 102.

52. Christian B. Keller, "Philanthropy Betrayed: Thomas Jefferson, The Louisiana Purchase, and the Origins of Federal Indian Removal Policy," *Proceedings of the American Philosophical Society* 144 (2000): 39–66.

53. Roosevelt, Message to Congress, Dec. 3, 1901, in James D. Richardson, ed., *A Compilation of the Messages and Papers of the Presidents, 1789–1902*, 12 vols. (Washington, D.C., 1903–6), 10:450.

54. Alan Trachtenberg, *The Incorporation of America: Culture and Society in the Gilded Age* (New York, 1982), 26.

55. Frederick E. Hoxie, "Exploring a Cultural Borderland: Native American Journeys of Discovery in the Early Twentieth Century," *Journal of American History* 79 (1992): 969–95, quotation on 974.

56. David Roberts, *In Search of the Old Ones: Exploring the Anasazi World of the Southwest* (New York, 1996), 86.

57. Deloria in Scott B. Vickers, *Native American Identities: From Stereotype to Archetype in Art and Literature* (Albuquerque, 1998), 159, 10–11.

58. Troy Johnson, ed., *Contemporary Native American Political Issues* (Walnut Creek, Calif., 1998), 11.

59. Ibid.

60. Reagan quoted in Gerald Vizenor, ed., *Crossbloods* (Minneapolis, 1990), xxiii.

61. White in David Hurst Thomas, Jay Miller, Richard White, Peter Nabokov, and Philip J. Deloria, *The Native Americans* (Atlanta, 1993), 261.

62. TJ, *Notes on Virginia*, 143.

63. Scot A. French and Edward L. Ayers, "The Strange Career of Thomas Jefferson," in *Jeffersonian Legacies*, ed. Onuf, 418–56, quotation on 418.

64. Vine Deloria Jr., *Custer Died for Your Sins* (1969; Norman, Okla., 1988), 95.

A Nation Imagined, a Nation Measured

The Jeffersonian Legacy

Kenneth Prewitt

Thomas Jefferson's greatness is celebrated by citing his extraordinary achievements from a list that numbers many more than the three he choose for his epitaph. Depending on the interest of the historian, the list of achievements can grow to great length. There is one achievement, however, that seems never to have made anyone's list. Jefferson, as secretary of state in 1790, supervised the first modern census in world history. Though by today's standards this was a primitive census, it initiated what has become the nation's longest continuous scientific project—an unbroken series of demographic portraits. Given Jefferson's well-deserved reputation as a political arithmetician and early demographer, it is odd that his role as the nation's first census director is so seldom noted. Jefferson's legacy, I argue here, is a nation *measured* as well as a nation imagined.

The first national census in America's history had, of course, many predecessors. The term itself dates to ancient Rome, where it referenced the registration of citizens and their property. The archaic definition of "census" is a poll tax. The New Testament census that

brought Mary and Joseph to Bethlehem was in the tradition of counting in order to tax the population. But if the term is Roman, the use
of a population count by the state predates Roman times. In the
fourth book of the Hebrew Bible, appropriately titled Numbers, the
Lord instructs Moses: "Take ye the sum of all the congregation of
the children of Israel, after their families, with the number of their
names, every male . . . from twenty years old and upward." That is,
count the number of those "able to go forth to war."

It is probable that taxation or military conscription, or both, gave
rise to other census operations indicated by archaeological records,
such as the *Nepohualco,* or "counting place," built by the Chichime-
cas a millennium ago. This site, near today's Mexico City, consists of
stones deposited by each inhabitant of the region, an early census
data bank. Other archaeological records from various ancient civi-
lizations indicate similar preoccupation by the state with carrying
out systematic counts. In these ancient records it is difficult to detect
all of the state purposes that might have been served by a census.
Certainly there was interest in economic data, as is suggested by
statistical records of harvest and grain storage. Ancient Chinese records, dating from the Han dynasty (206 BC to AD 220), indicate that
detailed population counts were made after each harvest.

But in the modern nation-state era, the American census in 1790
was the first periodic census, though it was followed closely by the
United Kingdom and France (1801) and then across the great century
of nation building: the Netherlands, shortly after its independence
in 1830; Sweden in 1855; Spain in 1857; Italy in 1861; the German empire in 1871; and the Russian empire in 1897. The postcolonial nations
of Latin America, Asia, and Africa followed in due course, and by the
end of the twentieth century only a handful of countries did not
have a regularly scheduled census.

The 1790 census supervised by Jefferson was the first national
census in America, but it had immediate predecessors in the colonial
era; eight of the original thirteen states had counted their populations, often numerous times, with New York (11 censuses prior to
1790) and the New England region much more practiced in this than
the middle Atlantic and southern regions, where some colonies had
not even one census prior to 1790.[1]

Colonial censuses aided British mercantile policies, being used to manage the flow and the composition of the population then settling the New World. There were efforts to maintain a desirable balance between free persons, bonded immigrants, and slaves. Colonial census numbers figured in the testy debates about dumping the unskilled and the poor on America's shores. Convicts were an issue, as inveighed against by Benjamin Franklin in the middle of the eighteenth century, leading eventually to the redirection of that traffic to Botany Bay. The religious composition was of concern; in its struggles with France, Britain was concerned to maintain a Protestant dominance in the mainland colonies. In this Britain was successful, and at independence only 1 percent of the population was Catholic.

The colonial leaders and the British parliament often saw population issues differently. As summarized by Aristide Zolberg:

> Both sides had similar notions regarding what sorts of people were desirable and undesirable; but whereas Britain was intent on ridding itself of convicts and paupers while seeking to retain the conforming and productive, the colonists were equally adamant to keep out the first and attract the second. Both sides shared the mercantilist understanding of population as the major source of wealth and power; but whereas this led Britain to try to keep the colonial population within bounds, it prompted the Americans to maximize their numbers by all possible means.[2]

Zolberg situates these debates in the context of colonial politics. "From the perspective of Britain," he writes, "the colonies were essentially economic undertakings, whose social, racial, or national makeup did not matter unless it occasioned problems of economic management or of external security, and even, in good Roman imperial tradition, facilitated rule by dividing the colonists." The Americans had a very different vantage point. For them, "the colonies were communities in the making, whose heterogeneous composition might be a source of conflict and possibly lead to disintegration, the more so if they were to be assembled into a single political entity."[3] Lurking behind differences over immigration was the explosive issue of independence.

Immigration debates in the colonial period foreshadow the issues that were to trouble the founders and subsequently trace through the nation's experience with massive immigration across the nineteenth century and yet again in the late twentieth and early twenty-first centuries. At the heart of these issues is a Jeffersonian concern: How can universal republican principles trump the different experiences and at times conflicting viewpoints that accompanied immigration? That there would be immigration was dictated by labor needs in the new nation, which opened its borders to, of course, the African slave trade and bonded servants in the eighteenth century, followed in the nineteenth century by land and job seekers from Catholic and Jewish regions of Europe, from China and Japan, and, today, from every impoverished region of the world. Given the population heterogeneity resulting from immigration, could the country really aspire to the liberal universalism so ardently proclaimed by the founding generation?

As early as 1751, Benjamin Franklin anticipated today's debates when he argues that the "importation of Foreigners" should occur only if employment opportunities expand and there are adequate "provisions for subsistence." Population size and the nation's resources must be kept in balance. He warns of the danger that proliferating foreigners "will gradually eat the Natives out" and hopes that high fertility among the present population (predominantly English and Protestant) will fill such "vacancies" that occur as the West is settled.[4] I note below that three decades later Jefferson puts his faith in a high native fertility that will be induced both by republican principles and by the bountifulness of the natural conditions of America.

Colonial censuses were, on the one hand, instrumental to British mercantilism and, on the other, fodder for revolutionary stirrings by those determined that in numbers and qualities the people should match the requirements of the envisioned nation based on liberal, republican principles. It was in service of implementing this vision that the first national census was designed.

Constitutional Purposes

The year 1790 brings something entirely new to census taking. It is to be a national census, one of the earliest tasks undertaken by the new government. And though the ancient uses of a census—

taxation and military preparedness—were of interest, what drove the census of 1790 and made it different from all previous censuses was its close association with establishing a republic based on principles of representation. This familiar story merits brief review. Recall the nation-building tasks that led to article 1, section 2 of the U.S. Constitution. Here we read that seats in the new House of Representatives "shall be apportioned among the several states which may be included within this Union, according to their respective Numbers." Following is instruction on how to calculate the Numbers (to which I return below), and then the sentence establishing the decennial census: "the actual Enumeration shall be made within three years after the first Meeting of the Congress of the United States, and within every subsequent Term of ten years, in such Manner as they shall by Law direct." The framers were here struggling with two challenges unique to the establishment of a republic at the edge of a vast, sparsely populated continent: how to establish a government based on the principles of federalism and how to avoid the dangers of colonialism.

As Henry Steele Commager tells us, the Americans of the Revolutionary generation "took the idea of federalism, which had never worked successfully, solved its most complex problem of the distribution of powers, and its most importunate problem of sanctions, and created the first successful and enduring federal government."[5] Separating law-making powers between the two legislative houses— the Senate based on equal representation for each state, and the House based on representation proportional to population size— was the compromise without which there would be no republic. The compromise could not, of course, be implemented without determining the respective numbers for each of the proposed thirteen new states—and thus the census of 1790.

But why a census every ten years? The framers meant to sustain their experiment in federalism, and they also sought to solve the problem of colonialism, which had undermined efforts to establish government based on the consent of the governed since the time of the Greek city-states. A colonial power, political theory argued, could not also be a republic. In treating some of its subjects as noncitizens, denying them the right to have rights, it contradicts the basic premise of a republic. (Slavery, a colonized group within the state, was of course also incompatible with the idea of a republic, as the framers well understood but effectively sidestepped.)

The new nation was especially susceptible to the temptations of colonialism—vast, rich, and sparsely settled lands lay just beyond the Alleghenies. Already a restless population was turning westward. The founding generation numbered among them many visionaries— Jefferson being one of the most articulate on this matter—who imagined a nation stretching to the Pacific. This vision posed a central constitutional question: Were the western territories to enter the Union as free and independent states or as colonies subject to the control of the Atlantic states? In favoring the former, though not without debate, the framers gave to the census its second significant nation-building task. Measure not just the growth of the population but also its westward movement and thereby regulate the pace at which the territories became the new states.

Though Jefferson was in Paris and not Philadelphia that summer of 1787, the Constitution reflected his belief that what set the American experiment apart from Britain's failure as an empire was the insistence on equal rights for all the territories that were to join the Union as states. Peter Onuf summarizes this Jeffersonian principle: "the new states all must be republican, independent of each other and the world yet bound together in perfectly harmonious and consensual union."[6] To keep the western territories as subject provinces would be to repeat the fatal mistake made by Britain. Jefferson had spelled out the principle of equality for the new western states in the Territorial Government Ordinance of 1784 (incorporated in the Northwest Ordinance of 1787). If "the Old World imagined the Enlightenment and the New World realized it," the census of 1790, Jefferson's census, was political engineering at its best.[7] It blended theory and practice, the idea of an expanding federal republic composed of states that themselves were republics, in the Jeffersonian sense, with the institutional means of realizing these aims that continues in an unbroken chain into the twenty-first century.

The Early Census

Prominently displayed in today's Bureau of the Census are likenesses of every director of the census, stretching across two centuries. Looming over this array is a portrait of Thomas Jefferson, proudly claimed by the bureau as the director of the first census. Though technically true, Jefferson's involvement in the administration of the 1790 census was minimal. The design of the first census was exclusively in the hands of the First Congress, convened in New York City in the spring of 1789. It turned its attention to the census early the following year and quickly made the decision that it would be conducted by the federal government rather than delegated to the states. There was, of course, little federal presence in the nation at large—revenue and customs officials, postal workers, a minuscule military, and judicial officials including U.S. marshals. The marshals undertook federal chores at the local level and worked on a fee basis, ideal traits for the ad hoc labor force necessary to conduct the census. In assigning enumeration to the marshals, the Congress, wittingly or not, initiated the principle that a nation needs information about itself and should provide this information as a public good.

There was early hesitancy about how much information to collect. James Madison wanted a more expansive census schedule than was eventually adopted, particularly urging the identification of occupations of the adult male population. Madison offered what, to him, was the commonsense rationale that "to accommodate our laws to the real situation of our constituents, we ought to be acquainted with that situation."[8] When the Senate rejected the proposal, he wrote to Jefferson that it had been dismissed "as a waste of trouble and materials for idle people to make a book."[9] That Jefferson shared Madison's interest is evidenced in his proposal a few years later, submitted on behalf of the American Philosophical Society, that the 1800 census collect "useful knowledge" beyond the bare minimum needed for apportionment. He recommended a nine-part occupational classification, a more detailed set of age categories, and data that would permit tracking immigration into the country.[10] Jefferson fared no better than Madison in urging more detailed information, and the 1800 census largely replicated that of 1790 in its limited focus.

The congressional debate about what to include in those earliest censuses points to a large truth about census taking: to count is also to classify. The categories made explicit by any classification scheme are seldom politically neutral. The congressional majority opposing a question on occupations felt that to allow an occupational classification would be to acknowledge separate interests, and that this posed a threat to the common good. Determining the relative size of different economic interests "conflicted with the traditional principle of a common good that embraced the entire community," writes Patricia Cline Cohen. "The object of wise governmental policy was to foster the happiness of society as a harmonious whole, a notion that arose from eighteenth-century ideas of an organic society."[11] The contrasting Madisonian view did eventually prevail when the 1820 census included a crude measure of manufacturing. "The common good was being broken into constituent parts, and the social order could now be comprehended through arithmetic."[12] Two hundred years later, as I note below, political arguments continue, with the focus on how (or whether) to break the population down into its constituent racial and ethnic parts. Today's measurement is intertwined with an "identity politics" that extends a Madisonian perspective well beyond anything imagined when the 1790 census was under discussion.

Jefferson and Political Arithmetic

It is perhaps ironic that Jefferson supervised the first census, which was one of the earliest instances of an energetic federal authority. His chief contribution to the conduct of the first census is telling, and it foreshadows his subsequent presidential engagement with territorial expansion. Though not provided for in the census statute, and not budgeted, Jefferson nevertheless extended the 1790 census to the Southwest Territory. This initiative paved the way for the early admission of Tennessee into the Union (1796), following a special mid-decadal census of the region. This special census was justified by pointing to the high base number counted in 1790, at Jefferson's insistence, and the assumption that growth since would have surely have reached a population of sixty thousand, the number set for admitting a new state to the Union. The special census confirmed this, and Tennessee became a state. Jefferson's initiative puts in practice one of the great promises of the Constitution: territories could quickly become equal members of the union when the census measures their numbers to the required level.

Excepting this initiative, Jefferson did not much intrude into the administration of the 1790 census. He did, however, energetically engage with how the 1790 count would apportion seats in the House of Representatives. When Jefferson released census returns to Congress in October 1791, it was quickly noted that neither the Constitution nor congressional statute had determined an apportionment formula. Debate was furious: because seats were indivisible, competing formulas for distributing the fractions would have a differential impact on the representation of particular states. The first presidential veto in the nation's history set aside an apportionment formula designed by Alexander Hamilton, thought by southerners to advantage the North. Jefferson had opposed Hamilton's design and advanced one of his own, which was adopted.[13] Virginia's delegation of twenty-one was the nation's largest. More than the size of Virginia's delegation was determined by Jefferson's success in controlling the nation's first apportionment formula. The formula advanced by Jefferson helped solidify the disproportionate influence of the South for decades to come. As Garry Wills has noted, Jefferson's intervention shifted a sufficient number of electoral votes to the slave-holding states to ensure not only Jefferson's election in 1800 but that of other candidates from slave states, including fellow Virginians Madison and Monroe.[14]

It should not surprise us that Jefferson prevailed in the debate to control the nation's first apportionment formula; it reflects his longstanding fascination and facility with numbers, and his use of that facility to political advantage. An early example is his ingenious calculation of Virginia's population in 1782, offered in his response to the inquiries of François Barbé de Marbois's on behalf of the French government. Jefferson writes that in the absence of "a perfect census of the inhabitants," he would turn to tax records. But these records having omitted "males between 16 and 21," he adds, "we must supply them from conjecture." His conjecture anticipated current statistical processes of interpolation and imputation by more than 150 years, and produced a population estimate for Virginia of 567,614.[15]

Jefferson's demographic skills were put to a more ambitious purpose in his now famous letter of September 1789 to James Madison, setting forth his principle that "the earth belongs in usufruct [trust] to the living." In asking what it is right, and wrong, for one generation to leave to another, Jefferson took up the exacting task of specifying the term "generation." As one scholar notes, the general notion that one generation could not bind the next was itself not original, but never had these claims been advanced "with the precision Jefferson was now able to supply; thanks to the authority of numbers, he was able to reduce generalities to a practical and workable law."[16] Madison had been through the difficulties of actually writing a constitution, and he doubted whether Jefferson's proposal was either practical or workable. Madison was properly skeptical toward the view that each generation should newly frame its own constitution. In his reply to Jefferson, however, Madison diplomatically cited the defeat of his simple recommendation to add an occupation question to the census as reason to doubt that Congress would agree to "so great an idea as that explained in your letter of September."[17]

What is compellingly interesting here, of course, is less the practicality of Jefferson's proposal to allow each generation to fashion for itself its political future than his willingness to move from high political theory to detailed demography. This anticipates by more than a century the arrival in American politics of the policy sciences and the effort to blend political theory and an empirical political science.

More generally, of course, the *Notes on Virginia* testifies to Jefferson's numerical inclinations: "Probably no one in America," James Cassedy writes, "was more imbued with the statistical spirit than was Jefferson. . . . If, as a scientist, he sought knowledge through experiment, he looked for it equally through observation and measurement of quantitative information. In virtually every area of his interests, he exercised an almost compulsive instinct to keep records of data."[18] To anticipate a point developed below, the endless measurements found in *Notes* were not solely the preoccupation of a scientist. Jefferson the politician-diplomat used his *Notes* as part of a larger effort to convince Europe that the great experiment across the Atlantic was not only a demographic success but also successful in agronomy, husbandry, manufacturing, and trade.

This last observation anticipates what was to become Jefferson's most important contribution to the new nation's demographic future, his faith in westward expansion. Later I consider in more detail the implications of that faith, but here I observe that as early as 1786 Jefferson is making a demographically based argument for geographic expansion: "we have lately seen a single person go and decide on a settlement in Kentucky, many hundred miles from any white inhabitant, remove thither with his family and a few neighbors; and though perpetually harassed by the Indians, that settlement in the course of ten years has acquired thirty thousand inhabitants." Jefferson is not content with this anecdotal reasoning but brings his numerical skills to bear on explaining the pattern we should expect: "The present population of the inhabited parts of the United States is of about ten to the square mile; and experience has shown us, that wherever we reach that, the inhabitants become uneasy, as too much compressed, and so go off in great numbers to search for vacant country. Within forty years the whole territory will be peopled at that rate. We may fix that, then, as the term beyond which the people of those [western] States will not be restricted within their present limit."[19] In this passage Jefferson gets one demographic trend as wrong as he gets the other one right. He correctly predicts the westward migration that was to define America in the nineteenth century. But his philosophical beliefs clouded his sociological reasoning, and thus he fails to see a second and equally critical demographic trend: the migration from rural to urban areas. This migratory constant had already redefined the Old World, to Jefferson's dismay, as it would redefine the New World in the nineteenth century.

Given these several early forays into demographic analysis, it is perhaps surprising that Jefferson did not take a more active interest in the 1790 census. It was Madison who more closely followed the first effort at national census taking, raising an alarm that continues to exercise politicians today—the possibility that a less than complete count in one region would politically disadvantage that region in comparison to areas in which the count is more complete. Madison worried that the southern states, particularly Virginia, being unfamiliar with census taking, would be undercounted. The census, he wrote, would be "so defective in the southern states as to give an undue preponderancy against them in the Legislature."[20] Madison is here anticipating a key feature of what today we recognize as the inevitable politics of census taking: an undercount that would differentially affect regions and population groups.

Numbers and the Blessings of America

There can be no nation without a population. And a nation that aspires to spread across an entire continent needs an ever-growing population to maintain the proper balance between land and people. In the litany of grievances Jefferson composed for the Declaration of Independence, King George stands guilty of suppressing population growth: "He has endeavored to prevent the Population of these States; for that purpose obstructing the Laws for Naturalization of Foreigners; refusing to pass others to encourage their migration hither, and raising the conditions of new Appropriations of Lands."[21] Franklin had anticipated this grievance in mid-century, when he elevated out-migration to that of a natural right: "God has given to the Beasts of the Forest and to the Birds of the Air a Right when their Subsistence fails in one Country, to migrate into another, where they can get a more comfortable living." He then makes the radical leap: "shall Man be denied a Privilege enjoyed by Brutes, merely to gratify a few avaricious Landlords?"[22] In this formulation, much more is at stake than the right of the colonies to grow in size. The "right to leave" challenges the notion that those born under the Crown owe it their lifetime allegiance.

Jefferson invokes this radical idea in his *A Summary View of the Rights of British America* (1774), a prelude to the Declaration. He builds on it to assert that allegiance is a matter of consent. That which is based on consent can be withdrawn if the conditions under which consent was granted are changed. The "right to leave" as a justification for rebellion does not survive the congressional editing that was to formulate the final wording in the Declaration. Jefferson himself, however, continued to believe that the argument carried weight, and "as a doctrine that persuaded Jefferson to act and others to support him, it contributed significantly to the formation of the revolutionary outlook."[23]

If population policy played a part in justifying the War of Independence, actual population numbers gave confidence to the revolutionary leaders, at least if they believed their own wartime propaganda. They "used demographic data," Margo Anderson writes, "to show that the infant United States had a large and growing population and could withstand war with England for many years." In contrast, "English commentators feared that their population was either stationary or declining."[24]

After the war, John Adams took up the theme of growth when he warned England against underestimating America: "the Americans are, at this day, a great people, and are not to be trifled with. Their numbers have increased fifty percent since 1774. A people that can multiply at this rate, amidst all the calamities of such a war of eight years, will in twenty years more, be too respectable to want friends."[25] Jefferson was advancing similar arguments in France, though now suggesting that the new nation's growth made it a necessary market for French goods: "for every article of the productions and manufacturers of this country [France] then, which can be introduced into the habit there [the United States], the demand will double every twenty or twenty-five years."[26]

When Jefferson reported that the 1790 census counted a population just shy of four million, Washington expressed disappointment. He had expected a number closer to five million. Washington found reasons for the presumed undercount (uncooperative citizens and indifferent enumerators) and asserted that the "authenticated number" would be far greater "than has ever been allowed in Europe, and will have no small influence in enabling them to form a more just opinion of our present growing importance than have yet been entertained there."[27]

Jefferson did his part by circulating census reports to America's diplomats. These indicated, in red ink, Jefferson's own population estimates, higher than those officially reported.

Population growth mattered for reasons other than war readiness or tax capacity. American Enlightenment thinking stressed population growth because more was assumed to be better, echoing Rousseau where he observes that "the most certain sign" of the prosperity of a political association and its members "is the number and increase of population."[28] Jefferson was not alone in his estimate that Virginia was doubling its population every twenty-seven years; similar claims were made by Jeremy Belknap for New Hampshire and Benjamin Franklin for Pennsylvania. Population growth could properly be attributed to the unique attractions of the New World; in Franklin's account: "the salubrity of the air, the healthiness of the Climate, the Plenty of good provisions, the Encouragement of early Marriages by the certainty of Subsistence in cultivating the Earth."[29]

Jefferson repeatedly sounds this theme, suggesting in his *Notes on Virginia* that men multiply not to become happy but because they *are* happy. He is not content with human population growth. He points out, again in the *Notes,* that the American deer, beaver, bear are more numerous as well as larger and heavier than their counterparts in Europe, further evidence that all species were favored by the benign conditions of the New World.

Jefferson is using the science of demography not just to account for or explain human happiness and welfare but also to show how they flow from the republican experiment. His fundamental demographic thesis, as Commager comments, holds that "a population which flourished and increased was both a product of and a tribute to the blessings which America enjoyed—blessings not only of Nature, but of government, economy, and society."[30]

Jefferson's blending of numbers with philosophy was not limited to demography. In his advocacy of the decimal system, he had in mind goals broader than rationalizing coinage or bringing order to accounting practices. Republican principles would be advanced because the "whole mass of people . . . would thereby be enabled to compute for themselves whatever they should have occasion to buy, to sell, or measure, which the present complicated and difficult ratios place beyond their computation for the most part."[31] The common citizen would not be dependent on tradesmen, and thereby would be able to exercise his own reasoning and judgment. More important, the government would be less likely to fool the populace. According to the author of a 1796 arithmetic textbook, the opaque British system of counting was "suited to the genius of their government, for it seems to be the policy of tyrants, to keep their accounts in as intricate, and perplexing a method as possible; that the smaller number of their subjects may be able to estimate their enormous impositions and exactions." Republican money, in contrast, "ought to be simple, and adapted to the meanest capacity."[32]

Demographic Forces Unleashed

Enlightenment philosophy notwithstanding, Jefferson's lasting contribution to demography was not his theoretical reflections or his cleverness at deploying arithmetic calculations in advancing political positions. What changed America's demography, and its demographic science, was a country of continental scope that was first imagined and then acquired through purchase, treaty, and military action across the whole of the nineteenth century. In the Ordinance of 1784, Jefferson had given specificity to what became the constitutional promise that the transmontane territories were to enter the Union as new states on equal footing with the original thirteen. At the convention itself this principle was contested. Gouverneur Morris pleaded that "the rule of representation ought to be so fixed as to secure to the Atlantic States a prevalence in the National Councils."[33] Delegates from the small states advanced a counterargument, recognizing that the dominance of the large-population eastern states could be checked by the steady admission to the Union of western territories. As noted above, a regular census was to ensure that new states would be represented on the same scale as the old. Political liberties would not be sacrificed in the westward movement—except, of course, those of slaves.

In rejecting the idea of a colonial empire to the west, the Northwest Ordinance and its constitutionally mandated instrumentality, the decadal census, set the conditions for Jefferson's boldest presidential act—the doubling of the nation's land mass with the purchase of the Louisiana Territory. There is no exaggeration in Jefferson's statement recruiting James Monroe to the task of negotiating with France: "on the event of this mission, depends the future destinies of this republic." That this was *not* to become a Jeffersonian agrarian republic, peopled by Anglo-Saxon farmers, is America's demographic story.

But of course the demographic story that does unfold is made possible only because of the America imagined by Jefferson. It is the imagined America that justified territorial expansion. "The West was the place where [Jefferson's] agrarian idyll could be regularly rediscovered, thereby postponing into the indefinite future the crowded conditions and political congestions of European society."[34] From the physiocrats, Jefferson took one of the central features of his political philosophy. An agricultural economy conformed "to the dictates of nature and nature's God," Commager explains, avoiding "the evils of colonies and wars and exorbitant taxes that plagued governments, and of the misery and luxury and vice that were the concomitants of great cities; added real wealth to the Commonwealth and nourished and safe-guarded the virtue of men and society."[35]

The economy that was to develop the West avoided few of these ills, certainly not colonization and wars. The colonization was not that of territory but of population groups forcefully relocated, purchased, conquered, or imported without citizen rights: African slaves, Mexicans, Native Hawaiians, Asian labor. Nor was the West settled peacefully, and the century's longest-running war, that against the Indians, can be traced to Jefferson's acceptance that the indigenous population might have to be forcefully relocated. He writes, in 1803, that the Indians "will in time either incorporate with us as citizens of the United States or remove beyond the Mississippi. The former is certainly the termination of their history most happy for themselves, but, in the whole course of this, it is essential to cultivate their love. As to their fear, we presume that our strength and their weakness is now so visible that they must see we have only to shut our hand to crush them, and that all our liberalities to them proceed from motives of pure humanity only."[36] Jefferson did not justify the forceful relocation of the Indian on racist grounds. In *Notes on Virginia* he had devoted a chapter celebrating the culture, intelligence, and spirit of the Indians, describing them as a noble race who faced an unfortunate fate. His romantic respect for the Noble Savage notwithstand-

ing, Jefferson was not what we today would call a "multiculturalist."
Writing to James Monroe in 1801, he noted that looking forward to
distant times, "our rapid multiplication will . . . cover the whole
northern, if not the southern continent, with a people speaking the
same language, governed in similar forms, and by similar laws." But
this America that he was imagining could not "contemplate with satisfaction either blot or mixture on that surface."[37] The multiplication
that Jefferson anticipated did of course come to pass, as did a common language and common law. But it came as a direct result of a
"mixture" unprecedented in world history. This is the complicated
story of nineteenth-century immigration, to which I turn in the next
section. It is a story that can be told because the West was acquired;
it did beckon, and if there were hostile Indians in the way, they could
be removed.

The "mixture" that immigration would introduce was, of course,
not yet on Jefferson's mind. When he expressed worries about a "blot
or mixture" on America's surface, he was answering Virginia governor Monroe's query on the merits of a western reserve for emanci-
pated slaves. This Jefferson strongly opposed. Onuf has written at
length and persuasively on how Jefferson came to see that the African populace was itself a nation, though not one that could share
the republican values on which the American experiment in self-
governance rested.[38] Jefferson writes in his *Autobiography,* "nothing
is more certainly written in the book of fate than that these people
[slaves] are to be free." He was just as certain that "the two races,
equally free, cannot live in the same government. Nature, habit, opinion has drawn indelible lines of distinction between them."[39] To protect the physical and moral character of (white) America—"our happiness and safety," as he wrote—the African would have to removed
by creating "an asylum to which we can, by degrees, send the whole
of that population from among us, and establish them under our
patronage and protection, as a separate, free and independent people, in some country and climate friendly to human life and happiness."[40] That country should not be America's West for that region
was firmly marked in Jefferson's mind as the frontier into which free
men would carry and then nourish republican values. Of course Jefferson's endorsement of Missouri joining the Union as a slave state

worked at cross-purposes here. His purpose was in service of a de-centralized republican scheme, but the consequence was the spread of slavery westward.

The outlines of the nation Jefferson imagined are now in view, at least speaking from the narrow perspective of demography. At its core was population growth and territorial expansion, the latter based on anticolonial republican principles. Its homogeneous population would engage in agricultural pursuits more than manufacturing and would be rural more than urban. Growth would primarily occur naturally, through fertility of those already settled in America, and less by fresh immigration. The territory would spread to the Pacific and would be added peacefully through treaty and purchase; free and equal states would join the Union as quickly as population numbers dictated. Despite both population and territorial expansion, fragmentation could be avoided because of a shared love of liberty and adherence to republican principles. This would be accomplished by removing from the nation, in reservations or distant colonies, those racial groups that either would not (Indians) or could not (African slaves) join white civilization.

The demographic realities unleashed by the decisions Jefferson did take—especially the Louisiana Purchase—dramatically altered the America he imagined and confidently expected, and this is the story of the nation that came to be measured.

A Nation Measured

There are two dimensions to the post-Jeffersonian demographic story, at times proceeding independently and at other times, as now, closely intertwined. One is about measurement and particularly the consistent use of racial classification as the accepted way to count and sort the population. The other is about internal migration, immigration, and related processes that remade the American population in the nineteenth and early twentieth centuries and then again in the late twentieth and early twenty-first centuries.

Both stories are foreshadowed by the 1790 census. This census, I have noted, was a simple one—not more than a half-dozen questions. But one of those questions generated an elementary racial classification that separated the white or European population from the black or African population. This sorting by race was required by one of the many compromises struck in 1787.

One of the difficult debates in Philadelphia was whether to base representation on population alone or on population plus wealth. The framers quickly fell into futile argument about how to measure wealth and realized that there was no sound method given the primitive nature of measurement. But in an awkward compromise they agreed that slaves were an easily measured indicator of wealth, and in the passage establishing the census stated that the count in each state "shall be determined by adding to the whole Number of free Persons, including those bound to Service for a Term of Years, and excluding Indians not taxed, three-fifths of all other Persons." Slaves, that is, were to count as six-tenths of a person for purposes of determining the population of each state. As Madison observed, the "Constitution therefore, decides with great propriety on the case of our slaves, when it views them in the mixt character of persons and property. This is in fact their true character."[41] This compromise was also to ensure a politically stronger South than would have occurred had slaves been left out of the count.

It is likely, however, that the census would have sorted by race even absent this constitutional compromise. There were social and philosophical reasons. Natural law and history had drawn "indelible lines of distinction," in Jefferson's words. To classify the population into racial groups would also help the new nation conduct its business. The census form that Madison ushered through the Congress—with its race, gender, and age distinctions—ensured a separate count of the population that mattered in the new government: adult white males. That is, voters, taxpayers, property owners, and, if needed, military recruits.

The 3.9 million Americans counted in the first census were overwhelmingly British and northern European (80 percent), with a significant African-slave minority (19 percent).

What I first emphasize about the distribution of population into these categories is the classification itself. Recall that the suggestion of Madison, subsequently supported by Jefferson, to create an occupation classification in the census was turned aside by the Congress. The census was *not* to be used to establish distinctions or differences.

An occupational classification would do political mischief. This congressional counterargument to Madison and Jefferson was, in fact, a profound insight into the power of the measurement system. Classification is arbitrary. It creates sharp differences where they would not otherwise occur. In the debate over occupational classification, for example, the opponents held that separating the population into agriculture, commerce, and manufacturing was artificial. Many Americans engaged in all three. Moreover, the critics suggested, "such categories undermined the notion of the common good, because they would inevitably encourage competition between groups."[42]

That the Congress understood the political implications of sorting the population into different economic groups makes the unhesitant use of a racial taxonomy all the more significant. It was unquestioned because it was natural and self-evident. Enlightenment thinking attributed observed physical and cultural differences to differences in the natural environment, and what could be more apparent than differences in skin color and facial features? That natural differences were soon to be rank-ordered into the superior and inferior was implicit of course in the justification of slavery. Racial hierarchy itself was part of the natural order.

The 1790 census of course was not the only expression of racial distinctions in the early Republic. The Northwest Ordinance had made it relatively easy to become a citizen in the new territories. Hoping to stimulate population movement, the ordinance "naturalized long-term alien inhabitants as U.S. territorial citizens, without any explicit discriminatory qualifications. French inhabitants, Catholics, the irreligious, free blacks, and individual Native Americans all could claim this new kind of national citizenship."[43] In 1790, however, as the new Congress debated citizenship issues, it restricted eligibility for naturalization to free white persons. Again, there were no distinctions of religion, language, or national origin; rather, there was an explicit exclusion based on race.

The confusion this introduced into Enlightenment political thinking about free and equal citizens is all too familiar. What denied citizenship—the fact that a man was a slave or that he was black? The argument went back and forth during the antebellum period, with northern state courts generally holding that free native-born blacks were citizens and with the courts of the slave states rejecting that proposition. The Supreme Court resolved the issue in the Dred Scott case (1857). The Negro could not be a citizen because, as Chief Justice Roger B. Taney wrote, they were "not intended to be included, and formed no part of the people who framed and adopted [the Constitution]."

It would of course be an exaggeration to attribute the racialization of American politics to the census. But the availability of a racial taxonomy—counting and sorting by race—was handmaiden to the politics of race that continue to the present. In one version or another, the classification of "European," "Negro," and "Indian" in the original census of 1790 has persisted, though the categories changed with the times. By 1820, it was necessary to add "free colored persons" to the classification scheme. After the Civil War, there arose interest in shades of color, and the census classified people as "Mulatto," "Quadroon," and "Octoroon." Asians first entered the census in the late nineteenth century. "Chinese" and "Japanese" are separately counted in 1890. "Filipinos," "Koreans," and "Hindus" are counted in 1920. Following statehood for Hawaii and Alaska, "Hawaiian" and "Part Hawaiian" appear on the 1960 census form, as do "Aleut" and "Eskimo." "Mexican" as a category appeared in 1930 but then was dropped following political pressure by the Mexican government. Mexicans in America were then counted as "White" until 1970. In the 1970 census, and in all subsequent ones, there is a "Hispanic" category, which in official statistics is considered an ethnicity rather than a race.

Throughout American history, starting with the 1790 census, the racial classification system played a central role in the regulation of relations among the races. Classification separated those entitled to full participation in society from those whose race was cause for exclusion. The slave system itself, and especially the attempt to balance admission to the Union of slave and free states in the first half of the nineteenth century, is one such instance. So were the relocation of Indians to reservations; the separate-but-equal doctrine; the design of Jim Crow laws; the denial of citizenship to Asians, the discriminatory immigration quotas in the 1920s; and the interning of Japanese Americans following Pearl Harbor.

More than a century and a half of discriminatory social policy designed to protect the numerical and political supremacy of Americans of European ancestry needed a classification system that assigned everyone to a discrete racial group. Census categories provided this classification, as did vital statistics and, eventually, the entire collection of administrative records in both the public and private sector. More generally, the census provided the basis for presuming that separate and distinct races constitute the true condition of the American population and can thereby provide the basis for law and public policy. Because there are measurable groups, there are traits that are differently distributed across these groups—including, of course, traits such as intelligence, social worth, moral habits. On this foundation was constructed a race-based legal code and social and economic practices that haunted the great republican experiment envisioned by Jefferson and his contemporaries.

Ironically, the civil rights legislation in the 1960s gave fresh momentum to racial measurement. Laws and policies were still to be based on racial classification, but in a 180-degree reversal the task is now to enforce those civil rights that prior uses of racial classification had denied.

The Civil Rights Movement and Racial Measurement

Where earlier policies had been discriminatory, new policies would right those wrongs. In this task, statistical proportionality became a favored legal and administrative tool. Across every sector of American life it has become commonplace to compare the proportion of a racial or ethnic minority group that has some advantage or suffers some disadvantage with the proportion of the white population similarly located. The census provides the denominator.

The civil rights movement did not start out with statistical proportionality in mind. It promised the end of social policy based on racial groupings. Echoing Enlightenment thinking, it celebrated universality and unity, not diversity. But discrimination did not easily give way. And soon the nation was enmeshed in a form of politics far removed from its traditional emphasis on individual rights. Equal opportunity became proportionate representation; individual rights became group rights; and nondiscrimination became affirmative action. Institutional racism entered the political vocabulary. Discrimination could be detected in housing patterns or wage rates. It could be measured, and statistical patterns were entered as evidence.

Moreover, groups other than African Americans bring their case forward on the basis of statistical proportionality: Hispanics, Asians, women, and the handicapped. In each instance, the census provides the denominator against which to assess who is being given equal treatment and opportunity, and who is not.

The racial classification system that gave rise to statistical proportionality as a tool of governance had a small number of discrete categories—"White," "Black," "Indian"—to which was added "Asian" and then, in 1970, "Hispanic" as an ethnic category. By 1990, every resident of the United States, according to the census, was one of four primary racial groups: "White," "Black/Negro," "Native Indian/Native Alaskan," "Asian," with a fifth residual, or "Other," option added on. Being of Spanish/Hispanic origin was presented as an ethnic not a racial distinction, on the assumption that a Hispanic could be of any race.

Census 2000 was to change this. It enlarged the four to five primary groups, by making "Native Hawaiian/Pacific Islander" a distinct group. And of much greater consequence, the census form in 2000 allowed respondents to mark "one or more" race. This multirace option is now being adopted across the entire federal statistical system and will gradually spread to the states and into the private sector. What for two hundred years had been a racial classification based on a handful of discrete groupings suddenly came to include sixty-three categories, or, when cross-classified by "Hispanic/Not Hispanic," 126 race/ethnic groups.[44]

This happened because Americans who claim more than one racial heritage felt that it was discriminatory to force them into one category. People could have more than one racial heritage. The argument that Madison's three-part occupational scheme was arbitrary—because one could be both a farmer and a man of commerce—reappears two hundred years later. This time, a simple adjustment fixed the problem: "mark one or more."

The end is not in sight. In racial classification, proliferation begets proliferation. To have gradually moved from three to four, five, and then, radically, to sixty-three measured race groups is to acknowledge that there is no natural limit. There is no prospect of returning to the simpler, discrete classifications of the nineteenth and twentieth centuries. The pressure to proliferate is given emphasis by the government's insistence that one's race is what one believes it to be. This is to underscore and legitimate identity politics. Identity politics is inherently self-proliferating as more and more subgroups believe there to be political advantage in a separate group identity. The republic of conflicting interests envisioned by Madison is now deeply planted in the measurement system, though in a manner that Madison and his contemporaries could not have envisioned.

I have summarized two hundred years of census history to make the now obvious observation. The nation imagined was not the nation that came to be measured. To ask whether American history would have been different had a racial taxonomy never been introduced in the census would take us deep into counterfactual reasoning. To refrain from racial measurement was in any case never seriously entertained. In the American experience, to sort by race is as natural as counting men and women, young and old.

It is not clear what will become of racial measurement or of the social policies to which it is anchored. The nation has a classification that has both too many and too few categories—too many for race-based policy making using statistical proportionality yet too few to accommodate the pressures of identity politics and the desire for separate recognition. The future of racial measurement will in large part depend on whether new immigrant groups resist or embrace racial classification. We return then to the Jeffersonian vision to see that a free republic, based on westward expansion, would produce a "nation of immigrants" more diverse than could be imagined in 1800.

Nineteenth-Century Immigration

The demographic picture as we start the journey of nationhood is given by the 1790 census. The native Indian population along the eastern seaboard had been killed or conquered, and by 1790 it constituted but a tiny fraction of the population. There is a much larger black African population numbering approximately one-fifth of the population. The largest group (49 percent) is of English descent, with approximately 20 percent of this group Irish and 12 percent from other parts of northwestern Europe.

This was not the homogeneous population often described. "By the standards of Europe," Zolberg notes, "the American colonies constituted a congeries of diverse communities which, if brought together into a single state, would constitute a uniquely heterogeneous mosaic."[45] The compositions of this mosaic varied from one region to another, New England then as now being the most homogeneous; the middle colonies being home to more Germans, Dutch, Celts, and French-Huguenot, with English constituting a comparative smaller share; and the South, of course, having the most racially diverse population. Cross-regional tensions often reflected these patterns, with New England resistant to non-English immigrants and other colonies variously xenophobic toward "foreigners," such as Moravians, Huguenots, or Germans. Franklin particularly inveighed against the Germans, for imposing their language and customs. He worried that German speakers "will soon so outnumber us, that all the advantages we have will not in My Opinion be able to preserve our language, and even our Government will become precarious."[46] These pre-independence tensions anticipate, of course, their much more virulent expression in the nineteenth century, when immigrants with their alien languages, faiths, and habits flow from every corner of Europe and even Asia.

It is religious tolerance that was particularly important in the seventeenth and early eighteenth centuries because so many had migrated to escape intolerance in their European countries. Religious diversity was, of course, within the Protestant tradition. Compared to the present concern with tensions among Christian, Muslim, Hindu, and Buddhists, or the nineteenth-century tensions between Protestants and Catholics and Jews, the earlier period with its largely Protestant population is sometimes viewed as homogeneous. But this is to overlook the intensity of religious faith and the differences in practice and outlook across the many Protestant churches: Anglican, Methodists, Baptists, Presbyterians, Congregational, Lutheran, and Quakers. After carefully reviewing the considerable ethnic and religious diversity in colonial America, historian Jon Butler concludes that in its diversity America at its independence was already the world's first modern society.[47]

It is against the backdrop of a nation already heterogeneous by European standards—and yet one promising to build its civic culture on principles of universalism and full participation (for free white males)—that the debates over immigration occur. These debates were vigorous in the early years of the Republic. Writing in 1787, Tench Coxe, later to become an ally of Jefferson's, caught the general sentiment that though immigration was necessary, it should not be too much or of the wrong kind. He writes: "how far emigration from other countries into this, ought to be encouraged, is a very important question. It is clear, that the present situation of America, renders it necessary to promote the influx of people; and it is equally clear, that we have a right to restrain that influx, whenever it is found likely to prove hurtful to us."[48]

Jefferson had taken a similar position in his Notes, where he writes of the "desire of America to produce rapid population by as great importations of foreigners as possible" but then also advises against "encouragement by extraordinary means." Here Jefferson, like his contemporaries, was concerned that too many of the wrong kind would come to America. To the extent possible, it was best to rely on natural fertility. There were reasonable demographic grounds for hoping that the western territories could be primarily peopled by the then-resident population. This resident population was young— about half were under sixteen and would soon reach fertility age. Jefferson's calculations led him to expect a doubling of Virginia's population every twenty-seven or so years. The belief that native-born Americans would expand in number and surge westward was quickly confirmed. By 1820, the number of Americans west of the Alleghenies, more than two million, was equal to the colonial population in 1776.

Jefferson's views on immigration were focused on whether strangers to the country would have it in them to embrace the values of republicanism. His worries are expressed in the Notes, where he observes that emigrants who had imbibed the "maxims of absolute monarchies" in their youth might bring those undesirable views with them, infusing into our laws a bias that will "render it a heterogeneous, incoherent mass."[49] Yet Jefferson also believed strongly in the socializing influence of the republic, and vigorously opposed the premise of the 1798 Alien Acts that called the loyalty of foreigners into question.

In his review of Jefferson's writing on immigration and naturalization, Zolberg comes to the balanced conclusion that Jefferson can rightly be called an "immigrationist," though one who would apply restrictions when immigration was likely to prove harmful to the nation. If Jefferson framed his views toward immigration with vast, rich agricultural land in mind, his archrival saw immigration as key to manufacturing. Alexander Hamilton, in his 1791 *Report on Manufactures,* noted that immigration from abroad would increase "the useful and productive labor of the country." As Rogers Smith writes, "Hamilton envisioned a fast-growing nation in which immigrants, women, children, and men of all ranks would be embraced as equals," all in the service of a manufacturing society.[50]

Neither Jefferson nor Hamilton could foresee the vast transformation that would result from the forces they had unleashed: first, new lands offering seemingly limitless opportunities for agriculturalists; then, rapid expansion of employment in a burgeoning industrial sector. In fact, the most astute observer of the early nineteenth century, Alexis de Tocqueville, generally viewed the new nation as demographically complete, a formed society whose population would grow through the natural processes of reproduction. Yet already Tocqueville, in an aside, draws worried attention to the surge of Irish immigrants to America's port cities, particularly New York and Philadelphia. Tocqueville offers an early glimpse of nineteenth-century immigration that would radically alter the nation's social and religious demography. Roman Catholics dominated immigration flows between 1820 and the Civil War period. The Irish, escaping economic deprivation as well as religious persecution, accounted for a major share. Emigration was further stimulated by political turmoil in northern Europe, sending Germans, French, Belgians, and Dutch to the American shores. Already in 1850 the Roman Catholic Church was the largest denomination in the country, though less numerous than all Protestant denominations combined.

The 1850 census was the first to introduce the distinction between native- and foreign-born. New York City was then more than half foreign-born, with similar high proportions in Chicago, Milwaukee, Detroit, St. Louis, and New Orleans. The nativist Know-Nothing Party in the years before the Civil War led an anti-Catholic cry. Romanism, insisted the nativists, undermined the Protestantism on which the nation had constructed its moral and political identity. And when nativists were not able to stem the flow of immigrants—which was encouraged by factory owners and shipping and railroad interests—their efforts focused on slowing down the naturalization process. If the external border could not be closed, internal borders should be created to prevent the political incorporation of undesirable population groups.

Immigrant flows were not limited to Europe. In the middle of the nineteenth century there was a sharp increase of Asian workers to the West Coast, drawn to the mines and railroad work that offered economic returns unheard of in China and Japan. Though citizenship was not part of the package, Asian labor was a boon to the American economy. Chinese men but not Chinese women were welcomed as workers. This was to prevent the Chinese from marrying and then having native-born children who would have a claim on citizenship. In the first instance of closing borders to immigrants, the Chinese Exclusion Act of 1882 and successor laws stopped Chinese immigration altogether; the 1907 Gentleman's Agreement between the United States and Japan had a similar effect on the flow of Japanese. These policies reflected both racist views and fears of wage competition—a mixture of motives that was to dominate immigration policy for decades.

Further dramatic demographic shifts resulted from the next surge of immigration, which began about 1880, peaking in the years before World War I. It was during this period that immigration from northern Europe fell sharply, to be replaced by large numbers of arrivals from southern and eastern Europe, including the first wave of Jewish immigrants. Anti-Semitism joined anti-Catholicism and anti-Asian sentiments in American politics.

Such prejudices were fueled by pseudoscientific racist theories when social Darwinism and eugenics became popular. The census was enlisted in constructing a race science that focused on defining who was nonwhite so as to protect the purity of the white race. "In general," writes Melissa Nobles, "to be 'white' was conceived as the complete absence of any 'negro or non-white blood,' down to the last drop and as far back generationally as one could go."[51] Racist quotas in the restrictive immigration laws passed in the 1920s were the culmination of four decades of efforts to control immigration and represented a last-gasp effort to reestablish the dominance of the population that had founded the Republic. But it was too late. The country had little choice but to try to figure out how it could become a pan-European nation.

The immigration narrative pauses with the restrictive immigration laws in the 1920s. Immigration dropped off sharply; and the few foreign-born who did arrive over the next four decades were again from northern and western Europe.

The nation's nineteenth-century demographic narrative is primarily but not entirely a story of immigration. In lesser numbers, the population also grew and altered its composition as a result of territorial wars and land purchase. The Mexican-American War in 1848 added the Southwest but also the nation's first large Mexican population, about eighty thousand people. The Spanish-American War in 1898 added the Puerto Rican islands and their people. When Hawaii was annexed in 1898, its native Pacific Islander population became Americans. Land purchase played its part. Jefferson's Louisiana Purchase in 1803 added a French Creole population; William Henry Seward's purchase of the Russian colony of Alaska in 1867 added the Inuit, the Kodiak, and other Alaskan natives. While population increases that resulted from conquest and purchase were not large, relatively speaking, they did add to the country's mixture of races, ethnicities, languages, and cultures.

Demographically, the story of the nineteenth and early twentieth centuries is one of increased diversification. The four million or so Americans at the time of the first census are from the British Isles and northern Europe, along with a sizeable minority of black, mostly enslaved inhabitants and a few Indians. Soon joining this demographic base are substantial numbers of new Europeans, at first primarily from Ireland and increased numbers from Germany but by the end of the century largely from southern and eastern Europe. Smaller additions include Creoles; native populations in Alaska and Hawaii; a native Mexican population in the Southwest; Caribbean-based Hispanics and blacks; and West Coast Asians.

Politically, the story of the nineteenth and early twentieth centuries is one of selective incorporation. Of the new demographic groups, it was the Europeans who were incorporated into the political life of the nation, though this was not easily achieved by Catholics and Jews. For groups separated out by their racial characteristics—Hispanics, Asians, African Americans, Native Americans, and Pacific Islanders—political citizenship was largely withheld. In this sense, the Republic had become what it had promised to avoid. There had been no outright colonization of territory, but significant numbers of inhabitants were treated as if they were colonized peoples. They were "stateless" in the sense that they did not have the right to have rights. The many ways in which this eroded the promise of a republic based on free and equal citizens is familiar history.

Late Twentieth-Century Immigration

A significant shift in immigration policy occurs in 1965 and continues with major legislative initiatives in the 1980s and 1990s. Earlier policy based on the 1920s legislation gave preference to national origin, designed to favor northern and western European immigration. It is now replaced with preferences that in no small measure are influenced by heightened civil rights sentiments. Reunification of families and hospitality to political refugees, along with the traditional emphasis on attracting workers with skills needed in the economy, have become the new criteria.

These new criteria led to massive shifts in the regions of the world sending immigrants to the United States. Europe is displaced. In 1850, more than nine of every ten foreign-born were from Europe. Even by 1900, this dropped only slightly (86 percent foreign-born are European), and still, in 1960, Europeans were 75 percent of the foreign-born. The drop-off was then sharp, as Asians and Latinos arrive in large numbers. More than half of the present foreign-born are from Latin America, more than a quarter are from Asia, and Europeans number fewer than one in five. These patterns show no signs of reversal.

It is these numbers, of course, that have given rise to heavy media attention about a more diverse America, with many stories proclaiming that the country will soon be a minority-majority nation. These stories misinterpret the data for they always exclude from the count of the white population a significant number of Hispanics who identify themselves as white. But the picture of a nation increasingly diverse in its ethnicity and national origins is correct. The nation is today composed of every world religion, civilization, culture, language group, and ethnicity. If in the nineteenth century America became history's first pan-European nation, it will in the twenty-first century become history's first panworld nation.

Demographic theory helps us see why. Jefferson and his colleagues placed their faith in the high fertility of the young population that had settled the eastern seaboard and would now move westward. This was a reasonable expectation. They can hardly be faulted for failing to anticipate the demographic transition. This term describes the change from high fertility/high mortality in the preindustrial period to low fertility/low mortality in the postindustrial period. Mass education and public health are the forces that reduce infant mortality and therefore fertility rates. The United States has experienced a demographic transition that by the latter decades of the twentieth century had led to less than replacement-level fertility in the white, native-born population.[52]

When this happens a country has two options: manage a population decline or adopt permissive immigration policies. The latter is sometimes known as "replacement migration." As defined by the United Nations: "replacement migration refers to the international migration that would be needed to offset declines in the size of the population, the declines in the population of working age, as well as to offset the overall aging of a population."[53] In the United States, when the native stock stopped reproducing at replacement level three decades ago, the adjustment in immigration policy was swift. Immigration plus higher than replacement-level fertility among the foreign-born added nearly 33 million residents between the 1990 and the 2000 decennial censuses, with especially high levels of growth among the working-age cohort. The present U.S. population is 10 percent foreign-born.

The source regions are the poorer, demographically young countries that send emigrants to the richer, demographically older countries. "If liberal immigration policy allows this process to play itself out," Jeffrey Williamson concludes, "mass migrations from emerging nations in the middle of their demographic transitions will always flood the advanced nations who have completed their demographic transitions. If restrictive immigration policy tries to choke off this process, then illegal immigration will try to circumvent it."[54]

Historically, emigration has been both age-selective and ambition-selective. It is the young with drive, energy, imagination, and determination who are more likely to strike out for new places and new possibilities. That was true of immigration from the Old to the New World in the nineteenth century and is generally the pattern today.

There are, then, demographic constants that suggest continued immigration to the United States. The world regions yet to complete their demographic transition are Muslim, Hindu, Buddhist, and Latin Catholic; they are culturally and linguistically and ethnically non-European. They are demographically young, low-wage areas. They have strong emigration pressures and no incentive for their home governments to prevent out-migration. Economic recession in the United States, and now anxieties about importing terrorism, may slow down immigration flows, but this will only be a pause. The demographic realities are powerful forces. The first political generation to learn that demography can trump political theory was that of the Jeffersonian Republicans. The West was settled by immigrants, who became city dwellers and factory workers in much greater numbers than they became yeoman farmers.

Conclusions

Jefferson's legacy is rich and extensive—covering issues of political philosophy, statecraft, diplomacy, religion, science, exploration, architecture, and education not even mentioned in this essay. The range of his legacy has been documented in a vast literature. My footnote to this literature derives from the fact that Thomas Jefferson supervised the nation's first census.

Since Jefferson's census in 1790, the United States has become history's most measured nation. The periodic census, taken every decade, is at the center of a far-flung measurement system that counts and sorts our political and economic life, our social organizations and demographic trends, our opinions and practices. How the nation views itself, and governs itself, is intricately linked to how it measures itself.

This comprehensive national measurement system gets its start in the early decades of the Republic. My effort has been to draw attention to several features that date from this early period: territorial expansion based on the principle of a republic of "republics" that would join the Union as their population growth warranted; the centrality of racial classification; and the continuous recording of the demographic diversification associated with immigration. Jefferson was central to all three of these narratives, and their interaction has made us the nation we are today.

Enlightenment thinking in the early Republic emphasized reason and the desire for liberty as universal human traits. But despite this celebration of what was common in human aspirations, the Constitution mandated separation of the population into distinct racial groupings. The census bolstered the assumption that race summarized differences that could not be blended, merged, or otherwise incorporated into the promise of universality. What begins as a distinction among the Europeans, Africans, and Indians is elaborated over the course of the nineteenth and early twentieth centuries to include new immigrant groups: Asians, Pacific Islanders, and Hispanics. The nation's classification system reflected and furthered the careful distinction between white and nonwhite.

Isaiah Berlin teaches us that a nation cannot achieve liberal values from a universalism that claims only one set of values to be true and all others false; and it cannot achieve liberalism from a relativism that allows each to have their own values, with none being judged either wrong or right. He writes: "all human beings must have some common values or they cease to be human, and also some different values else they cease to differ, as in fact they do."[55]

The nation's measurement system addressed the deep philosophical tension between universalism and diversity in a very particular manner. It assumed that race and ethnicity are among the deepest and most meaningful markers of diversity. From that flowed public policies that regulated the relations among different racial and ethnic groups, often in discriminatory ways.

Today, of course, issues of social justice have moved to the center of political debate and practice. We argue over the terms of social justice with the intensity that in the Jeffersonian period was reserved for issues of authority and liberty. Our contemporary politics of social justice now take up issues of social recognition and respect, even of group rights. Democratic theory, based on individualistic and egalitarian principles, is being pushed into unfamiliar territory. In no small measure, I trace these developments back to key decisions taken at the beginning: the population would be counted and sorted by race; it would inhabit a continent; it would be enlarged by the immigrant labor needed for this westward expansion.

NOTES

This essay is based on a lecture delivered as "Thomas Jefferson's West," Thomas Jefferson Foundation Distinguished Lecture Series, University of Virginia, October 10–13, 2001. I am indebted to the conference organizers and participants for correcting errors in the initial lecture, and for pointing me to issues and sources that led to important revisions in the text prepared for publication.

1. See Patricia Cline Cohen, *A Calculating People: The Spread of Numeracy in Early America* (Chicago, 1982).
2. Aristide Zolberg, *A Nation by Design* (Cambridge, Mass., forthcoming), chap. 1. Zolberg offers a rich analysis of the political economy of immigration in the colonial period, and the previous paragraph draws on this analysis.
3. Ibid.
4. J. A. Leo Lemay, ed., *Benjamin Franklin: Writings* (New York, 1987), 372–73. Quoted and further interpreted in Zolberg, *Nation by Design*, chap. 1.
5. Henry Steele Commager, *Jefferson, Nationalism, and the Enlightenment* (New York, 1975), 21.
6. Peter S. Onuf, *Jefferson's Empire: The Language of American Nationhood* (Charlottesville, 2000), 38.
7. Commager, *Jefferson, Nationalism, and the Enlightenment*, 3.
8. Quoted in Cohen, *A Calculating People*, 160.

9. For more detail on Madison's effort, see Margo J. Anderson, "(Only) White Men Have Class: Reflections on Early-Nineteenth-Century Occupational Classification Systems," *Work and Occupations* 21 (1994): 10–14.

10. For detail, see Carroll Wright and W. C. Hunt, *History and Growth of the United States Census* (Washington, D.C., 1900), 19–20. See also Michel L. Balinski and H. Peyton Young, *Fair Representation: Meeting the Ideal of One Man, One Vote* (New Haven, 1982), chap. 3.

11. Cohen, *A Calculating People,* 163.

12. Ibid., 164.

13. Margo J. Anderson, *The American Census: A Social History* (New Haven, 1988), 15–16.

14. See extensive review of the "slave power" literature in Garry Wills, "The Negro President," *New York Review of Books* 50 (Nov. 6, 2003), 45–51.

15. *Notes on the State of Virginia,* in Merrill D. Peterson, ed., *Thomas Jefferson: Writings* (New York, 1984), 213.

16. Herbert Sloan, "The Earth Belongs in Usufruct to the Living," in *Jeffersonian Legacies,* ed. Peter S. Onuf (Charlottesville, 1993), 296.

17. Quoted ibid., 301.

18. James H. Cassedy, *Demography in Early America: Beginnings of the Statistical Mind, 1600–1800* (Cambridge, Mass., 1969), 225–26.

19. Quoted ibid., 229–30.

20. Madison to Carrington, March 14, 1790, in William T. Hutchinson, William M. E. Rachal et al., eds., *The Papers of James Madison, Congressional Series,* 17 vols. (Chicago and Charlottesville, 1959–71), 13:105. For more detail, see William M. Fliss, "An Administrative and Political History of the Early Federal Census, 1790–1810" (master's thesis, University of Wisconsin, 2000). Fliss's thesis is also the source of earlier comment on the role of marshals in the 1790 census and more generally presents an excellent overview of how the first three censuses were administered and funded.

21. For a thorough account of how the conflict over immigration and naturalization influenced the movement for independence, see Zolberg, *Nation by Design,* chap. 1.

22. Lemay, *Franklin Writings,* 709, quoted in Zolberg, *Nation by Design,* chap. 1.

23. Ibid.

24. Anderson, *The American Census,* 11.

25. Adams to Matthew Robinson, March 2, 1786, in Charles Francis Adams, ed., *The Works of John Adams, Second President of the United States,* 10 vols. (Boston, 1850–56), 8:385.

26. Jefferson (TJ) to the Count de Montmorin, June 23, 1787, in Andrew A. Lipscomb and Albert Ellery Bergh, eds., *The Writings of Thomas Jefferson,* 20 vols. (Washington, D.C., 1903–4), 6:186.

27. Washington to Gouverneur Morris, July 28, 1791, quoted in Cassedy, *Demography in Early America,* 219–20.

28. Quoted in Commager, *Jefferson, Nationalism, and the Enlightenment*, 27.

29. Ibid., 45.

30. Ibid., 46.

31. Quoted in Cohen, *A Calculating People*, 128.

32. Erastus Root, *An Introduction to Arithmetic for the Use of Common Schools* (1796), quoted in Cohen, *A Calculating People*, 129.

33. Quoted in Edward S. Morgan, *The Birth of the Republic: 1763–89*, rev. ed. (Chicago, 1977), 139.

34. Joseph Ellis, *American Sphinx: The Character of Thomas Jefferson* (New York, 1997), 212.

35. Commager, *Jefferson, Nationalism, and the Enlightenment*, 47.

36. TJ to Governor William Henry Harrison, Feb. 27, 1803, quoted in Ellis, *American Sphinx*, 201.

37. TJ to James Monroe, Nov. 24, 1801, quoted ibid., 202.

38. Onuf, *Jefferson's Empire*, chap. 5.

39. TJ, *Autobiography* (1821), quoted ibid., 151.

40. TJ to Jared Sparks, Feb. 4, 1824, quoted ibid., 151.

41. Quoted in Melissa Nobles, *Shades of Citizenship: Race and the Census in Modern Politics* (Stanford, 2000), 27.

42. Ibid., 30.

43. Rogers Smith, *Civic Ideals: Conflicting Visions of Citizenship in U.S. History* (New Haven, 1997), 98.

44. Sixty-three are the number of separate categories that occur when all combinations of six are summed, using the familiar formula of two to the sixth power minus one.

45. Zolberg, *Nation by Design*, chap. 1.

46. Lemay, *Franklin Writings*, 473.

47. Jon Butler, *Becoming American: The Revolution before 1776* (Cambridge, Mass., 2000).

48. Tench Coxe, *An Enquiry into the Best Means of Encouraging Emigration from Abroad, Consistently with the Happiness and Safety of the Original Citizens* (1787), quoted in Zolberg, *Nation by Design*, chap. 2.

49. TJ, *Notes on the State of Virginia*, in Peterson *Jefferson Writings*, 85.

50. Smith, *Civic Ideals*, 141.

51. Nobles, *Shades of Citizenship*, 70.

52. Having below replacement-level fertility is an issue for most of the advanced economies of the world, all of which have experienced the demographic transition. The U.N. projects negative population growth for thirty-one European nations. For example, under current (median) U.N. projections, in the next half-century Italy's population will drop from 57 million to 41 million, and the Russian federation from 147 million to 121 million. Similar drops are projected for East Asia, where, for instance, Japan's population will shrink from 127 million to 105 million. Accompanying these population declines is population aging; a

third of the population in both Italy and Japan, for example, will be over sixty-five by midcentury. See *Replacement Migration: Is It a Solution to Declining and Aging Populations?* (Population Division of the Department of Economic and Social Affairs, United Nations Secretariat; ESA/P/WP.160, March 2000).

53. Ibid., 1.

54. Jeffrey G. Williamson, "Demographic Shocks and Global Factor Flows" (paper presented to the Federal Reserve Bank of Boston conference on "Seismic Shifts: The Economic Impact of Demographic Change," Chatham, Mass., June 11–13, 2001), 4.

55. Excerpt from Berlin's last essay, in *New York Review of Books* 45 (1998), www.cs .utexas.edu/users/vl/notes/berlin.html.

Oñate's Foot

Histories, Landscapes,
*and Contested Memories
in the Southwest*

Douglas Seefeldt

In EARLY JANUARY 1998, A THREE-AND-a-half-year-old bronze equestrian statue was vandalized at a visitor's center in Alcalde, New Mexico. While graffiti is presumably the most common form of damage inflicted upon public art, in this act the perpetrators worked without spray paint or markers, skillfully removing the right foot from the rider with a power grinder.[1] Like most attacks on public monuments, these vandals intended their act to be interpreted as a statement. In this case the befooting was a political statement, as this statue depicts Don Juan de Oñate (c. 1550–1626), celebrated by some as the "last conquistador." However, this leader of the first Spanish efforts at settlement into what is today New Mexico is a controversial figure, simultaneously remembered as noble by some, yet vilified by others who remember him as a colonial butcher who ordered the right foot removed from two dozen Acoma Pueblo male prisoners in February 1599.[2]

The vandals' timing was as calculated as their message for 1998 marked the four-hundredth anniversary, or *cuarto centenario,* of the arrival of Oñate and his six hundred pioneer colonists. The occasion inspired the organization of nearly two hundred projects throughout the state designed to celebrate New Mexico's Spanish colonial history and cultural legacy and address the prevalent Anglocentric view of the American past. Projects included public statues of Oñate in Santa Fe and Madrid, New Mexico, groundbreaking for a Camino Real museum in Socorro, and a Hispanic cultural center in Albuquerque.[3] The vandals used the attention given to the year-long celebration to their advantage by issuing a statement, accompanied by a photograph of the amputated bronze foot, that stated, "we see no glory in celebrating Oñate's fourth centennial, and we do not want our faces rubbed in it." Estevan Arrellano, the director of the visitor's center where the vandalized Oñate statue is located, replied, "give me a break—it was 400 years ago. It's O.K. to hold a grudge, but for 400 years?"[4]

Anniversaries like the Columbian *cuarto centenario* make excellent platforms for both commemoration and dissent. Plans presented to the Albuquerque City Council in the winter of 1997–98 by Hispanic leaders that proposed to spend $255,000 to construct another publicly subsidized memorial to Oñate in the city's Old Town met with vociferous protest from representatives of a variety of cultural groups including Mexican Americans, Native Americans, and Anglo Americans. Negotiations resulted in the monument design responsibilities being divided between two Hispanics and a Native American. Although the project was eventually approved, plans now call for a Holocaust memorial to be located at the original site intended for the Oñate memorial.[5]

While Oñate's colonization of the American Southwest as an actual event is long since past, controversies surrounding its interpretation continue to occur because publicly articulated views of the past remain contested so long as different groups remember different pasts and compete with others to shape public memory. As subaltern perspectives are encouraged to find voice in a shifting postcolonial discourse in the American Southwest, the reinterpretation of landscapes and memories reaches new audiences and becomes entangled in the larger questions associated with current debates over public memory and identity politics. This essay examines the fluid nature of the making of public memories, landscapes, and identities and the challenge of writing histories—on paper or in bronze—that are aware of these processes. History does not always adequately capture the multivocality and complexity of the Southwest's many cultures, their distinct places, myriad pasts, and evolving power structures that enable these groups to construct their own pasts. The significant challenge presented by these processes belies the seemingly clear-cut arguments espoused by many academic and public critics in today's climate of culture wars and other debates over memory and identity. Although the sculptor repaired the Oñate statue in Alcalde, the amputated foot was never returned and is still missing. Oñate's foot is a powerful symbol of the legacy of conquest reclaimed and held hostage, not unlike the very history of the region, by those attempting to reinterpret a disputed past commemorated by others in bronze.

Histories and Memories

The way groups create both private and public memory is an important part of social and cultural history. As David Thelen observes, "the historical study of memory opens exciting opportunities to ask fresh questions of our conventional sources and topics and . . . create[s] points for fresh synthesis." Investigations into memory construction can reveal how politics, culture, and ethnicity factor in the process. For as Thelen reminds us, "memory, private and individual as much as collective and cultural, is constructed, not reproduced." Individuals negotiate in and between groups to shape public memory at the community, state, and national levels.[6] Because individuals invested in a particular interpretation of the past influence the construction and negotiation of collective memories, the historical study of memory can shed light on the important role of persons and perspectives that might otherwise be overlooked. On the other hand, as Thelen cautions, memory can be a veritable minefield: "Since people's memories provide security, authority, legitimacy, and finally identity in the present, struggles over the possession and interpretation of memories are deep, frequent, and bitter."[7]

The key to the successful construction of memory is power. Therefore, contemporary social, political, and cultural values and interests are a significant part of the public memory negotiation process. Traditions and their attendant memories are arranged and rearranged to fulfill the particular needs of particular groups at particular times, often resulting in a process where competing memories exist side by side.[8] Historian Michael Kammen defines "collective memory" as what is remembered by the dominant culture, and "popular memory" as what is remembered by the common folk, while historian John Bodnar identifies two groups at work, the "official culture," concerned with social unity, continuity, and the status quo, and the "vernacular culture," concerned with diversity, special interests, and change. Bodnar contends that at the junction of these cultural expressions is "public memory," which he defines as "a body of beliefs and ideas about the past that help a public or society understand both its past, present, and by implication, its future."[9]

While such studies effectively portray public memory as a tool in the struggle between various groups for interpretive authority, they can oversimplify the variety of vernacular voices and the multiplicity of perspectives often found within seemingly homogeneous groups. Rather, as public historian David Glassberg argues, "there are multiple official histories as well as multiple vernacular memories."[10] In fact, sites of memory like the statue at the Oñate Monument and Visitor's Center do not really represent a homogeneous public memory or collective memory at all but rather a heterogeneous "collected memory," as historian James Young demonstrates in his study of Holocaust memorials. These memorials gather countless individual memories into a common space and assign them a common meaning. Or, as Glassberg observes, "Since it is nearly impossible to reach a consensus on the public interpretation of a historical event that anyone still cares about, public historical representations such as an exhibit, war memorial, or commemorative ceremony are often deliberately ambiguous to satisfy competing factions." Maya Lin's Vietnam Veterans Memorial in Washington, D.C., is perhaps the most recognizable example of what French historian Pierre Nora has termed *lieux de mémoire,* or sites of memory. According to Nora, these places are simultaneously material, symbolic, and functional; they are, "simple and ambiguous, natural and artificial, at once immediately available in concrete sensual experience and susceptible to the most abstract elaboration."[11]

Sites that interpret only one perspective are often the focus of prolonged debate and rancor—as aptly demonstrated by the former Custer Battlefield National Monument, now rechristened the Little Bighorn Battlefield National Monument—or, at the very least, are the subject of ironic condemnation.[12] As social and cultural attitudes change, so do public memories of past events, a revision fueled by present concerns of identity and heritage. According to geographer David Lowenthal, "the past is not a fixed or immutable series of events; our interpretations of it are in constant flux. What previous groups identify and sanctify as their pasts become historical evidence about themselves." Like the present, the past is always changing. Real and imagined, remembered and forgotten, multifarious events from the past can at once be carefully perpetuated and irreverently manipulated by tradition bearers or civic boosters. And because of this, Lowenthal warns, "when we identify, preserve, enhance, or commemorate surviving artifacts and landscapes, we affect the very nature of the past, altering its meaning and significance for every generation in every place." With each new ascendant layer of history applied to the cultural foundation of a constructed past, other perspectives become obscured. This process is significant, for as Lowenthal concludes, "every trace of the past is a testament not only to its initiators but to its inheritors, not only to the spirit of the past, but to the perspectives of the present."[13]

Pasts have been constructed in the American Southwest just as they have wherever and whenever humans strove to create a sense of place and validate particular memories. New Mexico's past is truly multidimensional, containing layer upon layer of distinctly different culturally specific landscapes and memories. The beliefs and attitudes about the past contained within these interlacing strata find expression in sites of memory through such diverse forms as statues, memorials, markers, plaques, national parks, national monuments, and even the most seemingly mundane vernacular landscapes. Each site of memory is the result of the combination of dynamic space containing a unique group of people and their particular landscapes, identities, and distinct memories of past events.

The Place of the Past

Most geographical interpretations of the past tend to frame a static ethnic history rather than a truly dynamic, hybrid past. A rigid categorization of human groups by their connection to the land can misrepresent the fluid nature of the ways various groups interact with their surroundings. Humans have always moved through dynamic physical space, pausing to make them into distinct places. To cultural geographer Yi-Fu Tuan, place is the result of getting to know undifferentiated space. So in a general sense, places are made when space and culture meet. Cultural variation is, of course, one of the primary factors that influences how place is imagined, constructed, and valued. While Tuan emphasizes that space and place can be defined only in reference to each other, they are certainly not synonyms. To demonstrate the interdependence of the two terms, Tuan employs an analogy that is particularly useful to the project of understanding cultural references to space and place: "If we think of space as that which allows movement, then place is pause; each pause in movement makes it possible for location to be transformed into place." Or, as eloquently put by writer Wallace Stegner: "A place is not a place until people have been born in it, have grown up in it, lived in it, known it, died in it—have both experienced it and shaped it, as individuals, families, neighborhoods, and communities, over more than one generation."[14]

To the cultural geographer, this process of place making results in what are termed "landscapes." Here the term "landscape" is used in its generic sense, as defined by Carl Sauer three-quarters of a century ago as "an area made up of a distinct association of forms, both physical and cultural." These forms are created by the lived experiences of specific cultures in specific places at specific times. Sauer explains landscape as process: "The works of man express themselves in the cultural landscape. There may be a succession of these landscapes with a succession of cultures. They are derived in each case from the natural landscape, man expressing his place in nature as a distinct agent of modification."[15] Tuan, elaborating on Sauer's man as agent of change concept, contends, "Landscape is more than nature superposed by the material expressions of human living. It signifies more to us than the sum of the material facts of hills and valleys, fields, roads, bridges, churches and houses; for besides scientific and economic appraisals, we have imputed to the landscape contents that can only be described as 'psychological, religious, esthetic and moral.'" To Tuan, the fact that landscape contains both objective (scientific and economic) and subjective (psychological, moral) characteristics means that it is an imaginary construct. The fact that landscape is not merely real, in a tangible sense, makes it necessary to distinguish between environment and landscape. Perhaps geographer Leonard Guelke puts it best: "The underlying idea is that a landscape is the creation of the historical mind—which is a product of the unique historical experiences of the inhabitants of the earth's regions."[16]

History is one effective way to connect stories of the past to landscapes of the present. In addressing the importance of cultural resource management, David Glassberg argues that "historical consciousness and place are inextricably intertwined; we attach histories to places, and the environmental value we attach to place comes largely through the memories and historical associations we have with it." The creation of sense of place is an important part of the struggle between groups for control of the past. Therefore place making is a way of constructing history, and sharing "place-worlds" is a way of reviving and revising the past. Ultimately, according to anthropologist Keith Basso, "we are, in a sense, the place-worlds we imagine."[17]

The Southwest has long been the setting for many such imaginary place-worlds. For more than three hundred years, from Christopher Columbus's first footfall in the Caribbean in 1492 until Mexican independence in 1821, Spaniards searched the Western Hemisphere for riches and wonders. Tales of Cíbola's seven cities of gold, Sierra Azul's vast veins of silver, and the Strait of Anian's passageway through the North inspired the rarely glorious, often tragic era of Spanish exploration of North America. While the Admiral of the Ocean Seas may not have found earthly paradise, and Vázquez de Coronado certainly failed to find streets paved with gold in Kansas, these intrepid frontiersmen, and the multitudes who followed them, encountered novel landscapes and inhabitants that inspired detailed description and often challenged their own cultural vocabulary. From Vázquez de Coronado's explorations in 1540 to the arrival of Oñate's colonists in 1598, Spanish explorers and military officers crossed western terrain in search of minerals and passageways only to return with little more than fantastic stories and crude maps of their encounters with the land and its peoples. But on these maps they inscribed new names for places already known to a wide variety of Native Americans; in this way, place naming is also history making.[18]

Histories Collide: New Landscapes and New Identities

Expedition journals provide important firsthand insights into how Spanish explorers perceived and imagined the lands of northern New Spain. In his study of how geographical images are created, geographer John Logan Allen contends that "since virtually all geographical lore is some mixture of empirical and non-empirical data and since neither the recording nor the interpreting of that data can be fully objective it follows that the processes by which images are formed must be, at least partially, subjective."[19] Visitors see natural surroundings differently than do an area's native residents. Tuan explains the tendency of the former to dominate the latter: "The visitor's viewpoint, being simple, is easily stated. Confrontation with the novelty may also prompt him to express himself. The complex attitude of the native, on the other hand, can be expressed by him only with difficulty and indirectly through behavior, local tradition, lore, and myth." Tuan argues that the visitor or outsider's perception of the environment is an aesthetic one that compares what it sees to some culturally specific idea of beauty. In contrast, those who have settled, and in the process have become native to an area, do not tend to make comparisons.[20]

Spanish explorers and colonialists brought a venerable, distinctly Western vision of time and space to northern New Spain beginning in the late sixteenth century. Long before Don Juan de Oñate won the coveted appointment to explore and colonize New Mexico in 1595, the far northern landscape of New Spain had captured the imagination of explorers and traders. Throughout the era of Spanish rule in this region (1598–1680, 1693–1821), many Hispanic governors, soldiers, and clerics—led by Native American guides—explored the vast *terra incognita* from their base of operations in Santa Fe. Their expedition journals contain firsthand descriptions of strange landscapes and curious inhabitants and expose the Spaniards' immediate impressions of the places and people they came into contact with in the contest for what was to them unknown land.[21]

The explorers' descriptions of commodities and the names they gave to particular places reveal the landscape attitudes and values they brought with them. Indeed, the vast majority of the Spanish explorers of the northern *Nuevo México* recorded observations of useful resources. On July 13, 1706, General Juan de Ulibarrí, sergeant major of the kingdom of New Spain, encountered the Arkansas River and its surroundings and made the following observations: "We arrived at the large river which all the tribes call the Napestle. . . . It runs from north to east. It is much more than four times as large as the Río del Norte [Rio Grande] and bathes the best and broadest valley discovered in New Spain. It has many poplar trees and throughout the upper part most beautiful open stretches. The plain on our side is a strand of a long league of level land and extremely fertile as is shown by the many plums, cherries, and wild grapes which there are on it."[22] Ulibarrí recorded impressions of a more cultivated landscape at the *rancherías* of El Cuartelejo, commenting on harvests of Indian corn, watermelons, pumpkins, kidney beans, and wheat: "because of the fertility of the land, the docility of the people, and the abundance of the herds of buffalo, and other game, the propagation of our holy Catholic faith could be advanced very much." The sergeant major wasted little time renaming and claiming these Indian agricultural settlements for the king of Spain.[23]

Some of these Spaniards saw Native American agricultural products as resources free for the taking. The journal of Antonio Valverde y Cossío's expedition, however, recorded how the captain protected Apache crops from his large retinue: "They found some fields of maize, frijoles, and squashes which the Apaches had planted. Moreover, as soon as the fields were noticed, the governor gave the order that under no circumstances should anything be seized, so that the military chiefs proceeded with great care."[24] Ulibarrí also "permitted no injury to be done" to the fields of corn, frijoles, and pumpkins planted by the Penxayes Apaches he encountered along the Río de Santa Ana.[25] These Spanish observers perceived a landscape that was filled not only with indigenous crops and game but one that, if protected rather than pillaged, also held the potential for the cultivation of both crops and Apache souls.

Timber, minerals, and other extractive resources also caught the eye of opportunistic Spanish explorers. In 1765, Juan Maria Antonio de Rivera described finding a mountain of metal: "We tethered the horses and climbed to the top where we saw such a variety of ore lumps, of various colors, as to be uncountable. Because of it one can say, without hesitation, that the whole mountain is composed of pure metal everywhere the eye can see." He also paid particular attention to commodities such as pasturage, water, and firewood during his two expeditions.[26] Francisco Atanasio Domínguez and Francisco Silvestre Vélez de Escalante also noted promising locations for future Spanish colonies. In one entry the fathers described a "very large meadow, which we named San Antonio, of very good land for farming with the help of irrigation, together with all the rest that a settlement requires by way of firewood, stone, timber, and pastures—and all close by."[27]

Spanish explorers and colonists saw some wildlife as curiosities. While governor of *Nuevo México,* Juan Bautista de Anza carried out orders to trap elk and ship them back to Madrid for exhibit in the royal zoological park.[28] Antonio Valverde y Cossío's journal described hunting distinctive local fauna as sport: "A bear came out of the thicket and threw the entire camp into an uproar. The people took great delight in teasing it for some time until they killed it." And again two days later he described the killing of a mountain lion, a wildcat, and another large bear. These Spaniards also saw other animals as commodities and recorded their abundance. Governor Valverde's men hunted deer, prairie hens, and, of course, the abundant bison.[29] Ulibarrí also noted enough bison to provision the entire camp and fish in the streams in abundance and variety.[30]

Explorers are driven, in part, by the fame that comes with being the "first" to discover and name something. These Spanish adventurers were no exception. Even expedition leaders engaged in punitive missions took the time to give every river, plain, and mountain a new name. Explorers are often motivated to risk life and limb by a desire to possess the landscape both materially and spiritually; their journals can provide a vista into such motivations.[31] In 1765, upon reaching the destination of his second expedition, Juan Maria Antonio de Rivera recorded his creation of the following memorial: "I left on the banks of the *Gran Río de el Tison* [Colorado River] in a new growth of white oaks, as a sign, a large cross with *viva Jesus a la Cabeza,* my name, and the year, at the foot, so that anyone can at any time benefit from our arrival there."[32] Whether searching for valuable minerals, food, and shelter along the trail, or envisaging future Spanish settlements in the wilderness, these explorers recorded the sources of essential commodities and mapped far northern New Spain, making known the unknown.

Humans see the environment through the lenses of their time and culture. One particularly evident example of these cultural filters can be found in the very different kinds of names that Native Americans and Europeans gave the land. Throughout the Southwest, Indian names tend to describe particular activities, such as *Pojoaque,* which means, "drink water place" in Tewa. Spanish explorers occasionally gave places descriptive secular names. However, many of the most descriptive labels were simply Spanish translations of Native American names, such as Río Colorado (red river), Río Florida (river of flowers), and El Lobo Amarillo (the yellow wolf). The majority of Spanish place names noted in these expedition journals, on the other hand, commemorated religious, political, and military people, places, and events from their own New World cultural history, such as Albuquerque, which is named for don Francisco Fernandez de la Cueva Enriquez, Duque de Alburquerque, the thirty-fourth viceroy of New Spain.[33]

Although some place names chosen by explorers honored political figures, most had religious significance, as demonstrated by Ulibarrí: "After we had quite descended the mountains, we reached, at the foot of it, a river which is very pleasant with groves of poplar and other trees. To this I give the name of Río de San Francisco Xabier under whose protection I was marching across unknown land, barbarously inhabited by innumerable heathens."[34] The secular often became the sacred, as it did when Valverde renamed the river the Apaches call "La Flecha" (the arrow), calling it "Nuestra Señora del

Rosario."[35] To Rivera and Anza, even event-associated names had religious significance: "That night we suffered a furious storm of wind and rain; because of that, and what was related before, we called this campground El Purgatorio," wrote Rivera.[36] After defeating hostile Indians, Anza returned to a simple campsite and transformed it into a site of memory by giving it a new name: "To this place the name of Río del Sacramento was given, this expedition having been dedicated to this most Holy mystery."[37]

Through the way they envisioned the land and the very names they bestowed on its features, these Spanish explorers effectively imposed their own unique cultural values on the indigenous landscape of northern *Nuevo México*. By recording and circulating their peculiar thoughts and impressions, these adventurers and their audience contributed to particular cultural constructions of place. The geographical features of imperialism mark such places. Spaniards imported foreign and invented new spatial systems, locational distributions, man-land relationships, social ecologies, and cultural landscapes in northern New Spain. As geographer D. W. Menig argues, these patterns and processes reflect the changes wrought and exacerbated by imperialism, including power shifts, dependency, culture changes, new economic relationships, and landscape transformation.[38]

The landscapes and memories—both real and imagined—that resulted from these colonial Spanish encounters with northern New Spain set the stage for identity politics and are in this sense directly connected to the current memory wars between Hispanics and Pueblo peoples in the Southwest. For many of the landscapes the Spanish explorers possessed and the subsequent colonials remade in their own image were often important places to a variety of Indian cultures—cultures that violently resisted the Spaniards' attempts to transform their indigenous cultural landscapes and memories.

Constructing Spanish Heritage in the Southwest

For much of the eighteenth century, Spanish colonists and the Pueblo populations of northern New Mexico feared nothing more than Comanche raids. The thinly populated, remote villages and hamlets of the colonists proved no match for the terror of Comanches on horseback as they, like the Spaniards, expanded their territory and seemingly plundered at will. Many northern Pueblos fared no better. Because of its reputation as a trading center, Taos Pueblo was a favorite target. The Spanish colonial government was quick to respond, sending what few troops it had in New Mexico to chase down the raiding parties. Captain Antonio Valverde y Cossio led one of the region's earliest recorded punitive expeditions against marauding Utes and Comanches in the fall of 1719. After a Comanche raid on Pecos in 1746 left twelve dead, Governor Codallos and five hundred soldiers and Indian allies surprised the Comanches at Abiquiú the next year, killing over one hundred, capturing over two hundred more along with one thousand horses. After another defeat at the hands of Governor Codallos in 1748, the Comanches, seemingly broken, were allowed to trade at Taos. This peace would not last long, for by 1751 the Comanches were raiding villages and Pueblos again. The pattern of raids followed by punitive expeditions would continue for the next three decades. The success or failure of these retaliatory expeditions often determined whether a governor would finish his term or be replaced.[39]

By the mid-1770s, there arose a series of Comanche leaders so feared and hated that their nicknames live to this day in folk drama, on mountains, rivers, and now, even on a highway rest area.[40] A series of Jupe Comanche leaders known by the name "Cuerno Verde" is mentioned in reports of three eighteenth-century Spanish skirmishes: the first occurred at Ojo Caliente on August 30, 1768, where "one who wore as a device a green horn on his forehead, fixed in a headdress or on a tanned leather headpiece" was killed by townspeople defending their plaza;[41] the second clash, led by Don Carlos Fernández, occurred in 1777; the third battle, led by Lieutenant-Colonel Juan Bautista de Anza, took place in 1779.[42] The final event proved to be the end of the mortal Cuerno Verde figure and the beginning of an enduring legacy that spread across the region through the folk tradition.

The Spanish-speaking villagers of what is now northern New Mexico and southern Colorado almost immediately canonized the legendary Cuerno Verde's demise in drama. The 515 octosyllabic verses of Los Comanches have been recited regularly by actors on horseback at Taos and elsewhere throughout the far northern region of what was northern New Spain from some time between 1779 and 1800 to the present. On fiesta day in many small *placitas* in northern New Mexico, crowds gather at the village square to witness the staging of this drama, born out of the struggle of eighteenth-century Spanish colonial villagers to survive in the harsh environment of droughts and Comanche raids. On one side of the plaza are villagers dressed as Spaniards on horseback led by General Don Carlos Fernandez. On the other side are villagers dressed as mounted Comanches. The production begins with Cuerno Verde, chief of the Comanches, boasting:

> Don your war paint, sound the war drums,
> We must bring them to our feet.
> I shall go and seek this general,
> This foolhardy, impious man.
> Let him meet me in this battle
> And survive me if he can.
> Who is he, what do they call him,
> Whomsoever he may be.
> I, *Cuerno Verde,* challenge him
> To come and combat me.

Don Carlos Fernandez, the Spanish general, answers the Comanche:

> Bide your time, Oh bloody heathen,
> I will come without your call.
> Your challenge is not needed
> I will meet you one and all.
> But first, tell me, who are you,
> And whence those idle boasts.
> Hearken to these words I utter,
> You and your savage host.[43]

Los Comanches is a local development of the traditional *Juegos de Moros y Christianos* (Jousts between Moors and Christians) performed frequently in Spain and its colonies. As is common in the colonial Southwest, from an Old World tradition came a New World variation: Moors were replaced with Comanches, and Christians with an army of soldiers, settlers, and Indian allies. The action of the play itself is based largely upon Don Fernández's 1777 engagement of the Comanches on the Staked Plains near Las Orejas del Conejo. The only variation is the death of the second Cuerno Verde, who reportedly survived the 1777 battle only to succumb to Governor Anza two years later in the mountains of southern Colorado.[44] *Los Comanches* is one of only two secular historical folk dramas known to have originated in New Mexico, the other being *Los Tejanos,* a play that tells the story of General Manuel Armijo's expedition from Texas to New Mexico in 1841.[45]

It is important to emphasize that Hispano folk dramas—both sacred and secular—are a part of the seasonal fiesta or festival, and are not stand-alone events. As folklorist Roger Abrahams notes, "the distinction between folk drama and other festival entertainment is one that seems to be fabricated by scholars." He defines folk drama as a traditional activity that uses dialogue and action to tell a story that the audience already knows, such as the events related to the death of Cuerno Verde in the play *Los Comanches.*[46] However tempting it may be to seek similarities throughout the Spanish-speaking world and to draw sweeping generalizations about the role of folk drama in the lives of the community, the very nature of the art form makes it flexible and allows particular groups to articulate their own concerns and celebrate their unique experiences and achievements. This explains why a play like *Los Comanches,* part of a *santo patrón* fiesta, would not play in California, Arizona, or Peoria for that matter. Those places have their own Cuerno Verdes to venerate.

In New Mexico, Spanish-speaking people who identify with the Spanish colonials and seek to establish Spanish American, or "Hispano," cultural heritage employ such invented or recovered traditions as folk dramas and historical pageants in their efforts to create public memory. Two such seasonal public festivals that commemorate historical events include the Fiestas del Valle de Española, where the Hispanic community pays tribute to the first Spanish colonial settlement of New Mexico by Oñate in 1598, and the Santa Fe Fiesta, an event that celebrates the reentry of the Spanish into New Mexico in 1692. Beginning in earnest with the arrival of the Santa Fe Railroad in 1880, later-arriving Anglos joined with local Hispanos to construct Spanish heritage in New Mexico through the invention or revitalization of Spanish-influenced architecture, arts and crafts, literature, drama and pageantry.[47] The first Santa Fe Fiesta was presented in 1919 as a tourist attraction designed by Anglo boosters to attract other Anglos to the region to enjoy a southwestern lifestyle that included Indian and Mexican cultures. However, as anthropologist Sarah Horton has demonstrated, throughout the twentieth century Hispanic leaders have "re-appropriated" the Santa Fe Fiesta from the tourism promoters and have shaped its message to one that celebrates Hispano pride in their colonial New Mexico heritage by highlighting historical figures like Don Diego de Vargas. As people feel threatened they tend to become self-conscious about their identity, and as Horton points out, "the fiesta's celebration of Hispano heritage only increased in importance as the number of Hispano residents of Santa Fe steadily declined during the 1990s." In fact, as many Hispano residents are well aware, the 1990 census reported an Anglo majority in Santa Fe for the first time since the city's founding in 1610.[48]

Hispanic history is actively preserved and prominently displayed in numerous museums, universities, and state government facilities throughout New Mexico.[49] But the Santa Fe Fiesta's historical figure of Don Diego, representing the heroic glory of Spanish imperialism, strives not to preserve the past but rather to perpetuate historical fantasy, as does the ahistorical figure of the Fiesta Queen, symbolizing the idealized myth of pure Castilian blood. These fantasies, Horton argues, project the image "of time and bloodlines forever frozen at the moment of Spanish colonization."[50] But in New Mexico, as in much of the American West, culture is not static, but rather a fluid process constantly transformed by those using dynamic places and malleable pasts to create public memories and develop associated ethnic identities. Historians and other public intellectuals also participate in this process by contributing their authoritative voices to the negotiation of public memory and the recent surge in contentious debates over ownership of the past.[51]

Playing Politics with Pueblo Pasts

Writing in 1993, Ted Jojola, director of Native American Studies at the University of New Mexico, identified two concurrent abuses of images of Pueblo Indian culture by non-Indians:

The Pueblo Indians of New Mexico have been the subjects of a specific kind of mythologizing since the Spanish colonists arrived in the sixteenth century, but particularly so since the 1920s. There have been two distinct and often parallel aspects of this imagemaking. One is promulgated by social scientists in the fields of anthropology, ethnography, and history. The other is touted by entrepreneurs of tourism and popular culture. Among social scientists, New Mexico became a "living laboratory." Among entrepreneurs and state boosters, New Mexico became a "living backdrop." In both instances, however, the interpretations were and are dominated by outsiders (non-Pueblo) who seek, for their own affirmation, a primitive and exotic human landscape.[52]

Both kinds of "imagemaking" can reckon as their forefathers the heinous racist and the well-intentioned ethnographer. The "living laboratory" type of mythologizing is an important topic that is outside the purview of this paper but ought not to be ignored. It is Jojola's second type of image making, the "living backdrop" type of mythologizing, that can best be seen in the cultural appropriation of Pueblo imagery by Anglos and Hispanos in such public events as the historical pageants of the Santa Fe Fiesta.

The increasing conflict between interest groups for control of the interpretation of the past may appear to suggest a current conceptual crisis in the fields of history and anthropology. But in truth, generations of historians and anthropologists have been and continue to be concerned with the misrepresentation of the past due to the lack of subaltern voices in historical representations of the past.[53] "Identity politics," "essentialism," and "nativism"—terms often used in a derogatory manner—are just a few of the labels that scholars and subjects bandy about in their attempts to conceptualize, rationalize, and criticize representations of the past. Identity politics employ gender, class, and ethnicity to define self, status, and culture. Essentialism holds the position that there is only one authentic experience, often claiming an insight particular to identity. Nativism specifically asserts the primacy of birthright in the process of understanding and interpreting a particular worldview, and "nativistic" is a term used to describe a particular indigenous versus colonial position. In short, identity is inclusive and can be appropriated in a politically correct manner, whereas essentialism and nativism are much more unambiguously exclusive.

The controversy surrounding Ramón Gutiérrez's multiple prize-winning book *When Jesus Came, the Corn Mothers Went Away: Marriage, Sexuality, and Power in New Mexico, 1500–1846* is an intriguing example of the recent stalemate in the contest for legitimate interpretation of American Indian pasts. The book's generally positive academic reviews from its initial publication in April 1991 to its later well-articulated criticisms—in print and in public forums by both Pueblo and non-Pueblo scholars after mid-1993—reveal the roles of essentialism and identity politics in the struggle between scholar and subject for control of the past.

At the beginning of his study, Gutiérrez suggests its significance, especially to Pueblo Indians, by declaring: "This book, then, is profoundly a project in point of view. It gives vision to the blind, and gives voice to the mute and silent. The conquest of America was not a monologue, but a dialogue between cultures, each of which had many voices that often spoke in unison, but just as often were diverse and divisive."[54] This topic, one sure to appeal to a wide range of scholarly readers, reflects Gutiérrez's sensitivity to the plight of the Pueblo people, both at the hands of the Spaniards and the chroniclers who have come before him. In a postpublication interview, the author explained that he wanted "to show American historians that there was a vibrant center of social, cultural, and economic activity in the Rio Grande valley."[55] This was Gutiérrez's first book, a study that began as a promising doctoral dissertation completed in 1980 at the University of Wisconsin. *When Jesus Came* was awarded at least ten academic prizes, the most for any book published by Stanford University Press, and the acclaim launched Gutiérrez's career in spectacular fashion. The book arrived at a time when the "new western history"—as the press described the views of several younger western historians whose work focused more on race, class, gender, and the environment than did that of previous generations—had its moment in the public mind. Although in many ways the subject of Gutiérrez's book fits squarely into the tradition of the "old western history," many academics championed it as a worthy example of a new way of thinking about the western past, assigning it in their courses in sufficient number to require a prompt second printing.[56]

Although academic book reviews range from exercises in congratulatory back patting to vicious displays of petty backstabbing, in this case the scholarly review process played a key role in securing *When Jesus Came*'s position as an academic sensation. No fewer than twenty-three book reviews and review articles appeared in a variety of professional journals in the first three years after its publication, indicating the subject's appeal beyond the limited circle of friends and foes. Contained within this corpus are many serious disagreements with the methods employed and analysis put forth by Gutiérrez, but overall the reviews tend toward the congratulatory.[57]

Some reviewers did assess the book in less than glowing terms.[58] However, rather than critiquing content and analysis, most of the negative comments from the earliest reviewers focused on matters of personal preference or issues of professional style that can be boiled down to three main themes. First, some reviewers complained that Gutiérrez employed too much sociological jargon and statistical analysis, and that his thesis was obscured with overabundant factual detail.[59] Second, several reviewers asserted that he failed to compare his findings to similar work on marriage, sexuality, and gender in other parts of Latin America.[60] Third, many of his peers observed that a radical change in focus and style from the first two parts of the book to part 3 results in poor integration of the overall work and made his main theme difficult to follow.[61]

In contrast, three of the most distinguished reviewers—scholars who have made careers working among the various sources that Gutiérrez used to construct his book—share a common complaint that the author's facts "claim more than the sources warrant"; that "there are occasions when he overinterprets or claims too much for his limited data without acknowledgment"; and that he tends "to make a good story better." "Some readers will wonder," one these reviewers wrote, "if Gutiérrez provides an accurate picture of colonial life."[62] At first, however, the preponderance of ringing endorsements seemingly outweighed these negative comments to those multitudes that bought or assigned the book in their classes.

Obligatory general praise may be a convention of the genre of academic reviews, but many of these early reviewers misjudged or unwittingly endorsed some of Gutiérrez's fallacies of method and analysis that would draw later critics' fire.[63] The lone exception in reviews published prior to the spring 1993 backlash from Pueblo intellectuals is one by Patricia Seed. Writing in the *American Historical Review,* she astutely noted, "indigenous voices are predominantly represented by official records and hence are not present in an unmediated way in the sources."[64] Nearly all of the other reviewers missed this crucial point: by relying solely upon outsiders' descriptions of intimate sexual and social behavior recorded by early ethnographers and other non-Pueblos, Gutiérrez left the voices of the Pueblo peoples out of his telling of their history. Seed's concerns were soon reinforced by other non-native scholars and several Native American public intellectuals who had a more immediate connection to the quest for understanding the complexity of this particular past.

No Pueblo scholars were solicited to contribute reviews of Gutiérrez's book in academic journals or major newspapers, the established public forums for scholarly discourse. In the spring of 1993, however, during the annual meeting of the Organization of American Historians, several Pueblo voices were finally heard when a collection of statements by various Pueblo and non-Pueblo scholars was delivered.[65] Later that same year, two public meetings were held at the University of New Mexico where panels of Pueblo intellectuals again expressed their objections to the portrayal of Pueblo culture at the time of Spanish contact in *When Jesus Came.* Gutiérrez himself attended the second of these events, responding in person to the criticisms from the forums that one observer—University of New Mexico anthropologist Sylvia Rodríguez—characterized as "remarkable for their sheer emotional intensity."[66] One member of the group specifically addressed the failure of the academic review process, observing, "the gathering controversy over the book is provoking a more careful consideration of its merits, but that discussion will appear too late to influence the judging of the book in the ten prestigious competitions it has won."[67]

The Pueblo complainants focused on the issue that most of the academic reviewers had missed, namely that "absent a strong articulation by the Pueblo people themselves in the form of oral history, documented statements, and/or research conducted by Pueblo scholars, and a carefully laid thesis, one cannot and should not claim to be offering a historical dialogue that includes a Pueblo voice." Many others echoed the opinion that for Gutiérrez's approach to be more "authoritative," "representative," "ethical," "legitimate," and above all, "valid," he should have used living Pueblo people as informants.[68] According to Rodríguez, Gutiérrez replied to his critics that being a historian and not an ethnographer, he chose not to consult Pueblo informants, claiming that oral historical memory is not valid beyond five or six generations.[69] One critic sums up this divergence in methodological approaches by noting that Gutiérrez "may not write history the way it used to be written, but we still practice our Pueblo ways the way they were handed down. Of course, he will not understand, because that part is not written." Also called into question was Gutiérrez's practice of applying ethnographic information from one pueblo to all the pueblos. As one respondent objected: "studying Indians as research objects denigrates us. Assuming that alleged sexual behaviors can be put forth as public information is humiliating to us! The Gutiérrez book does both." Or, as another summed it up, "needless to say, Gutiérrez's arrogance has no boundaries, not with any kind of customary or ordinary respect, anyway." One critic went so far as to cast the author's motive for writing the book as little more than self-serving careerism: "But more than anything, it has benefited Ramón Gutiérrez, who, after all, used the American educational system to achieve yet another American dream."[70]

Unsubstantiated generalizations, objectification of subjects, and an arrogant approach are surely among those sins historians should avoid at all costs. These transgressions, among others, appear on Alison Freese's virulent lampooning list titled "New Western History Methodology as Practiced by Ramón Gutiérrez in *When Jesus Came, the Corn Mothers Went Away*."[71] As Sylvia Rodríguez observed in her treatment of this controversy, "more than a trace of bitterness, personalism, and even demonization of Gutiérrez has crept into much of the Native American public discourse about the book and, interestingly, has surfaced as well among Anglo Indianist critics such as Freese herself."[72] Another problematic theme comes across in the Pueblo critics' accusations that *When Jesus Came,* and Ramón Gutiérrez in particular, are guilty of intentionally perpetuating a procolonial view of New Mexico history.[73] Simon Ortiz vociferously asserted this point:

> The treatise by Gutiérrez has been accorded the highest recognition by contemporary Western historians, and one wonders why. There is only one explanation: to justify European dominion over the indigenous Americans since 1492 and to continue to deny the massive genocide of Indian people, the theft of their lands and the further perpetration of theft, and the loss of vast portions of their Indian cultural integrity. Because the lie is told within the context of unquestioned and accepted Western cultural knowledge and with the tacit approval of Western historians, it must be assumed there is nothing noxious about it.[74]

Gutiérrez refuted the idea that he wrote *When Jesus Came* in order to "justify European domination over the indigenous Americans" in his introduction: "This is not a history of Spanish men or of Indian men, or of their battles, triumphs and defeats. It is a history of the complex web of interactions between men and women, young and old, rich and poor, slave and free, Spaniard and Indian, all of whom fundamentally depended on the other for their own self-definition."[75] Indeed, as Patricia Seed pointed out in her review, "this volume orients itself in terms of a vibrant area of contemporary interdisciplinary concern with an attempt to revive the histories of colonialism with a particular sensitivity to how colonial subjects are constructed by both themselves and by colonizing powers."[76]

By shifting our focus from issues of fact or fallacy in *When Jesus Came* toward the political rhetoric of "self-definition," perhaps we can shed some light on its controversial reception. At the center of the essentialist's objections to what are perceived to be cultural appropriations of places and pasts is the question of identity. Who is allowed to interpret Pueblo pasts? Several Pueblo educators, writers, and administrators raised the issue of Ramón Gutiérrez's own ethnicity in the following statements:

The author claims, in this case, to be an "insider" by virtue of being a native New Mexican.

As a scholar who claims, as I have been informed, *genízaro* (peasant Indo-Hispano heritage) ancestry, he does not bring anything other than absurd attention to Pueblo culture. . . . As Pueblo people, we know the truth about European colonization and the establishment of dominion over our land and people.

Can he remove the lenses of a twentieth-century Chicano or Hispanic and be able to tell his story objectively? I cannot accept his book as an authoritative source. Any information on Pueblo community life—what we are about and what we perceive our past to be—should come from those people who are from the Pueblo communities themselves. . . . I do not recognize any authority from any culture except ours for a discussion of those foundations.

He is, for all practical purposes, an outsider to these teachings and therefore is very limited in understanding or interpreting the customs and practices that are unfamiliar to him.

In my opinion, he is obsessed with sexuality and places that personal obsession on the Pueblo people. . . . He is a product of the western European world of Puritanism that is still obsessed with sexuality.[77]

As Sylvia Rodríguez succinctly emphasizes in her review, "not merely is the *truthfulness* of Gutiérrez's claim to 'give voice to the mute and silent' challenged, but his very *right* to utter such a claim."[78]

Beyond the questions of truthfulness or right, Gutiérrez should have realized that if his primary aim was truly to "give voice to the mute and silent," no amount of archival research could prepare him, as an outsider, to speak for those who are, in fact, anything but mute. After all, the main thrust of the Pueblo critics' protest seems primarily to protect both the medium and the message of their various local traditions by controlling the messenger. Rodríguez describes this situation best: "The Pueblos have long claimed the exclusive right to transmit, represent, and evaluate authentic Pueblo culture. So in one sense, their objection to Gutiérrez's tale is nothing new and entirely predictable. But in today's context of postcolonial, postmodernist, and feminist debates about positionality, viewpoint, authority, power, and voice, the issue resonates more loudly than ever before."[79] As

Patricia Seed notes in her review, this kind of essentialist reading of what is a shared past can cause a condition where "the equally complex story of accommodation and the forging of a hybrid order is thus obscured in the strongly drawn story of subaltern cultural resistance and survival."[80] This is significant because by insisting on strictly essentialist criteria, or any other identity politics–oriented agenda in our quest to understand the past—be it through the lens of tradition or history—we will most certainly obscure its complexity. The politics involved in the very ways we understand the past are an essential part of the historian's challenge. Or, as historian Steve Stern puts it, "the quest for a higher understanding untainted by politics is a profoundly misleading illusion."[81]

Gutiérrez erred by claiming special essentialist status as an insider to interpret the story he sought to tell, while simultaneously ignoring or overlooking indigenous sources of information. As Sylvia Rodríguez astutely points out, essentialism and identity politics cut quite thin: "The very hybridity of their perspectives, not unlike that of Gutiérrez himself, is what generates the original urge to question or give voice to the subaltern. This impulse, and the projects it gives rise to, cannot but provoke reaction and challenge from those subaltern to the interlocutor, whoever she or he may be."[82] The long-standing mingling of Spanish and Indian blood in the Southwest may have created a hybrid cultural geography and a recognizable region, but the numerous combinations of ethnic identity that even the Spanish colonials grappled with by defining *castas* in the sixteenth and seventeenth centuries provide seemingly endless opportunities for sub-subaltern identities and alternative perspectives on the past.[83]

Gutiérrez's methodology attempted to force the round pegs of the various complex Pueblo social systems into the square holes of an alien theoretical framework. Ultimately, he should neither be blamed nor credited for calling the methods of history into question; that was not his intention. His controversial book simply provided the stage for various players to act out their roles and brought greater attention to the long-standing debate over who can legitimately interpret the past.

Beyond Essentialism, or, Toward "a Truly Honest American History"

Identity politics are de rigueur in academe. Today, in any discussion of the past, who it is that tells us about the people, places, and events, is seemingly just as important as what we are being told. Much of today's academic and public rhetoric—from both dominant and subaltern groups—would have us believe that this is a new phenomenon, one born out of either a deteriorating postcolonial cultural hegemony and the attendant legitimization of subaltern perspectives. However, words printed on a page or uttered from the podium are not solely responsible for today's contentious academic essentialist climate. Larger social and cultural influences have contributed significantly to this trend for some time, from such sweeping changes as the cultural passages through romanticism, realism, modernism, and postmodernism, to the national mobilization for World War II, the public discomfort over the Cold War, as well as this century's ongoing struggles for civil rights and environmental responsibility.

Other contributing factors are that the Southwest is intimately associated with the much larger mythos of the American West, and many of the Old West's most cherished myths have failed to withstand the tests of these changing times. For example, most of us now know that the West was not simply a masculine proving ground for Anglo immigrants to become Americans. Recent scholarship has demonstrated that women, ethnic minorities, and other foreigners often found opportunities in the West. Even bison and American Indians—those most "western" of Old West images—have managed not only to survive the millennium but to thrive while other "traditional" western resources and peoples such as underground mines and cowboys are vanishing from view. Taken together, the innumerable experiences of a wide variety of races, classes, ethnicities, and genders reveal an altogether different West, one that calls for reinterpretation both within the academy and without.

From the nineteenth-century emergence of the "frontier" folklore of Davy Crockett and Buffalo Bill Cody later popularized by turn-of-the-century modern mass media, to the mass-market saturation of Old West, Civil War, and general military history magazines, books, and films—created by both professional historians and popular writers—the popularity of frontier and westward expansion themes has ensured that the romantic history of the American West continues to thrive. But to be fair, the blame for this perception should not rest solely on interpretations developed outside of the academy. As late as the last two decades of the twentieth century, scholars of the American West had just begun to "catch up" to the rest of their American history colleagues by making cautious first attempts at developing multicultural frameworks for significant research questions. Through these studies, western scholars are only now constructing detailed analyses of the region's past that integrate the perspectives of Native Americans and others who had for so long appeared as tokens or have been left out of the story of the West entirely.[84]

By the early 1990s, however, the most dramatically revisionist works failed to present a truly multivocal perspective on western history, preferring instead to tear down traditional methods, sources, and interpretations and replace them with similarly monovocal alternatives. Alan Trachtenberg found this to be the case in his critique of the 1991 National Museum of American Art exhibit The West As America: Reinterpreting Images of the Frontier, 1820–1920. He contends that "what was missing was the effort to construct a different way of thinking about the nation itself, one which would take diversity and multiplicity as much into account as distortion and ideological rhetoric." Trachtenberg suggests a litany of alternatives, including vernacular art by Native Americans, graphics by opponents of the Mexican War, art produced by working cowboys and homesteaders, art produced by blacks on the range, art produced by Hispanics in the Southwest and California, and graphics by the Wobblies. "Too often," he concludes, "the curators simply repudiated official art, instead of reaching beyond it to a positive alternate vision."[85]

This was not a phenomenon limited to the field of western art, for as the decade wore on, scholars working in other fields called for radical departures from the methods, sources, and subjects of even the new western history. For example, a 1992 article by Antonia Castañeda threw down a gauntlet by proclaiming that "most feminist scholars write the history not of women, but of white women in the West." She challenged historians of all fields to "examine their assumptions as well as their racial, class, and gender positions as they redefine historical and other categories of analysis." Castañeda cited the profound lack of history doctorates taken by women of color as one of the primary reasons for a lack of scholarly studies treating women of color in the nineteenth-century West.[86] This argument, while reflecting the recent influence of essentialism and identity politics pervading graduate programs in women's history, Indian history, and many other fields in the humanities, does accurately reflect the pressing need to represent more voices in the histories of the American West.

But are these additional voices to simply articulate the "useful" histories akin to those created by Carl Becker's metaphorical "Mr. Everyman?" Pragmatic rather than malicious, this Mr. Everyman is not out to deceive, "but he necessarily takes the facts as they come to him, and is enamored of those that seem best suited to his interests or promise most in the way of emotional satisfaction." Becker concluded that while each of us professional historians has a bit of Mr. Everyman in us, we must strive to be more than simply our own historians.[87] In 1974, Alfonso Ortiz, an anthropologist from San Juan Pueblo, admitted that the extreme reaction by some Indian peoples against history written by non-Indians bothered him, but he suggested that "it should bother historians more, for it shows that some Indian people have come to distrust historians to the extent that they feel a need to assert total sovereignty over their traditions and their past." Ortiz recognized that many Indians feel that they must proclaim: "'You, whitey, you ripped me off, therefore I am not going to let you come onto my reservation; furthermore, I am going to write my own history and do my own thing.'"[88] While Ortiz believed that there certainly has been ample justification for adopting this position, he cautioned that "to continue such a split between Indians and historians would be tragic, for it would preclude a new dialogue, a kind of creative mutually rewarding partnership between Indians and sympathetic historians." Instead, he prescribes collaboration as the means to "a truly honest American history."[89] The goal of this collaboration is to create a synthesis of Indian traditions and non-

Indian histories that promises a much richer reading of what is a multivocal past.

Several legal attempts to protect indigenous cultural definition and identity have emerged in recent decades. Such legislation includes United Nations efforts to establish rights for indigenous peoples across the globe, and United States federal legislation such as the Native American Graves Protection and Repatriation Act of 1991 (P.L. 101-601) and the American Indian Religious Freedom Act of 1978 (P.L. 95-341). Ted Jojola asserts that these legislative achievements serve primarily "to lay the foundation for the development of a patent on culture and historical interpretation."[90] Hoping to build upon these gains in federal recognition of tribal sovereignty, some Indian scholars and professional organizations are working to extend such protections to Indian intellectual property. Organizations like the Native American Archives Coalition are seeking to establish a set of guidelines designed to protect Indian interests by controlling access to tribal archives by promoting "an awareness of Native Americans' concerns regarding the appropriate use of Native American records, especially with respect to privacy rights, intellectual property rights, and cultural property rights."[91] Historians may soon be facing similar kinds of access restrictions that anthropologists and archaeologists have been accustomed to for the past decade. Establishing one's own political identity, be it via ethnicity, gender, class, or any combination thereof, is key to self-definition, but should it be the dominant characteristic through which access to the materials necessary for understanding the past is determined?

Anthropologists attribute the genesis of nativism, or "culturalism," to the eighteenth-century German *Kultur* theories developed to define and empower a people who were disenfranchised by the rising cosmopolitan Franco-Anglo imperial civilization.[92] Marshall Sahlins notes in his work *How "Natives" Think: About Captain Cook, For Example,* "now, two hundred years later, a marked self-consciousness of 'culture' is reappearing all over the world among the victims and erstwhile victims of Western domination—and as the expression of similar political and existential demands." Nativism is a global issue of utmost importance to historians and anthropologists working today. Sahlins astutely noted the irony of this trend, whereby, as "a response to the planetary juggernaut of Western capitalism, their struggles recreate, if on a wider scale and in more critical form, the opposition to bourgeois-utilitarian reason that first gave rise to an understanding of cultures as distinct forms of life." Sahlins suggests that rather than being liberated by hitching their cart to this post-modernist theory, proponents of a nativist agenda find "at this transitional moment, the notion of culture is in jeopardy: condemned for its excessive coherence and systematicity, for its sense of boundedness and totality. Just when so many people are announcing the existence of their culture, advanced anthropologists are denying it." Sahlins goes so far as to proclaim: "'Culture,' it seems, is in the twilight of its career, and anthropology with it." It is becoming increasingly apparent that in addition to anthropology, we might add history, ethnohistory, American Indian history, and any other kind of identity history to Sahlins's list as well.[93]

At the same time, postmodernist cultural anthropology is questioning the very possibility of objective truth. Adam Kuper observes, in reference to nativism, that "this line of argument feeds readily into a current political discourse that links identity, culture and politics." He further warns of the dangers inherent in a literal interpretation of the postmodernist agenda: "We must beware lest the question of whom we study, who should make the study, and how it should be conducted is answered with reference to the ethnic identity of the investigator."[94] Public debates between academics over identity politics and essentialism can be as exceptionally ugly as they are useless to the project of understanding the past. This is not to say that we cannot derive some benefit from examining them, but rather that we must be careful not to get so caught up in the debates that we lose sight of our larger project.[95]

What then is the future of the past? Kuper suggests one possible course of action: "What is required is a reconsideration of the whole project of which nativism is simply the culmination. We must ask fundamental questions about the nature of ethnography and its uses. We must remember that there are alternative definitions of our project available."[96] Sahlins expands on this idea, suggesting "one cannot do good history, not even contemporary history, without regard for ideas, actions, and ontologies that are not and never were our own.

Different cultures, different rationalities."[97] History and tradition are two distinctly different ways to understand the past, but they are not incompatible. They should not be placed in opposition to one another, nor should one be used to verify the validity or accuracy of other. Furthermore, historians must recognize that although the American government often treated all Indian people as if they were one culture, there are significant differences from group to group that preclude the idea of a singular Indian history or methodology. As Ortiz observed: "each tribe, band, or community has its own sovereign history. . . . [L]ikewise, each people has its own traditions and viewpoint to the past."[98] One must make the important distinction between acknowledging that every social unit has its own way of interpreting the past and concluding that only Indian people should write Indian histories, characterized by the increasing tendency toward exclusive essentialism as demonstrated by the specific identity-related criticisms leveled at Ramón Gutiérrez discussed above and toward other more recent non-Indian scholars who attempt to study Native American pasts.[99]

What then is the next step? In his article "Significant to Whom?: Mexican Americans and the History of the American West," David Gutiérrez proposes that scholars of the social history of the West are currently in a position to create "a fundamental reconfiguration in the ways minority peoples are conceived of, categorized, and analyzed in history and contemporary American society." There is little to be gained by simply describing the differences between communities or contributing essentialist renderings of these communities. Instead, he argues, "close attention to the structures that internally stratify and divide communities must be a central component of any project that aspires to render human *all* of the historically subject peoples who have lived and now live in the West."[100] Projects of this sort promise to reveal the complexity of the human experience, effectively rendering moot the questions of a so-called minority people's significance and makeing obsolete the production of "recognition histories" that simply acknowledge their contributions to the American past.

In her recent book *Something in the Soil: Legacies and Reckonings in the New West*, historian Patricia Nelson Limerick points out that stories and memories have also transformed the West. Obscured by a litany of other more conspicuous agents of change, such as plowing, irrigating, grazing, mining, and developing, these narratives have, according to Limerick, "piled themselves up into moraines, deltas, and heaps of memory" at conspicuous places like National Parks, battle sites, and both natural- and human-made wonders. The American West, she contends, "is composed of layers and layers of accumulated human activity and thought." These "strata of memory," as she calls them, serve to orient her personal and professional explorations of the western past.[101]

As Limerick and others have shown, historians of all stripes need to stop arguing about where the West is or is not, who did what first, and who is and is not eligible to write what kind of history, and try to move together toward a greater understanding of how the very perception of the western past is created—and always has been created—by multiple voices for numerous reasons. In order to do this most effectively we should focus on local variations in the struggle over identity and the construction of public memories that occur in the distinct places that various humans have made from the western spaces they have encountered. By combining the theory and methods of the academic study of history and memory with the experiential work of public history and public memory, the fluid nature of the ongoing construction of the past emerges from what previously appeared to be a static set of accepted facts. Rather than a focused narrative of national or regional themes that necessarily leave out multiple perspectives, the western past is more akin to an interrelated web of individual and group memories: memories in the landscapes; landscapes containing values; values embedded in stories; stories told in public; public memories continually constructed and debated.

NOTES

1. The $108,000 sculpture, created by "Sonny" Rivera of Albuquerque, New Mexico, is a central feature of the Rio Arriba County's $1.5 million Oñate Monument and Visitor's Center opened on April 29, 1994. For national and international reporting on the vandalism, see James Brooke, "Conquistador Statue Stirs Hispanic Pride and Indian Rage," *New York Times,* Feb. 9, 1998, sec. A; Tina Griego, "A Foot Note to History: Amputation of N.M. Statue Underlies 400-

Year-Old Grudge," *Denver Rocky Mountain News,* June 21, 1998, sec. A; and Mary Dejevsky, "Ancient Relations Fail to Get Off on the Right Foot," *Independent* (London), July 22, 1998.

2. The prisoners taken at Acoma were charged with "wantonly killing" Oñate's nephew, Don Juan de Zaldívar Oñate—*maese de campo general* of the expedition—two other officers, eight soldiers, and two servants. For English translations of documents pertaining to the Oñate period, including an account of the trial and sentencing of the rebel Acomans, see George P. Hammond and Agapito Ray, eds. and trans., *Don Juan de Oñate, Colonizer of New Mexico, 1595–1628,* 2 vols. (Albuquerque, 1953), 477–79. Captain Luis Gasco de Velasco reported to the viceroy on March 22, 1601: "More than six hundred prisoners were taken. Twenty-four Indians had their feet cut off as punishment; all those more than twenty years of age were taken as slaves; those younger were put under surveillance for twenty years" (Hammond and Ray, *Don Juan de Oñate,* 615). Oñate was himself tried and stripped of his command and banished from New Mexico for his cruel actions toward the native inhabitants.

3. Ibid., and James Brooke, "An Anniversary Brings Pride and Resentment," *New York Times,* May 3, 1998, sec. 1.

4. As reported in Brooke, "Conquistador Statue Stirs Hispanic Pride and Indian Rage."

5. Ibid.; Scott Baldauf, "New Mexico's Year of Fiestas Dampened by a Divisive Past," *Christian Science Monitor,* May 27, 1998; Griego, "A Foot Note to History"; and Patrisia Gonzales and Roberto Rodriguez, "Bridges Needed to Unite Cultures," *Denver Post,* April 4, 1999, sec. G.

6. David Thelen, "Memory and American History," *Journal of American History* 75 (1989): 1117, 1119, introducing a special issue on memory and American history. See also the influential essays in Eric Hobsbawm and Terence Ranger, eds., *The Invention of Tradition,* (Cambridge, UK, 1983), 1.

7. Thelen, "Memory and American History," 1126–27.

8. See Michel-Rolph Trouillot's *Silencing the Past: Power and the Production of History* (Boston, 1995) for a fascinating study of the role of power in the production of historical narratives.

9. Michael Kammen, *Mystic Chords of Memory: The Transformation of Tradition in American Culture* (New York, 1991), 5–10; John Bodnar, *Remaking America: Public Memory, Commemoration, and Patriotism in the Twentieth Century* (Princeton, 1992), 13–16, 17. Other important works in this vein include Pierre Nora, "Between Memory and History: *Les Lieux de Mémoire,*" trans. Marc Roudebush, *Representations* 26 (1989): 18–19; Benedict Anderson, *Imagined Communites: Reflections on the Origins and Spread of Nationalism,* rev. ed. (New York, 1991); John R. Gillis, ed., *Commemorations: The Politics of National Identity* (Princeton, 1994).

10. David Glassberg, "Public History and the Study of Memory," *Public Historian* 18 (1996): 11–14.

11. James E. Young, *The Texture of Meaning: Holocaust Memorials and Meaning* (New

Haven, 1993), xi–xii; Glassberg, "Public History and the Study of Memory," 13–14.

12. The legacy of the Custer/Little Bighorn Battlefield was the topic of a dynamic symposium held at the national monument in 1994 and continues to be the focus of intense debate as a monument to the Indian participants is under development. See two essays in *Montana: The Magazine of Western History* 42 (1992): Robert M. Utley, "Whose Shrine Is It?" 70–74; and Douglas C. McChristian, "In Search of Custer Battlefield," 75–76. On inaccuracies at national monuments, see James W. Loewen, *Lies Across America: What Our Historic Sites Get Wrong* (New York, 1999); and John Seelye, *Memory's Nation: The Place of Plymouth Rock* (Chapel Hill, 1998).

13. David Lowenthal, "Age and Artifact: Dilemmas of Appreciation," in *The Interpretation of Ordinary Landscapes: Geographical Essays,* ed. D. W. Meinig (New York, 1979), 103, 124, 125. See also Lowenthal's *The Heritage Crusade and the Spoils of History* (Cambridge, UK, 1998); *The Past Is a Foreign Country* (Cambridge, UK, 1985); and "Past Time, Present Place: Landscape and Memory," *Geographical Review* 65 (1975): 1–36.

14. Yi-Fu Tuan, *Space and Place: The Perspective of Experience* (Minneapolis, 1977), 5–7; Wallace Stegner, "The Sense of Place," in *Where the Bluebird Sings to the Lemonade Springs: Living and Writing in the West* (New York, 1992), 201. See also Lewis Binford, "The Archaeology of Place," *Journal of Anthropological Archaeology* 1 (1982): 6, 28: "I am interested in sites, the fixed places in the topography where man may periodically pause and carry out actions."

15. Carl O. Sauer, "The Morphology of Landscape," *University of California Publications in Geography* 2 (1925): 25–26, 37.

16. Yi-Fu Tuan, "Man and Nature: An Eclectic Reading," *Landscape* 15 (1966): 31; Yi-Fu Tuan, "Thought and Landscape: The Eye and the Mind's Eye," in *The Interpretation of Ordinary Landscapes: Geographical Essays,* ed. D. W. Meinig (New York, 1979), 90, 100; Leonard Guelke, "Historical Geography and Collingwood's Theory of Historical Knowing," in *Period and Place: Research Methods in Historical Geography,* ed. Alan R. H. Baker and Mark Billinge (Cambridge, UK, 1982), 194.

17. Glassberg, "Public History and the Study of Memory," 17; Keith H. Basso, *Wisdom Sits in Places: Landscape and Language among the Western Apache* (Albuquerque, 1996), 7.

18. John L. Allen, "Exploration and Creation of Geographical Images of the Great Plains: Comments on the Role of Subjectivity," in *Images of the Plains: The Role of Human Nature in Settlement,* ed. Brian W. Blouet and Merlin P. Lawson (Lincoln, Neb., 1975), 5; Donald A. Barclay, James H. Maguire, and Peter Wild, eds., *Into the Wilderness Dream: Exploration Narratives of the American West, 1500–1805* (Salt Lake City, 1994); William Brandon, *Quivira: Europeans in the Region of the Santa Fe Trail, 1540–1820* (Athens, Ohio, 1990); George P. Hammond, "The Search for the Fabulous in the Settlement of the Southwest," in *New Spain's Far*

Northern Frontier: Essays on Spain in the American West, 1540–1821, ed. David J. Weber (Albuquerque, 1979); John L. Kessell, "'To See Such Marvels with My Own Eyes': Spanish Exploration in the Western Borderlands," *Montana: The Magazine of Western History* 41 (1991): 68–75.

19. Allen, "Exploration and Creation of Geographical Images of the Great Plains," 3.

20. Tuan further contends that "occasions to voice environmental values seldom arise; values are implicit in the people's economic activities, behavior and style of life" (Yi-Fu Tuan, *Topophilia: A Study of Environmental Perception, Attitudes, and Values* [Englewood Cliffs, N.J., 1974], 63–64, 67–68).

21. Several surviving Spanish journals and letters record the daily activities of punitive and exploratory expeditions into the region of northern *Nuevo México.* The discussion below relies on the documents collected in Alfred Barnaby Thomas, ed. and trans., *After Coronado: Spanish Exploration Northeast of New Mexico, 1696–1727; Documents from the Archives of Spain, Mexico, and New Mexico* (Norman, Okla., 1935). For a general overview of Spanish exploration into the region, see Thomas, "Spanish Expeditions into Colorado," *Colorado Magazine* 1 (1924): 289–300; Joseph J. Hill, "Spanish and Mexican Exploration and Trade Northwest from New Mexico into the Great Basin," *Utah Historical Quarterly* 3 (1930): 2–23; and J. Manuel Espinosa, "Governor Vargas in Colorado," *New Mexico Historical Review* 2 (1936): 179–87; Frederic Athearn, *A Forgotten Kingdom: The Spanish Frontier in Colorado and New Mexico, 1540–1821,* 2d ed., Cultural Resource Series, no. 29 (Denver, 1992). For an overview of the current state of many of these resources, see Lawrence A. Clayton, ed., *The Hispanic Experience in North America: Sources for Study in the United States,* (Columbus, Ohio, 1992).

22. Ulibarrí journal, July 29, 1706, in Thomas, *After Coronado,* 65–66.

23. Ulibarrí journal, Aug. 11, 1706, ibid., 72–73.

24. Valverde journal, Sept. 22, 1719, ibid., 113.

25. Ulibarrí journal, July 25, 1706, ibid., 64. The 1680 Spanish legal code, Recopilación de Leyes de los Reynos de las Indias, stipulated that no grants or grazing permits would be issued in the proximity of Indian lands to ensure that Spanish livestock would not destroy their crops (Myra Ellen Jenkins, "Taos Pueblo and Its Neighbors, 1540–1847," *New Mexico Historical Review* 41 [1966]: 95).

26. Rivera journals, July 19, 1765, in Thomas, *After Coronado,* 141–43; June 29, 1765, ibid., 103; Oct. 8, 1765, ibid., 192. See also ibid., 95–97, 184–86, 190.

27. Domínguez journal, Aug. 7, 1776, in Ted J. Warner, ed., *The Domínguez-Escalante Journal: Their Expedition through Colorado, Utah, Arizona, and New Mexico in 1776* (Salt Lake City, 1995), 10.

28. Kessell, "To See Such Marvels," 74.

29. Valverde journal, Oct. 2, 1719, in Thomas, *After Coronado,* 121; Oct. 4, 1719, ibid., 123; Oct. 3, 1719, ibid., 122; Oct. 16, 1719, ibid., 129.

30. Ulibarrí journal, Aug. 15, 1706, ibid., 67; Aug. 2, 1706, ibid., 75.

31. Kessell, "To See Such Marvels," 69.

32. Rivera journal, Oct. 21, 1765, in Austin Nelson Leiby, "Borderland Pathfinders: The 1765 Diaries of Juan Maria Antonio de Rivera" (PhD diss., Northern Arizona University, 1985), 220, 227. According to Leiby, "Long Live Jesus at the Head of the Cross!" led many of the Spaniards into battle during the Reconquest of Spain from the Muslims.

33. T. M. Pearce, ed. *New Mexico Place Names: A Geographical Dictionary* (Albuquerque, 1965), xi-xii, 5.

34. Ulibarrí journal, July 21, 1706, in Thomas, *After Coronado, 62.*

35. Valverde journal, Sept. 22, 1719, ibid., 113.

36. Rivera journal, Oct. 14, 1765, ibid., 206.

37. Anza journal, Aug. 31 1779, ibid., 131.

38. D. W. Meinig, "Geographical Analysis of Imperial Expansion," in *Period and Place: Research Methods in Historical Geography,* ed. Baker and Billinge, 72–74.

39. Hubert Howe Bancroft, *History of Arizona and New Mexico* (San Francisco, 1889), 234–36, 249.

40. "Colorado's Newest Rest Area—Cuerno Verde," *Milestones* (Sept./Oct. 1995): 1–2. Newsletter published bimonthly by the Colorado Department of Transportation. Cuerno Verde Rest Area project files, Public Information Office, Colorado Department of Transportation, Denver, Colorado. This topic is the subject of a forthcoming journal article by the author and is discussed in a conference paper, "Constructing Comanche Pasts: Public Memory and the Cuerno Verde Rest Area," presented at the Western History Association annual meeting, San Antonio, Tex., Oct. 2000.

41. Alfred B. Thomas contends that "Chief Greenhorn was not killed on this occasion. He met his death at the hands of Governor Anza in 1779" (Thomas, *The Plains Indians and New Mexico, 1751–1778: A Collection of Documents Illustrative of the History of the Eastern Frontier of New Mexico,* Coronado Cuarto Centennial Publications, 1540–1940, vol. II, ed. George P. Hammond [Albuquerque, 1940], 166–67). Elizabeth A. H. John disagrees, concluding "that the fallen chief left a son who dedicated his own life and those of his followers to vengeance for his father" (*Storms Brewed in Other Men's Worlds: The Confrontation of Indians, Spanish, and French in the Southwest, 1540–1795* [Lincoln, Neb., 1975], 469), and recent scholars endorse her position. See Thomas W. Kavanagh, *The Comanches: A History, 1706–1875* (Lincoln, Neb., 1996), 79, 92; and Stanley Noyes, *Los Comanches: The Horse People, 1751–1845* (Albuquerque, 1993), 62, 323 n. 2.

42. Alfred B. Thomas, *Forgotten Frontiers: A Study of the Spanish Indian Policy of Don Juan Bautista de Anza, Governor of New Mexico, 1777–1787* (Norman, Okla., 1932), 66–71. In addition to leading settlers to Alta California, Anza is remembered for defeating Cuerno Verde on Sept. 3, 1779, and for creating lasting peace and alliance pacts with the various Indian peoples while governor of the Province of New Mexico (1777–87). For studies of Anza's tenure as governor, see Thomas, *Forgotten Frontiers*; and Ronald J. Benes, "Anza and Concha in New

Mexico, 1787–1793: A Study in New Colonial Techniques," *Journal of the West* 4 (1965): 63–76.

43. Gilberto Espinosa, trans., "Los Comanches," *New Mexico Quarterly* 1 (1931): 136.

44. Aurelio M. Espinosa, *The Folklore of Spain in the American Southwest: Traditional Spanish Folk Literature in Northern New Mexico and Southern Colorado*, ed., J. Manuel Espinosa (Norman, Okla., 1985), 219; see also Aurelio M. Espinosa, "Los Comanches: A Spanish Heroic Play of the Year Seventeen Hundred and Eighty," *University of New Mexico Bulletin*, Language Series, 1 (1907); Gilberto Espinosa, trans., "Los Comanches," 133–46; A. L. Campa, "Los Comanches: A New Mexican Folk Drama," *University of New Mexico Bulletin*, Language Series, 7 (1942); and Beatrice A. Roeder, "Los Comanches: A Bicentennial Folk Play," *The Bilingual Review/La Revista Bilingüe* 3 (1976): 213–20. For general studies of New Mexican folk drama, see works by A. L. Campa: "Religious Spanish Folk-Drama in New Mexico," *New Mexico Quarterly* 2 (1932): 3–13; and "The New Mexican Spanish Folktheater," *Southern Folklore Quarterly* 5 (1941): 127–31; works by John E. Englekirk: "Notes on the Repertoire of the New Mexican Spanish Folktheater," *Southern Folklore Quarterly* 4 (1940): 227–37; "The Source and Dating of New Mexican Spanish Folk Plays," *Western Folklore* 16 (1957): 232–55; and Edwin B. Place, "A Group of Mystery Plays Found in a Spanish-Speaking Region of Southern Colorado," *University of Colorado Studies* 18 (1930): 1–8.

45. For more on this drama, see Aurelio M. Espinosa and J. Manuel Espinosa, "Los Tejanos: A New Mexican Spanish Popular Dramatic Composition of the Middle of the Nineteenth Century," *Hispania* 27 (1944): 291–314; and Aurelio M. Espinosa and J. Manuel Espinosa, "The Texans: A New Mexican Spanish Folk Play of the Middle Nineteenth Century," *New Mexico Quarterly Review* 13 (1943): 299–308.

46. Roger D. Abrahams, "Folk Drama," in *Folklore and Folklife: An Introduction*, ed. Richard M. Dorson (Chicago, 1972), 355.

47. Charles Montgomery, *The Spanish Redemption: Heritage, Power, and Loss on New Mexico's Upper Rio Grande* (Berkeley and Los Angeles, 2002), and his article, "The Trap of Race and Memory: The Language of Spanish Civility on the Upper Rio Grande," *American Quarterly* 52 (2000): 478–513. For the appropriation of Spanish colonial culture by Anglo artists and writers in particular, see also Dean Rehberger, "Visions of the New Mexican in Public Pageants and Dramas of Santa Fe and Taos, 1918–1940," *Journal of the Southwest* 37 (1995): 450–69.

48. Sarah Horton, "Maintaining Hispano Identity through the Santa Fe Fiesta: Re-Appropriating Key Symbols and Resisting Anglo Dominance," *Kiva* 66 (2000): 251, 254–55. Other important works on the Santa Fe Fiesta include Sarah Horton, "Where is the 'Mexican' in 'New Mexican'? Enacting History, Enacting Dominance in the Santa Fe Fiesta," *Public Historian* 23 (2001): 41–54; Chris Wilson, *The Myth of Santa Fe: Creating a Modern Regional Tradition* (Albuquerque,

1997); and Ronald L. Grimes, *Symbol and Conquest: Public Ritual and Drama in Santa Fe, New Mexico* (Ithaca, N.Y., 1976).

49. Jon Hunner, "Preserving Hispanic Lifeways in New Mexico," *Public Historian* 23 (2001): 29–40.

50. Horton, "Maintaining Hispano Identity," 263–64.

51. For a discussion of this trend, see Steve J. Stern, "Paradigms of Conquest: History, Historiography, and Politics," *Journal of Latin American Studies* 24 (1992): 1–34.

52. Jojola, "*When Jesus Came, the Corn Mothers Went Away: Marriage, Sex, and Power in New Mexico, 1500–1846*, by Ramón Gutiérrez," in *American Indian Culture and Research Journal* 17 (1993): 141.

53. In fact, Native Americans writers, whom cultural scholar Scott Michaelsen terms "organic intellectuals," have written and published accounts of their own people from the very emergence of the discipline of American anthropology, often in collaboration with non-Indian ethnographers (Michaelsen, *The Limits of Multiculturalism: Interrogating the Origins of American Anthropology* [Minneapolis, 1999]).

54. Ramón A. Gutiérrez, *When Jesus Came, the Corn Mothers Went Away: Marriage, Sexuality, and Power in New Mexico, 1500–1846* (Stanford, Calif., 1991), xvii.

55. Liz McMillen, "Hot Young Author and a Fresh Slant on U.S. History Add Up to Much-Honored Book on American Southwest," *Chronicle of Higher Education* (Dec. 2, 1992): A8.

56. These awards include the Herbert E. Bolton Prize in Latin American History and the Frederick Jackson Turner Prize from the Organization of American Historians, two of the most prestigious prizes in the field of history. McMillen, "Hot Young Author," A8; Sylvia Rodríguez, "Subaltern Historiography on the Rio Grande: On Gutiérrez's *When Jesus Came, the Corn Mothers Went Away*," *American Ethnologist* 21 (1994): 892; John R. Wunder, "What's Old about the New Western History: Race and Gender," pt. 1, *Pacific Northwest Quarterly* 85 (1994): 57.

57. *When Jesus Came* is variously described as "theoretically sophisticated": John L. Kessell, *Pacific Historical Review* 62 (1993): 364; Patricia Nelson Limerick, "Stop Dancing or I'll Flog Myself," *New York Times Book Review* (July 12, 1992): 21; David J. Weber, *Western Historical Quarterly* 22 (1991): 473; "profound": Sarah A. Radcliffe, *Journal of Historical Geography* 18 (1992): 490; Roberto M. Salmón, *Journal of American History* 78 (1992): 1410; and as an "important," a "major," and a "significant" contribution: Peter L. Steere, *American Indian Quarterly* 16 (1992): 574; Susan Kellogg, *Hispanic American Historical Review* 72 (1992): 430; Muriel Nazzari, "Relations between the Sexes in Spain and Its Empire," *Journal of Women's History* 4 (1992): 147. The praise ranges from the stolid: "impressive," "thoroughly rewarding," and "a useful addition to the historical record": Barbara Bush-Slimani, "American Eves," *History Today* 42 (1992): 59; Asunción Lavrin, *The Americas* 49 (1992): 95; S. J. Kleinberg, *Journal of American Studies* 28 (1994):

93; to the exuberant: "unquestionably a work of great importance," "a model of scholarly expertise and erudition," "one of the best ever written on the Pueblo culture," and "the influence of *When Jesus Came* will extend beyond New Mexico and the Southwest": Sarah Deutsch, *Journal of American Ethnic History* 13 (1994): 98; Herman W. Konrad, *Canadian Journal of History* 26 (1991): 542; Alvin R. Sunseri, *Journal of the West* 32 (1993): 105; Albert L. Hurtado, "The Underside of Colonial New Mexico: A Review Essay," *New Mexico Historical Review* 68 (1993): 188.

58. Examples of faint or qualified praise include: "it is a useful addition to the scant literature on these general topics"; "Despite the problems, *When Jesus Came the Corn Mothers Went Away* deserves careful attention as an innovative, thoughtful, and persuasive study"; and "an important and provocative, if slightly flawed, contribution to the historiography of the Southwest": Paul E. Hoffman, *The Historian* 54 (1991): 158; Jesus F. De La Teja, *Southwestern Historical Quarterly* 97 (1993): 385; Vista K. McCroskey, *Social Science Quarterly* 73 (1992): 712.

59. McCroskey, 712; Bush-Slimani, 59; Nazzari, 147.

60. Particularly comparisons to Patricia Seed's book *To Love, Honor, and Obey* (1988). Nancy A. Hewitt, *William and Mary Quarterly* 50 (1993): 607; Kellogg, 430; Nazzari, 147; Patricia Seed, *American Historical Review* 97 (1992): 968.

61. Bush-Slimani, 59; De La Teja, 385; Hoffman, 158; Nazzari, 147; Cynthia Radding, *Ethnohistory* 41 (1994): 468.

62. Ralph H. Vigil, "Inequality and Ideology in Borderlands Historiography," *Latin American Research Review* 29 (1994): 163; Weber, 471; Kessell, 364; Hurtado, 187.

63. Most notably, several reviewers believed that Gutiérrez had ample documentation in a solid base of sources: see Konrad, 542; Radding, 468; and Salmón, 1410. Some claimed that he represented a wide range of perspectives by using methods and sources from many disciplines: see De La Teja, 384; Steere, 573; and Weber, 474. One reviewer went so far as to proclaim *When Jesus Came* as "ethnohistory at its most detailed, fascinating and well-researched" (Radcliffe, 488). Others wrote that Gutiérrez "successfully combines the story of the invaders with 'the vision of the vanquished'" (McCroskey, 712), and that "the analysis in this book is sensitive to time and place and clearly reconstructs a historical panorama of New Mexico that is long overdue" (Salmón, 1410).

64. Seed, *American Historical Review* 97 (1992): 968.

65. S. Rodríguez, "Subaltern Historiography on the Rio Grande, 892. The commentaries were compiled by the Native American Studies Center at the University of New Mexico (hereafter UNM) and published later that year as, "When Jesus Came, the Corn Mothers Went Away: Marriage, Sex, and Power in New Mexico, 1500–1846, by Ramón Gutiérrez," in *American Indian Culture and Research Journal* 17 (1993): 141–77 (hereafter this collection of commentaries is cited as Native American Studies Center compilation). The contributors include: Ted Jojola (Isleta Pueblo), director, Native American Studies, associate professor, School of Architecture and Planning, UNM; Alison Freese, information special-

ist, Native American Studies Center, UNM; Simon J. Ortiz (Acoma Pueblo), writer; Joe Sando (Jemez Pueblo), director, Institute of Pueblo Indian Study and Research Center, Albuquerque, New Mexico; Roxanne Dunbar Ortiz, professor of Ethnic Studies, California State University, Hayward; Susan A. Miller (Seminole Nation of Oklahoma), doctoral student, University of Nebraska, Lincoln; Rina Swentzell (Santa Clara Pueblo); Penny Bird (Santo Domingo Pueblo), education consultant, NM Department of Education, Indian Education Unit, Santa Fe, NM; Glenabah Martinez (Taos Pueblo), chair, Social Studies Department, Rio Grande High School, Albuquerque, NM; Jimmy Shendo (Jemez Pueblo), student resource specialist, Native American Studies, UNM; Diana M. Ortiz (Acoma Pueblo), Center for the New West, Albuquerque, NM; and Evelina Zuni Lucero (Isleta / San Juan Pueblo), writer and instructor, UNM.

66. S. Rodríguez, "Subaltern Historiography on the Rio Grande," 892.

67. Susan A. Miller, in Native American Studies Center compilation, 162–63.

68. Lucero, ibid., 176; Bird, ibid., 169, 171; Freese, ibid., 145; Jojola, ibid., 165; D. Ortiz, ibid., 174; R. Ortiz, ibid., 161; Swentzell, ibid., 166–67.

69. S. Rodríguez, "Subaltern Historiography on the Rio Grande," 898.

70. Shendo, in Native American Studies Center compilation, 173; Martinez, ibid., 171; Swentzell, ibid., 169; D. Ortiz, ibid., 174; S. Ortiz, ibid., 151; D. Ortiz, ibid., 174.

71. Freese, ibid., 150.

72. S. Rodríguez, "Subaltern Historiography on the Rio Grande," 895.

73. Bird, in Native American Studies Center compilation, 170; Jojola, ibid., 165–66; R. Ortiz, ibid., 158; S. Ortiz, ibid., 151.

74. S. Ortiz, ibid., 151.

75. Gutiérrez, When Jesus Came, xvii–xviii.

76. Seed, American Historical Review 97 (1992): 967.

77. Jojola, in Native American Studies Center compilation, 143; S. Ortiz, ibid., 151, 152; Martinez, ibid., 172; Bird, ibid., 169, 170; D. Ortiz, ibid., 173; Swentzell, 167, 169.

78. S. Rodríguez, "Subaltern Historiography on the Rio Grande," 895.

79. Ibid., 898.

80. Seed, American Historical Review 97 (1992): 968.

81. Stern, "Paradigms of Conquest," 6.

82. S. Rodríguez, "Subaltern Historiography on the Rio Grande," 898.

83. See such recent works as James F. Brooks, Captives and Cousins: Slavery, Kinship, and Community in the Southwest Borderlands (Chapel Hill, 2002); Curtis Marez, "Signifying Spain, Becoming Comanche, Making Mexicans: Indian Captivity and the History of Chicana/o Popular Performance," American Quarterly 53 (2001): 267–307; Anne Fairbrother, "Mexicans in New Mexico: Deconstructing the Tri-Cultural Trope," Perspectives in Mexican American Studies 7 (2000): 111–30; and Joseph A. Rodríguez, "Becoming Latinos: Mexican Americans, Chicanos,

and the Spanish Myth in the Urban Southwest," *Western Historical Quarterly* 29 (1998): 165–85.

84. The literature is vast. Important recent syntheses include Patricia Nelson Limerick, *Legacy of Conquest: The Unbroken Past of the American West* (New York, 1987); Richard White, *"It's Your Misfortune and None of My Own": A New History of the American West* (Norman, Okla., 1991); Walter Nugent, *Into the West: The Story of Its People* (New York, 1999); and Robert V. Hine and John Mack Faragher, *The American West: A New Interpretive History* (New Haven, 2000).

85. Alan Trachtenberg, "Contesting the West," *Art in America* 79 (1991): 121.

86. Antonia I. Castañeda, "Women of Color and the Rewriting of Western History: The Discourse, Politics, and Decolonization of History," *Pacific Historical Review* 61 (1992): 533, 507–8. Castañeda reports, "statistics reveal that between 1975 and 1988 there were 192 doctoral degrees in history awarded to women of color: 8 to Native Americans, 42 to 'Asians,' 101 to African Americans, and 41 to 'Hispanics.'"

87. Carl Becker, "Everyman His Own Historian," presidential address delivered before the American Historical Association, 29 December 1931, *American Historical Review* 37 (1932): 230.

88. Ortiz's commentary was part of a symposium held at the annual meeting of the American Historical Association in December 1974. Alfonso Ortiz, "Some Concerns Central to the Writing of 'Indian' History," *Indian Historian* 10 (1977): 20, 21. On the state of the field, see Donald L. Parman and Catherine Price, "A 'Work in Progress': The Emergence of Indian History as a Professional Field," *Western Historical Quarterly* 20 (1989): 185–96; R. David Edmunds, "Native Americans, New Voices: American Indian History, 1895–1995," *American Historical Review* 100 (June 1995): 717–40; Donald Fixico, ed., *Rethinking American Indian History* (Albuquerque, 1997); Russell Thornton, ed., *Studying Native America: Problems and Prospects* (Madison, Wis., 1998); Devon A. Mihesuah, ed., *Natives and Academics: Researching and Writing about American Indians* (Lincoln, Neb., 1998); and Donald Fixico, *"Bury My Heart at Wounded Knee* and the Indian Voice in Native Studies," *Journal of the West* 39 (2000): 7–15.

89. A. Ortiz, "Some Concerns Central to 'Indian' History," 21.

90. In addition to being director of Native American Studies, Jojola (Isleta Pueblo) is an associate professor of planning in the School of Architecture and Planning at the University of New Mexico. Jojola also lists the Indian Arts and Crafts Act of 1990 (P.L. 101-644) and the Native American Languages Act of 1990 (P.L. 101-477), to which one could add the Tribally Controlled Community College Assistance Act of 1978 (P.L. 95-471) and the Indian Arts and Crafts Enforcement Act of 2000 (P.L. 106-497) (Jojola, in Native American Studies Center compilation, 142).

91. Founded in 1997 by members of the Society of American Archivists, the Native American Archives Coalition is a division of the Archivists and Archives of Color Round Table of the Society of American Archivists. Native American

Archives Coalition, "Proposed Mission Statement," April 10, 1999, www
.landclaimsdocs.com/conferences/pdf/nativeamericanarchivescoalition.pdf.
See also Devon A. Mihesuah, "Suggested Guidelines for Institutions with Researchers Who Conduct Research on American Indians," *American Indian Culture and Research Journal* 17 (1993): 131–39.

92. Adam Kuper, "Culture, Identity, and the Project of a Cosmopolitan Anthropology," *Man* 29 (Sept. 1994): 545.

93. Marshall D. Sahlins, *How "Natives" Think: About Captain Cook, For Example*
(Chicago, 1995), 13–14.

94. Kuper, "Culture, Identity and Cosmopolitan Anthropology," 542–43, 545.

95. For some recent public examples, see Donald A. Grinde Jr., "Teaching American Indian History: A Native American Voice," *Perspectives* (newsletter of the
American Historical Association) 32 (1994): 11; James Axtell, "'Personal Ven-
detta' Undermines Native American Goals," ibid., 31–32; Donald A. Grinde Jr.,
"Donald A. Grinde, Jr., Replies," ibid., 32–33; Francis Paul Prucha, "The Challenge of Indian History," *Journal of the West* 34 (1995): 3–4; and Vine Deloria Jr.,
"The Struggle for Authority," *Journal of the West* 34 (1995): 3–4.

96. Kuper, Culture, Identity, and Cosmopolitan Anthropology," 547.

97. Sahlins, *How "Natives" Think,* 14.

98. A. Ortiz, "Some Concerns Central to 'Indian' History," 17.

99. See Richard White, "Using the Past: History and Native American Studies,"
chap. 9 in *Studying Native America: Problems and Prospects,* ed. Russell Thornton
(Madison, Wis., 1998), 217–43.

100. David G. Gutiérrez, "Significant to Whom?: Mexican Americans and the History of the American West," in *A New Significance: Re-envisioning the History of
the American West,* ed. Clyde A. Milner (New York, 1996), 78, 82; emphasis in
original.

101. Patricia Nelson Limerick, *Something in the Soil: Legacies and Reckonings in the
New West* (New York, 2000), 13–14.

Contributors

Jeffrey L. Hantman is associate professor of anthropology and director of the Interdisciplinary Program in Archaeology at the University of Virginia. He is the author of numerous articles on the archaeology and native history of Virginia, with a particular focus on colonial-era cultural interactions between Indians and colonists in the Chesapeake region. He is currently writing a book summarizing more than a decade of archaeological, ethnohistoric, and ethnographic research on Monacan Indians of Virginia, to be published by the University of Virginia Press.

Jenry Morsman is a doctoral candidate at the University of Virginia. He proposed the university's Lewis and Clark Bicentennial Project in 2000 and directed it until 2002. Morsman is currently an instructor at Middlebury College while completing his dissertation on the Mississippi River in the development of the United States, 1783–1860.

Peter S. Onuf is Thomas Jefferson Foundation Professor of History at the University of Virginia. He is the author and editor of numerous works on Thomas Jefferson and the era of the early American

Republic, including *Jefferson's Empire: The Language of American Nationhood* (University of Virginia Press, 2000) and (with Leonard Sadosky) *Jeffersonian America* (Blackwell's, 2002). Onuf is now completing a book with his brother Nicholas G. Onuf, *Nations, Markets, and War: An Essay in Modern History,* forthcoming from the University of Virginia Press.

Kenneth Prewitt, currently the Carnegie Professor of Public Affairs at Columbia University, directed the U.S. Census Bureau from 1998 to 2000. He has recently published *Science and Politics in Census Taking* (Russell Sage Foundation and Population Reference Bureau, 2003), has a second census-related book in press, and is starting a book on racial and ethnic classification in America's national statistical system.

Douglas Seefeldt, assistant professor of history at the University of Nebraska, Lincoln, was director of the University of Virginia's Lewis and Clark Bicentennial Project from 2002 to 2004 and served on the advisory board of the Lewis and Clark Exploratory Center of Virginia. As a 2001–3 Woodrow Wilson Postdoctoral Fellow in the Humanities, he taught in the Media Studies Program and conducted research at the Virginia Center for Digital History. He is currently working on a book that examines the changing landscape of the 1857 Mountain Meadows massacre site and the contested place of its various monuments in public memory.

Alan Taylor is a professor of history at the University of California at Davis. He is the author of *Liberty Men and Great Proprietors: The Revolutionary Settlement on the Maine Frontier* (1990); *William Cooper's Town: Power and Persuasion on the Early American Frontier* (1995); and *American Colonies: The Settlement of North America* (2001). *William Cooper's Town* won the Bancroft, Beveridge, and Pulitzer prizes in American History. His current project is *The Divided Ground,* which examines the Canadian-American borderland in the wake of the American Revolution, with a special emphasis on native peoples.

David Hurst Thomas has served since 1972 as Curator of Anthropology at the American Museum of Natural History (New York). A specialist in Native American archaeology, Thomas has written thirty books, edited ninety additional volumes, and written more than one hundred scientific papers. His most recent book is *Skull Wars: Kennewick Man, Archaeology, and the Battle for Native American Identity* (Basic Books, 2000). In 1989, Thomas was appointed as a founding trustee of the National Museum of the American Indian (Smithsonian Institution) and elected to the National Academy of Sciences.

Index